CRITICS PRAISED ROBERT J. DVORCHAK'S STUNNING FULL-DISCLOSURE ACCOUNT OF THE JEFFREY DAHMER SERIAL KILLINGS

MILWAUKEE MASSACRE

"A sordid, frightening tale of weird sexuality and crime, one that should chill the heart of the most jaded reader."
—*Florida Sun-News*

"The most straightforward account of the lot . . . if someone felt compelled to read one of the Dahmer books, this is . . . the pick of the litter."
—*Cleveland Plain Dealer*

"Well-researched and well-sourced."
—*Milwaukee Magazine*

"With such vivid descriptions, the only thing this book lacks is a scratch-and-sniff facility."
—*Northwest Evening Mail*

NOW HE BRINGS US A DIFFERENT KIND OF NIGHTMARE.

SOMEONE IS STALKING ME

QUANTITY SALES

Most Dell books are available at special quantity discounts when purchased in bulk by corporations, organizations, or groups. Special imprints, messages, and excerpts can be produced to meet your needs. For more information, write to: Dell Publishing, 1540 Broadway, New York, NY 10036. Attention: Special Markets.

INDIVIDUAL SALES

Are there any Dell books you want but cannot find in your local stores? If so, you can order them directly from us. You can get any Dell book currently in print. For a complete up-to-date listing of our books and information on how to order, write to: Dell Readers Service, Box DR, 1540 Broadway, New York, NY 10036.

SOMEONE IS STALKING ME

ROBERT J. DVORCHAK

A Dell Book

Published by
Dell Publishing
a division of
Bantam Doubleday Dell Publishing Group, Inc.
1540 Broadway
New York, New York 10036

ISBN: 0-440-21454-8

Printed in the United States of America

Published simultaneously in Canada

October 1993

10 9 8 7 6 5 4 3 2 1
RAD

"The white man will never be alone. Let him be just and deal kindly with my people, for the dead are not altogether powerless."

—Duwamish Indian Chief Seattle

CHAPTER 1

Any chance that Saturday night would be routine ended when the phone rang at 6:40 P.M. at the Marshall Police Department. It was February 9, 1991. Joe Delapas had reported to work about four hours earlier on the second shift, answering the phone and working dispatch. The call came in on the department's general number, not the emergency 911 line on which everything is recorded. But it was urgent nonetheless. A Michigan Bell telephone operator was on the line with a distressed man, who had picked up his phone and hit "zero" instead of dialing a number. In such cases, operators are instructed to patch the call through to the police jurisdiction nearest the point of call. And now Delapas was on the phone with a sobbing man who was trying to get help. But because he was having a hard time making sense, it took Delapas a few moments to figure out what was going on.

"My wife is in the driveway hurt, and my two kids are in the car," the man cried.

Delapas needed some particulars—address, location,

the nature of the problem—but the caller kept repeating the same line over and over. His wife was hurt and his kids were in the car.

After repeated inquiries, Delapas learned the call was coming from 16240 Division Drive, the road just south of town that divides Marshall Township and Fredonia Township in Calhoun County, a mostly rural area in south central Michigan. Marshall police didn't have jurisdiction out there; this was a job for the Calhoun County Sheriff's Department. Using standard procedure for an emergency call, Delapas ordered the man to stay on the line while he momentarily put him on hold. The policeman then dialed the Marshall Fire and Ambulance Service to get help for an unknown medical emergency. Then he was back on the line with the caller, who was screaming and crying: "Why did this have to happen?" Delapas told him to stay on the line until help arrived.

Paramedic Jeffrey Caison was in the first hour of his thirteen-hour shift when he took the call from Delapas. Caison figured this was a heart attack. Most of the hundreds of "unknown trouble" calls he had answered in his two years as an emergency medical technician turned out to be heart-related. Caison fired up the ambulance and was on his way with his partner, Richard Terrell, whose round-the-clock shift had begun twelve hours earlier. The ambulance ran "code red"—lights flashing and siren wailing—from the station, located just south of Marshall's traffic circle that surrounded the town's centerpiece Greek Revival fountain. The commotion stirred a few of the residents on the streets of Marshall, a picturesque pocket of Middle America 7,000-strong, known for its antique shops and historical architecture, where a penny still buys twelve minutes of time on its Michigan Avenue parking meters.

By southern Michigan standards, February 9 was a mild winter's evening. Arctic fronts, as biting as a hawk's beak, can swoop down through Canada and across Lake Michigan to grip the prairie-like flatlands in the state's midsection. But on this Saturday the temperature climbed to a high of 43 degrees by late afternoon. Patches of snow, the stubborn remnants of a long-gone storm, still lingered around the edges of farm fields displaying the dun-colored stubble of dead cornstalks. The sun had set at 6:04 P.M. And it was in the dying twilight that the ambulance roared down South Kalamazoo Avenue.

The cops were on the way too. A crackling police radio got the attention of Sheriff's Deputy Guy Picketts, who was picking up some equipment at home. A trouble call on Division Drive was addressed to Deputy William Lindsay, but Lindsay was off on police business in Battle Creek, fifteen miles to the west. Picketts advised dispatch he would handle the call. This was familiar ground for him. He once resided in the farmhouse at 16240 Division Drive before he enlisted in the Navy in 1966. He wondered what could be going on at the old homestead, a five-hundred-acre farm that Frank Zinn had owned since the 1940s. Picketts jumped into his police cruiser, a white Ford Crown Victoria LTD with black and gold trim, and punched the gas pedal. At full horsepower, he headed south on Kalamazoo Avenue, where he passed the ambulance. At Division Drive, he turned right and sped about another mile before turning left onto a dirt-and-gravel driveway leading to a two-story frame farmhouse replete with a chain swing on a columned front porch. There, at the head of the drive, was a silver Jeep Wagoneer. A human form lay face up on the ground. He could see two tots strapped in their car seats in the back, and the older of them was crying. Rushing from the car, he saw the woman on the ground, who looked as if she had slipped and fallen, except she wasn't moving. A dab of blood oozed from her nose. Approaching, Picketts glanced around for signs of potential trouble, and then knelt and checked her carotid artery for a pulse. He failed to find one. Then he heard a faint voice coming from inside the house.

"Help my wife. Help my wife," a man said.

"Help is on the way," Picketts shouted back.

The voice belonged to Bradford J. King. He was the one who had called the Marshall Police Department, and he had stayed on the phone until help arrived just as Officer Delapas had ordered him to. Delapas didn't hang up until he heard the sound of sirens coming from King's end of the line. Picketts saw a man emerge from the house to an enclosed porch; he was dressed in outdoor clothes—Army-like fatigue trousers, a camouflage T-shirt, a hat and hunting boots. Picketts hoped King could provide some answers.

The two kids were bewildered and immobile inside their car seats in the Jeep. The way the Jeep was parked, they could see only what was happening to the front and the sides. The older had seen his mother disappear below the window line, but he couldn't have understood she had been shot. The infant was too young to realize anything. All the older one said later was, "My mommy fell down. My mommy's hurt." Because of the restraints of the car seat, they couldn't see the barn or anything behind them.

The ambulance roared into the driveway at 6:54 P.M., right on Picketts's tail. Standard procedure dictates that the police check the area for trouble before the paramedics jump into action. The last thing anyone wants is someone threatening those who are concentrating on saving a life. Caison took those few moments to radio headquarters that he and Terrell had arrived. Picketts signaled the paramedics by pointing downward—the standard sign for a body on the ground—and headed toward the back porch of the house where he heard King's voice.

Paramedics are always racing a clock. If they can get to the scene within five minutes, they have a reasonable chance of jump-starting a heart to get blood into the brain before the lack of oxygen kills its ability to function. Any longer delay increases the victim's chances of being clinically dead. From what the paramedics observed, the woman's body hadn't been moved. Her head was turned to the right, and her airway hadn't been cleared. Terrell detected a single pulse-beat when he placed his fingers on a vein in the woman's neck, and he heard one final breath—a dying exhale as it turned out—when he cleared the woman's windpipe. Her airway was blocked by blood and saliva, which gathers if a stopped heart prevents the body from pumping blood away from the lungs. In a practiced series of emergency moves, Terrell inserted a tube down the woman's throat through the pink, frothy saliva to get air inside her lungs. Caison compressed the woman's chest, trying to get her heart started again with external help. As part of the cardiopulmonary resuscitation, he then applied a machine that generates an electric jolt. The current is designed to convert the rapid, uncoordinated contractions of the heart muscle back into a regular heartbeat. This defibrillator works only when its two terminals contact bare skin, so Caison cut away the woman's sweat shirt—a gray one adorned with the U.S. flag and saying "Operation Desert Storm—These Colors Don't Run." He also opened her jeans so he could place one pad against her chest and the other against her hip.

That's when he spotted the bullet hole in her chest.

Caison called to Deputy Picketts, who was halfway between the body and the house when word of a gunshot wound stopped him in his tracks. Picketts turned to confirm the entry wound, then confronted King, who by this time had come outside the house to the back porch.

"Do you have any weapons?" Picketts asked.

"I have a shotgun," King replied.

"Is there anyone else on the property?"

"No."

"Stay right where you are."

Picketts faced a whole different situation now. He dashed to his cruiser and radioed in the new information; a shooting requires that supervisory personnel be on the scene. He also retrieved a camera to start recording the scene as part of his basic police work. A crime scene doesn't stay uncontaminated for long. Everyone who enters the area brings something into it, and everyone who exits takes something away. If used correctly, the camera can preserve the scene more precisely than anyone's memory.

Something else caught Picketts's eye—the hayloft door of the barn was slightly open. The woman was down between the barn and the house, and the loft was a perfect ambush point. Picketts made a mental note to get up there as soon as he could.

Sergeant Harold Badger, who was in charge of the jail and the road patrol this Saturday night, arrived at seven o'clock to take charge of the scene until the county's two detectives got there. While looking over the paramedics' shoulders as they toiled, Badger noticed a second bullet hole. This second shot hit just above the vaginal area.

Two things were already clear—this was no accident, and these wounds weren't self-inflicted.

The shooting jarred the sheriff's department, which in the past decade had averaged one murder investigation per year. The woman on the ground was Diane Newton King, the thirty-four-year-old, high-octane television news anchor for WUHQ-TV Channel 41 in nearby Battle Creek. Everybody knew her as the energetic personality who delivered the morning news at this ABC affiliate. The authorities knew something more. Six months earlier, she began receiving phone calls at work from a star-struck fan who sought her advice on how to get into journalism. The anonymous admirer also wanted to get together for lunch. Diane was more annoyed than concerned with this come-on until she found a hand-delivered letter in her mailbox on October 30. It was made of words cut out of a magazine—the kind of message kidnappers use to deliver ransom notes—and said ominously, "You should have gone to lunch with me." The frightened woman informed the sheriff's department about the letter and the calls, and the Kings had set up an elaborate security ritual just in case this anonymous admirer pressed his obsession. A sickening shudder went through more than one cop just then—this stranger's attraction had become fatal.

The traffic in the Kings' driveway got heavier by the minute. If there is a suspected heart attack, standard procedure calls for additional paramedics to back up the original crew at the scene. There's just too much work to be done, and extra hands could make the difference between life or death. One of the three extra paramedics who responded was Robert Mansfield. He was at home and off duty, but two signals spurred him into action. His police scanner monitored the report of a "trouble" call at the same instant that his beeper went off. The voice pager gave him the address, and he was off. Mansfield's car is equipped with a flashing red light and siren. In less than four minutes, he was at the King household. Since he was told this was a heart attack, and most heart attacks happen inside the house, Mansfield raced to the door and encountered Bradford King on the back porch.

"Where are you going?" King demanded.

"I'm here with the ambulance. I'm here to help," Mansfield said.

"You can't go in there," King replied.

That was a weird response, Mansfield thought. Usually, agitated family members beg the paramedics to hurry up, to do this or do that, just do something. This guy was brushing him off. It was no time to argue, either.

"I'm here to help," Mansfield repeated. "Where is everybody?"

King pointed toward the Jeep Wagoneer, and Mansfield sprinted off to assist his colleagues.

Diane King lay parallel to the driver's side of the car, with her head pointed toward the front and her arms outstretched. With the exception of that one breath and heartbeat, she had no vital signs. The paramedics worked nonstop, but a thought crossed their minds, too. Usually, family members make pests of themselves, asking how bad things are and generally getting in the way. King stayed on the porch, about forty feet away, and didn't seem very interested in moving. And the kids were still in the back seat, illuminated by the dome light. The older child, Marler, was just a month shy of his third birthday. He was at the age where children never stop talking or moving. Now, strapped in a car seat on the driver's side, he put his face over to the window to look at the paramedics, then looked over at his three-month-old sister, Kateri. Both of them were crying.

The paramedics toiled in vain on the lifeless form lying in the dirt. Nothing can match the exhilaration paramedics feel when they cheat death and save a life. And nothing feels worse than losing that contest. Diane King's last hope—and it was only a ghost of a hope—was getting her to an emergency room. She was placed onto a backboard, then loaded into the ambulance for a final rush to Oaklawn Hospital in Marshall. Caison turned the ignition at 7:08 P.M., fourteen minutes after he had arrived, and drove off on a six-minute dash. Sergeant Gary Morgan, responding to the trouble call, was just pulling up to the Kings' driveway when he was asked to escort the ambulance to the hospital. While the paramedics restocked their supplies, Morgan stood by the emergency room doctor who pronounced Diane King dead at 7:17. Morgan stayed with the body until the county medical examiner released it to the Craig Kempf Funeral Home, just across the street from the hospital.

Morgan now had police work to do. He put into plastic evidence bags the woman's gray sweat shirt, blue jeans, black scarf, white bra, red panties, and Nike sneakers. He made sure the items and the body were in a secure place, so no one could tamper with what was now evidence in a criminal investigation.

The journey to what should have been the safety of her driveway began about four-fifteen P.M. for Diane. She was returning from a three-day visit at the home of her mother, Freida Newton, in the Detroit suburb of Sterling Heights. She was expected that night at a party to be given by her boss at WUHQ-TV. And she wanted to spend some time alone with her husband—something that had become increasingly rare since the birth of their second child in November.

Diane spent the afternoon showing her cousin, Elaine Wash, how to make baskets from strips of paper and cloth. The two women worked for hours—they were both good talkers—and Diane's two tots played with her mother and stepfather. Originally, Diane planned to leave the children with grandma to have Saturday night alone with her husband. Then Brad would drive back and pick them up on Sunday. But she changed her mind at the last minute, and both kids and Diane were packed and ready to head home at four-fifteen.

"Boy, is your father going to be surprised to see you kids," she said.

The party was to start at seven o'clock. But there was another reason for leaving early. Ever since the star-struck fan had placed that note of cut-out letters in her mailbox, Diane tried to make it home before dark whenever possible. She always called ahead to alert her husband when she would be home, too, so she wouldn't be alone when she got there. Her stepfather was on the phone when she had everything packed, so Freida promised to make the call later.

Diane hugged and kissed her mother in the driveway, and she drove off with the kids belted securely in their car seats. Freida paused to pick up a toy tractor and other playthings—it was warm enough for Marler to play outside—and put them in her garage before going into the house. Once inside, Freida dialed the number in Marshall and told her son-in-law with as much civility as she could muster, "Diane's on her way home now." It was open knowledge Freida and Brad never did get along.

Diane maneuvered the Wagoneer down St. Joseph's

Road and right onto Metropolitan Parkway to Telegraph Road on her normal route toward Ann Arbor, where she picked up Interstate 94 west toward Marshall. It doesn't take long to leave behind the suburban sprawl and ease into the open countryside of southern Michigan.

Diane was wearing a patriotic Operation Desert Storm sweat shirt her stepfather bought from a paralyzed Vietnam veteran. It was emblazoned with the U.S. flag and a map of Saudi Arabia. February 9 was the twenty-fourth day of the Persian Gulf War, and the nation's attention had been riveted on a patch of desert half a world away. Diane paid particular attention, not only because she was in the media but because she was an Army veteran. Allied jets were bombing the turrets off Iraqi tanks bunkered down in Kuwait and southern Iraq. Ragtag mobs of Iraqi soldiers were surrendering. American commanders crowed that Saddam Hussein no longer had the fourth largest army in the world. Marines and Army armored units awaited the order to start the ground war. And Michiganders were eager for news of Army Specialist Melissa Rathburn-Nealy of Grand Rapids, who had been missing since January 31. She was the first American woman to be taken a prisoner of war since World War II. The latest reports had her being moved to the Iraqi town of Basra, perhaps as a human shield. The war was on everyone's mind. Local papers were filled with ads, pictures of yellow ribbons, and messages of support for hometown troops. In this deployment, the nation's heartland wasn't going to let its sons and daughters fight without support.

It takes two hours and fifteen minutes to drive the 120 miles to Marshall. Diane exited the interstate and drove down the quiet country roads to Division Drive, a lane she had driven hundreds of times since she moved out here ten months ago. This is the kind of place people seek to escape big-city crime and grime, and no place in America could look more safe than this farm, where the nearest neighbors on either side are several hundred feet away. She left the pavement for the dirt-and-gravel lane leading to the farmhouse. Probably she called to her young son, "Wake up, Marler. We're home. We're going to see daddy now." It was still light out, just as she had planned. The driveway runs between the house and the barn. The barn, painted red and trimmed with white, once housed workhorses but was now used for storage.

When Diane got out of the Wagoneer, she never noticed the dull-gray barrel of a rifle protruding from the hayloft on the second floor. A crack pierced the silence, and a bullet one-fifth inch in diameter tore through her sweat shirt and slammed into her chest. The sliver of metal stung and burned as it tore through her heart. It lacked the shocking power to knock her backward, but she crumpled when her legs lost the ability to support her. She fell back with her arms outstretched. A bolt on the rifle ejected the spent cartridge, which disappeared into the shreds of straw littering the hayloft's floor. Another round was chambered. Some seconds later, with Diane King flat on the ground, a second shot rang out.

A couple of hundred yards down Division Drive, Tanya Scott was in the process of packing her car for a move to a new home. While standing on her porch, she heard two gunshots. She didn't think much of it, certainly not enough to consider calling the police. Gunshots from hunting were not uncommon out here. She finished loading her car and left her driveway about 6:45 P.M.

In the gloaming, Diane was bleeding to death on the cold, hard ground. Purplish stains from the hole in her chest soiled the sweat shirt that said "These Colors Don't Run." Even if she had been inside an emergency room at that moment, no one could have saved her. Blood frothed to Diane's nose as she took her final labored breaths while looking up at a darkening sky.

Her bewildered son, trapped in his car seat and unable to fend for himself, saw his mother fall from sight. In two minutes, three at the most, Diane Newton King was dead.

CHAPTER 2

"Good morning, everyone."

With that trademark opening line and a smile, Diane Newton King connected to her viewers each day. She was as much of a part of Michigan mornings as a bowl of cornflakes—which, in fact, had been invented at the turn of the century by W. K. Kellogg when Battle Creek earned its name in history as "Cereal City." WUHQ's television market has 880,000 potential viewers, and Diane's voice was the first one a lot of them heard in the morning. Personable and down-to-earth, she was a good fit in this section of Middle America. In two years of delivering the news, she had attained a degree of celebrity. When she walked through the shopping mall, people would turn and exclaim, "Oh look, it's Diane King." She often served as hostess for community parades and ice shows and pageants. Regular viewers felt as if they knew her. It seemed more like she was talking to them across the kitchen table than from a TV studio, and folks who tuned in said they felt like offering her a piece of toast or a cup of coffee as she talked. Her voice carried a tone of authority and believability. She could change emotions with authenticity, and what she said could set a tone for the day. That's why she liked to end most of her newscasts with an upbeat story.

The red light went on for her first newscast at 6:57 each morning. It was a three-minute segment leading in to ABC's *Good Morning America,* and it gave her the chance to give the local news first. Then, from a studio in Manhattan, Joan Lunden and Charles Gibson interviewed their daily guests while Mike Schneider delivered the national news. Twice during the *GMA* show, King also did a pair of five-minute segments, called cut-ins, at 7:25 and 8:25 A.M. But to get her newscast in shape for the opening segment, King had to rise in the wee hours of the morning to get to the studio by five A.M. She checked the morning newspapers, scrolled the news wires at the station, and fashioned her news script. Everything had to be accurate—and concise enough to fit into her allotted time slots. And she had to look good on camera, so her hair, makeup, and nails had to be done just right.

WUHQ did not have a noon, evening, or nighttime news program, just Diane in the morning. After her last cut-in, she lined up interviews during the day or figured what news events or news conferences to cover. Her workday was supposed to end at one P.M., but because she was the station's only reporter, she almost always stayed over, sometimes four to nine hours over. Behind the glamour that people associate with the TV media, there's a lot of unseen sweat and drudge work.

"One day, everybody's going to know me from one end of the world to the other," Diane told her older sister, Darlene Goins, when she got into TV work. She was a fighter and a pusher, and she wanted to be famous and successful.

Diane's role model was Barbara Walters. She loved to tackle tough stories that could make a difference in people's lives. For one report she put together an in-depth look at a garbage-incineration plant in Grand Rapids. Another time she examined the consequences of disposable diapers clogging up landfills. She reported on overcrowding at the Calhoun County Jail, where five or six inmates were housed in a single cell. And she was an advocate for the downtrodden fighting the bureaucracy. She once took up the cause of a woman trying unsuccessfully to tap into a program for her mentally handicapped child. Diane pushed the case to the director of mental health services for Calhoun County, and got services delivered that had previously been denied. In the lives of that woman and child, she made a difference. Her job as a reporter was summarized in this creed: comfort the afflicted and afflict the comfortable.

"She was a ball of fire," said Kristina Mony, an intern who worked with King for more than a year and who became a close friend as well. "She taught me so much, not only about journalism, but about life and morals and values. She said it was one thing to be the head and shoulders of the news, but it was another to do stories that touch people's lives. I have never met anybody like her and I probably never will again. She loved her job and she loved her kids. She sounds like a superwoman and she was. She was very independent. She didn't want to depend on anyone for anything."

Diane also didn't take no for an answer. Once, she asked the station to send her to Peru to do a story on the disappearing rain forests. WUHQ said no, they couldn't afford the trip, so she took her case to places like National Geographic for money. In a letter sent in October of 1989 she wrote on WUHQ letterhead:

> This letter is a request for a $5,000 grant for WUHQ-TV 41 News Prime Time to produce a documentary on Peru's disappearing rain forest and the great dangers that threaten mankind if these forests continue to be destroyed.
>
> The Binder Park Zoo in Battle Creek, Michigan, is sponsoring a trip to the Peruvian Amazon to study rain forest conservation and the Amazon's complex natural habitat, thereby educating participants in global ecology. WUHQ-TV would like to accompany that group on a one-week expedition.
>
> We are an ABC affiliate which is privately owned and has limited funding. A project of this magnitude requires a great deal of preparation. Therefore, your immediate attention to this request is vital.

The trip never came off. But Diane was so sure she was going that she and Kristina got their medical shots and bought khaki safari shorts and luggage for the expedition. Kristina's file on the project was titled "The Amazon Women."

But if she couldn't go on grand expeditions to South America, Diane did figure out ways to make trips in Michigan. In July of 1989 she and Kristina made a three-day, two-night bicycle tour of the peninsula along Lake Michigan. She produced the series of stories she wanted, even though to get them she had to sleep out in the rain one night and ride a bike for three days until her thighs ached.

"She told me to choose your battles. You can't fight everything in the world," Kristina said. "And she told me to always have a purpose, always have a dream. Her dream was to be a network anchor."

Diane kept a personal file at work, saving every article she found on her passions—Native Americans and women in the media. As part of her duties, Diane also produced documentary shows. She discovered her first one right under the station's nose. WUHQ is located six miles outside downtown Battle Creek on Dickman Road. The three-story, red brick building was once headquarters for Fort Custer, a military training post named for George Armstrong Custer, who lived briefly in Monroe, Michigan, and led a Michigan brigade in the Civil War before he was killed fighting the Sioux with the U.S. 7th Cavalry at Montana's Little Bighorn River in 1876. One can only imagine how Diane, a Native American, felt about working in a place named after a soldier who lived and died fighting her ancestors. Established in 1917 and dedicated by Custer's widow, Elizabeth, Camp Custer was a place for World War I doughboys to train under the stern eye of drill sergeants before they crossed the Atlantic to fight the Germans in France. The camp was expanded to a fort in World War II, and it served as a detention center for German prisoners of war who were retrained for jobs. Now it is home to a 770-acre military cemetery, and among those buried under military headstones are sixteen German POWs killed in a train accident while en route to Fort Custer from a work detail on a sugar beet farm near Blissfield, Michigan.

WUHQ's thick-walled offices could withstand a bomb blast, but it was hard to create any warmth out of something that was so militarily drab. The newsroom was in the basement and offered a view of the turnaround in the front driveway. There were desks for King, the news editor, the cameraperson, and the station engineer, plus a desk in the middle of the room where the TV intern sat. A blue Channel 41 insignia hung on the wall behind Diane's desk, which was adorned with a gold-plated, white-marble award she had won. She also had a Wayne State University coffee mug and an unframed snapshot of her husband, Brad, and her son, Marler, tacked to a corkboard. The building's first floor housed the offices of the president, vice president, marketing and sales directors, and receptionist. Up one more flight of stairs was the engineering room and bare-bones studio where Diane did the news. It was hardly an elaborate set, equipped only with a desk, and Diane hated it. The backdrop could be either blue or gray—its lone concession to cosmetics.

Diane was relatively new in the media, but she was living out a fantasy. After years of working other jobs, King had decided on entering the TV business, and she got her break in Colorado at the age of twenty-nine.

"She wanted to be a reporter. It was her dream in life. . . . She was so gung ho," said Cindy Zebelman, a friend in Denver. "She wanted to be an example. She wanted to show women and Indian boys and girls that they too could be on TV."

Once Diane got started, she had a meteoric rise.

If Diane didn't know the inside workings of TV news, she made up for it with spunk and ambition. She was the type of person who did everything wholeheartedly, whether it was pursuing a career, a relationship, Native-American studies, or just plain fun. "If she made up her mind to do something, she'd just do it. She was that way ever since she was a child," said her mother, Freida. She had once considered a military career in the Army and had been commissioned a second lieutenant. And although she had an associate degree in physical education from Mount Ida College in Massachusetts and a degree in communications from Wayne State University in Detroit, she hadn't used it as much of a springboard. She worked in banks, department stores, and restaurants before she decided to take control of her own destiny.

Part of the impetus came from the self-fulfillment boost she got from Erhard Seminars Training, or "est," named after self-help guru Werner Erhard, who led the enlightenment movement in the 1970s but later disappeared after running afoul of the Internal Revenue Service. The est movement started in California, with a basic message of accepting yourself and taking charge of your life. Some people were turned off by its mysticism and drill sergeant–style training sessions, but the philosophy had appealed to such celebrities as Yoko Ono, singer John Denver, and yippie-turned-yuppie Jerry Rubin. Devotees said est gave them a kind of "kick in the butt" to go in the direction they wanted to go anyway. They said est encouraged them to speak up for what they believed in. It was a message Diane found appealing.

Just before Diane got her first TV job, she was working as an enrollment manager for Werner Erhard and Associates in Englewood, Colorado. She had met her husband, Bradford, through a mutual friend in est while they were living in Michigan. Brad was a former cop who wanted to be a trainer in Erhard's program, and he was on Erhard's staff in Ohio and Colorado. Diane's family, with its blue-collar roots, thought est was an oddball if not cultish thing to get into. But then again, Diane was full of surprises. Her life seemed to be a prolonged exercise of finding out who she was, and by extension, discovering who she wasn't.

One day, out of the blue, Diane phoned Reynelda

Ware Muse, the black anchorwoman who had been at Denver's KCNC-TV since 1968. Diane gushed about how much she admired Muse, then begged for just a few minutes to seek advice. The idea of getting paid to appear on camera and do something she enjoyed sure beat running a cash register in a department store.

From time to time, Muse had heard the pleadings of wannabe Diane Sawyers or Connie Chungs looking for a break to get on the air. Most didn't have a chance or a clue. But something in Diane's voice—perhaps a tone of sincerity and determination—brought out Muse's supportive side. Muse told Diane about the hard realities she was up against. Starry-eyed reporters usually start straight out of college, shopping for openings with their audition tapes produced in school studios, or get their foot in the door with an internship. They work for peanuts in small markets, gaining experience that they can eventually exchange for better paychecks at bigger stations. Only a fraction make it big and enjoy network-type salaries. It's like the major leagues in baseball—millions play the game on sandlots, the good ones get to perform for money in the minors, the cream of crop rises to the big show, and the best of the best make megabucks. Diane was starting out in tee ball.

With no on-air or practical experience, Diane couldn't possibly hope to wriggle into a market as big as Denver's. Muse told her she'd have to slave away in an entry-level job in a smaller city, maybe even starting in radio, busting her tail to make any kind of an impression. Ahead lay long, demanding hours and holidays and weekends spent working in the office rather than at home. Plus, King could expect cutthroat competition and nasty internal politics. In this business, people with prickly egos claw their way to the top. There was no need to watch for back stabbers; media people are quite capable of stabbing each other in the front.

"Everything was against her. She was making such a late start, it seemed impossible. It's very, very difficult to make a transition into this business from another field. I told her the worst. But nothing that I said deterred her. She was a woman who knew what she wanted. She was aggressive and tenacious," Muse recalled. "She was determined to get into the business. You meet so many people who want to do things, and after a while you can discern who has what it takes. When the smoke cleared from what I said, she was still standing. I was impressed by that."

King was quite a package: intelligent, iron-willed, and intrepid. She may not have been the best speller or most polished writer in the world, but she got by on her personal motto: "Fake it till you make it." She also had the intangibles for TV's glamour side, that is, looking and sounding good on camera. TV news is a mixture of journalism and a Hollywood-type glitz. Like moviemaking or modeling, it offers the lure of visibility and celebrity, plus the news business gives one the chance to pry and probe in front of a camera. Little wonder King—with her interest in reporting and her desire to make the world a better place—found it so seductive. Plus, she was athletic and attractive, photogenic enough to have entertained ambitions of being a fashion model.

Ever since she was a kid, though, Diane had never thought of herself as truly pretty. That was one reason she drove herself so; she tried extra hard to be the best, and she masked her insecurities with an outward boldness. She was five feet two inches tall, 137 pounds, and had a radiant smile showing off teeth recently straightened by braces. She had black hair to go with her deep brown eyes and dark features. She also dressed impeccably, even if her taste for fashionable clothes exceeded her means to pay for them. "I have a beer budget and champagne tastes," she joked to family and friends.

King's Native-American heritage was an asset in the eyes of employers seeking to avoid an all white-male image. She was the third of five children of an English father and a Mohawk mother. As a child, she was called "half-breed" and taunted for having dark skin. But she converted the pain of bigotry into determination to succeed. She was her family's shining star. "At some point in her life, she decided she was going to be somebody," said her youngest sister, Denise. "And if she made up her mind on something, she'd figure out a way to get it."

It helped to have a supportive husband, Bradford, eleven years her senior. Having endured one failed marriage, he was willing to sacrifice his own ambitions for his wife's career. He was content to let her have the limelight. If people derisively called him Mr. Diane King, so be it. This was the time for women to make it in the corporate world, and traditional roles were being redefined. He had one unmistakable physical characteristic—his shaved head. Male-pattern baldness had claimed the hair on the top of his pate, and a razor finished the job on the sides and back—because that's the way Diane wanted it.

Before she even landed a job, Diane typed a note of thanks to Reynelda Muse on May 22, 1985, for having taken the time to suggest some media contacts. It was an action typical of her savvy personality. She wrote

> I must say you were right when you said that people in this business were very helpful and supportive. Once again, thank you for everything. I will get

this job, and I'm not stopping until I get exactly what I want.

Less than three months later, King cracked open the door on her new career. She was hired as a production assistant and researcher who lined up guests for programs at KRMA-TV Channel 6, the public television station in Denver. It was the bottom rung, but it was a start. In reality, she was hardly more than a glorified gofer working behind the scenes. Others in the same job as King worked as unpaid volunteers; she was fortunate enough to be drawing a paycheck, even if it was a meager $8,000 a year.

Given this opportunity, Diane made the most of it. And while she was working hard at her duties, she began assembling an audition tape—something to make a commercial station want to hire her. She was still a raw talent that needed some polishing if she expected to make it in the business. Diane was a perfectionist who demanded total effort from herself. She required the same things of others, and she was rather blunt sometimes in telling them if they didn't measure up. She had learned in est to be confrontational and speak up for what she believed.

"She was very direct. And sometimes you have to tone that down a bit when you're working with other people. There's a lot of teamwork required in producing a television show. Broadcasting is a competitive business. And you can easily alienate people along the way," said Lin Mrachek, the executive producer who hired her. "Diane was still learning, and not at a stage of total confidence. She was so different from most people who take life a little less seriously than she did."

One time Diane had a stormy exchange with the owner of a clothing store who had donated a suit for a host on KRMA. The owner called the station's general manager to complain when the clothes weren't returned, and Diane was told to write a letter of apology. "She didn't feel she was in the wrong, so she didn't totally apologize when she wrote her letter," Mrachek said. "We rewrote the note and had to tell her, 'Diane, you better sign this.' "

Within sixteen months, Diane landed her first on-air job, and the networking she did with Reynelda Muse paid handsome dividends. Muse's station had just hired a reporter from KJCT-TV in Grand Junction, Colorado, which meant there was an opening in a small market that Diane might want. Out of 213 TV markets in the country, Grand Junction is the 187th smallest. And Muse was right about the pay; King's entry-level job paid about $13,000 a year. KJCT's reporters were either straight out of a journalism school or working in their first broadcast job. King may have been older than the other rookies, but station manager Jan Hammer was impressed with her energy and her audition tape. And KJCT had never hired a Native American before.

"We thought she had great potential. She was ambitious, hard-working, and energetic. At the same time, she was open, friendly, and approachable. She was very much a people person. She was someone you'd like to get to know," Hammer said. "She had all the qualities you look for in a reporter. She was the most aggressive reporter we've ever had."

At first, Diane went alone to get started in Grand Junction, leaving Brad 240 miles away in Denver to tie up loose ends. The temporary separation was a price that had to be paid to further a career, and her career came first. They still had four months left on an apartment lease in Denver, and Diane had rented another place in her new town. Brad wasn't working, so there was a strain on the marriage as well as the budget. It was a familiar theme in their relationship.

"I saw it as a low point in his life. He was separated from his wife and he was unemployed. All he talked about was how much he missed Diane. He wanted to do his part in the partnership," said Alex Galant, a friend in Denver.

But within four months, Brad was on his way to Grand Junction. Galant and another friend, John Van Vleet, helped Brad pack up the moving van. By this time, Diane was well on her career path.

On the job, she did it all—the police beat, city hall, and enterprise reporting. She disdained the fluffy-type features, the kind of brainless stuff that gives TV news the image of being short on substance and long on style. Diane preferred to dig into investigative pieces on such topics as the radioactive tailings in uranium mines. She did so many uranium stories that friends nicknamed her Millie Mill Tailings.

On another story, Diane exposed a loophole in the security system at the Grand Junction airport. As part of a cost-saving measure, the airport would shut down the machine that's supposed to detect if passengers are carrying guns or knives after the last flight out. But passengers mingled in the secure area until the last flight in, which was three hours later. Airport officials made a sweep of the area every morning to check for weapons, but Diane wasn't convinced the procedure was foolproof. Why couldn't someone smuggle in a weapon during the night, innocently walk through the machine without tripping the alarm and then retrieve the weapon before boarding a flight? One day, when the metal detector was shut down, she smuggled in three pieces of metal, which could have just as easily been guns or knives. She taped them under a washroom sink, under a pay telephone and under a shoeshine chair. Only one of the metal bars was found in the security sweep, and the Federal Aviation Administration ordered a reevaluation of the airport's security. That's the kind of reporting Diane loved: breaking open a story on her own and getting results from it.

Diane also loved her new locale, as much for its raw, rugged beauty as for its neighborliness. Located in western Colorado, twenty-five miles from the Utah border, Grand Junction is a town of 30,000 residents, and the population in the greater Grand Valley is about triple that. The valley—rich in ranching, mining, and recreation—is on the western side of the Continental Divide, or the western slope of the Rocky Mountains. To the north is a mountain range called Book Cliffs. To the east is the Grand Mesa, a flattop tableland with steep rocky sides. To the south is the Colorado National Monument featuring Red Rock Canyon, a miniature version of the Grand Canyon. The Grand Junction Valley area has become a Shangri-La for retirees, featuring two hundred lakes for fishing and swimming, mountains for hiking or biking and skiing, streams for white-water rafting, plenty of seclusion for communing with nature, and a sky as blue as a robin's egg. The area had its problems, not the least of which was drug trafficking for big-spenders at the Rocky Mountain ski resorts, but it offered a comfortable pace of life, free of big-city congestion, dirt, and traffic. All in all, it seemed a good place to raise children, and Diane embraced the idea of motherhood.

Diane and Brad had their first child on March 6, 1988. A name can have special significance, and Diane named her son Marler—her maiden name. It was a tribute to her father, George Herbert Marler, who died in 1966 from complications after a Michigan doctor botched some surgery. Diane was ten years old when he died, and his death punched a big void in her life. The Newton in Diane's name came from her stepfather, Royal Newton. Taking his name as hers was Diane's way of telling her stepfather that, after some rough spots, she had accepted him into the family.

Nothing seemed beyond King's grasp. She was a woman without boundaries. "If you talk about someone who wanted it all in terms of career and family, it was Diane. She wanted it all and thought she could have it all," said Jan Hammer. "But there was another side to her. She wasn't the self-assured person people thought. To those who were really close to her, she expressed not so much a feeling of inadequacy but a feeling of being insecure. She needed support. She needed to know she was moving forward, that she was on the right track. She was unsure of herself."

King also became a mentor in her own right. At KJCT, she helped Debbie Rich, a colleague of hers in the Junior Service League, get a job in TV news. She thought Rich had the smarts, looks, and gumption to be in the news business, so she encouraged her to try it.

"Diane was very willing to get someone started in the business. She told me everything, just to help. She taught me a lot," Rich said. "She was a very determined woman. She had her mind set on what she wanted to do."

Diane also enhanced her reputation as a stern taskmaster. In the newsroom, she demanded everything of herself and expected nothing less from the supporting cast. She ordered her crew to shoot certain scenes exactly the way she wanted. The same went for the snippets of quotes, or sound bites. She hadn't mastered the technique of softening criticism, and some people—especially men who didn't like being bossed by a woman—resented her for it. And she bumped into one of those corporate double standards: men who were aggressive and assertive are seen as take-charge types; women who have the same characteristics are perceived as something else.

Diane also had a real ego clash with one of the other women reporters, Monica Rogers. They may have been on the same team, but they sure got on each other's nerves, especially after Monica got the evening anchor job over Diane. The newsroom became the arena for more than one cat fight. And friends pulled Diane aside and told her the internal clashes just weren't worth it.

"Diane was a person who could push you to the edge," said Mike Moran, KJCT's news director who had to mediate some of the squabbles. "She was not afraid to tear into me. She'd do that often. She was not afraid to tell you exactly what she thought."

On the other hand, Diane liked to take young people under her wing. Lesley Tucker left college early to work in the sales department at KJCT. The first person she met in Grand Junction was Diane Newton King, who encouraged her to get into the news end of the business.

"She was like a big sister to me. Diane was a caring, thoughtful, and enthusiastic person. She always had an encouraging and positive thing to say. She would always say, 'Go for it. Just do it.' We've never had as good a reporter as her in this town. She was always digging for news. She worked so hard to get where she was. She often told me, 'No matter what, I'm going to make it.' She said it was never too late to do what you really wanted to do," Tucker said. "She was strong-willed, sometimes bullheaded. But I never saw anything bad about her."

Diane also made a big impression as host of KJCT's public affairs show called *News 8 Forum.* The Colorado Media, Agencies and Clients Association singled out one segment in 1989 as the state's best public affairs program. She won a Starward, which was in the form of an Oscar, with her name etched on it as the producer.

People were starting to notice her. But she was constantly looking to improve. When told her writing could use a little work, Diane sought out a private tutor to help her with scripts. She sent tapes back to Reynelda Muse and sought out tips on how she could be better. If she felt she had a weakness, she went after it with a vengeance.

The hard work paid off. Just two years after getting the on-air job at KJCT, Diane advanced another step. She was hired by WUHQ in Battle Creek, Michigan, as the morning news anchor in the nation's thirty-eighth largest market. Her duties, beginning February 13, 1989, also included special projects and documentary shows. Plus, she was going back home to Michigan—as a success and a celebrity. The first one in her family to earn a college degree, Diane had grown up and gone to high school in the Detroit suburb of Sterling Heights. If Diane kept going—and she had no reason to believe she couldn't—maybe she could land a job with a Detroit station or the networks. Life in the fast lane was exhilarating. And the pay was getting better. Now she was earning $22,600 a year, up from her starting salary of $13,000 at KJCT. She also hoped the move would benefit Brad. Grand Junction didn't have the widest array of job opportunities. Brad worked at all sorts of odd jobs—delivering morning newspapers, flipping burgers in a greasy spoon, clerking in a jewelry store, selling men's clothes in a fashion store, running the cash register at a twenty-four-hour gas station/convenience store and counseling patients at St. Mary's Hospital. But none of these things befitted a man with a master's degree in criminology who was working on his doctorate. Maybe he'd have better luck in Michigan.

Diane and Brad left a lot of friends behind when they packed up their belongings in a moving van. They had Sunday brunch with Lesley Tucker and her boyfriend. And before departing, they invited their closest friends for a farewell meal at the Gatehouse, a bed-and-breakfast where they spent their final night in Colorado. Debbie Rich was there with Mike Moran, plus the news and sports anchors at KJCT. Her colleagues had mixed emotions. They were happy to see her move up in the world but sorry she had to say good-bye. Diane and Brad shed tears when they left. Their time in Colorado had been the happiest of their lives. Before they put the Rocky Mountains in their rearview mirror, they stopped in Denver to say good-bye to other friends. She wanted to take advantage of this job opportunity; she only hoped that the relationship between her family and Brad would improve.

In Michigan, Diane's determination carried her. She did everything that was asked of her and more. After her first year, she was rewarded with a glowing appraisal by Larry Neinhaus, who as WUHQ's news editor, was her immediate supervisor. The appraisal covered her strengths and pointed out areas she needed to work on:

> No regrets, Diane. Your hiring was a good decision. I was looking long and hard for someone with personality and talent to fill the morning anchor po-

sition here at 41. You fit the bill nicely. You continue to be a fresh, upbeat informant for morning TV watchers. The warm smile and bubbly personality are perhaps your greatest assets. This station benefits most from the positive image you project.

As expected, your on-air delivery has improved much in this first year. You are appearing more confident, comfortable, and credible. And your writing has improved in large measure. Obviously, continue to work on delivery and writing skills. In particular, I've noticed that you have apparent difficulty in writing to video. You need to take more time in preparing scripts so the voice-over and video "mesh" well. In addition, the timing for sound bites is too often "off." These are minor adjustments that need to be made to insure a clean, smooth, visually appealing show. I would suggest you come in a bit earlier in the morning to prep yourself.

One of your attributes that gives me greatest satisfaction, Diane, is your aggressiveness. While you can be a "royal pain in the behind," I'd much rather see that than apathy or passiveness. I like your determined approach to researching projects like community mental health. Applied to future projects, that kind of "drive" will get us where we need to go a whole lot quicker. Your aggressive style and ambition will help us to be more productive than we have been of late. I look forward to seeing more of that commitment.

One more word on aggressiveness. I encourage you to practice a lot more tolerance and patience with fellow news staffers. While I realize you have your agenda, keep in mind that others have their respective agendas too. In particular, try to understand the needs of [the new camerawoman], and refrain from placing too many demands on her as she tries to learn a new skill. Patience and consideration will pay dividends . . . guaranteed.

A note on productivity. Let's work harder at getting daily news shoots scheduled in advance. Try to get on the phone first thing in the morning to set up potential interviews. I'll try, as well, to be of greater assistance to you. We all need to be more productive with our time . . . especially as we look to increased demands down the road. We need to make more efficient use of our time.

A final note, Diane. You have a fragile ego. You are not the easiest person to criticize. Please know that any criticism I offer . . . seldom though it may be . . . is intended to help us perform as a department and team.

Thanks, Diane, for your continuing positive contributions!

Not bad for a year's work.

And when the station offered a $1,000 raise after the first year, Diane pressed for more. Feeling she was underpaid, Diane asked Kristina Mony to check around at other stations in the area. She was sensitive to the fact that women often get paid less than men for doing the same work. Discovering that her salary was lower than that of other reporters and anchors in the area, she demanded an increase of $6,000.

Her arguments failed to persuade her bosses, who gave her only $1,000. But, from a purely practical standpoint, Diane needed more money. A year after returning to Michigan, she became pregnant with her second child. Brad wasn't so keen on the idea, but Diane really wanted another baby. Over the next several months, she proudly told everyone she came in contact with—politicians, business leaders, civic officials, people on and off the job—about the impending birth. But Diane's pregnancy included the unpleasant side effect of severe morning sickness. Sometimes, immediately after she finished a cut-in, she sprinted in high heels down the hallway and down the stairs to throw up in the first-floor women's room. If she went out to film interviews during the day, she always carried soda crackers to settle her stomach. And keep her less cranky.

On November 20, two days before Thanksgiving, she gave birth to a baby girl. Although she had planned a "natural" childbirth, the baby was delivered by cesarean section, just as Marler had been. And once again, King picked a name that had special meaning. The newborn was named Kateri Tekakwitha King, after a Mohawk who inspired a wave of Catholic fervor among her people three centuries ago. Kateri Tekakwitha was the daughter of a Mohawk chief and an Algonquin mother who had been converted to Catholicism by French missionaries. Like so many Indians who had no immunities to European diseases, Tekakwitha and her family contracted smallpox. Her mother and father died when she was four, and she was left scarred and weakened. Tekakwitha took a vow of virginity and devoted her life to teaching prayers to children and helping the sick and the aged. On her deathbed, her last words were "Iesos konoronkwa"—"Jesus, I love you." Two Jesuit priests and her Indian friends said the ugly smallpox scars disappeared from her face. She died in 1680 at the age of twenty-four and was buried on the site of the reservation where Diane's grandmother and mother were born. Known as the Lily of the Mohawks, Tekakwitha was declared venerable in 1943 and was beatified in 1980 by the Roman Catholic Church. She is one step away from sainthood, and Diane loved her story so much she wanted it to be part of her daughter's life. For Kateri's baptism, King planned to dress her daughter in a traditional Indian buckskin outfit. She couldn't wait for the child to grow so she could share with her the story of her namesake.

The birth announcement had an Indian flair. It read

> Another special blessing . . .
> Another Special Baby!
> But this time the Creator sent a girl . . . as beautiful as our son Marler.

Despite the demands of career and family, Diane also had a strong social conscience. She would do stories on a particular issue she cared about, then get personally involved in volunteer work. She had been president of the Denver chapter of the National Organization for Native American Women, and had worked at a Catholic Outreach soup kitchen in Colorado. At her first job at KRMA, she helped with a program called *Senior Showcase* and did community work for senior citizens. While in Grand Junction, she researched a story and got involved in Partners, a program similar to Big Brothers or Big Sisters. It pairs adult role models with troubled teens. Most of the kids are referred by the Colorado Department of Social Services, or juvenile courts and schools. They usually come from a single-parent household with a history of child abuse, drug or alcohol abuse, and minor crimes. The minimum commitment to be a Partner to one of these troubled kids was three hours a week for at least one year. Diane and Brad did such a good job with one kid that they were selected as "Partners of the Year." Because of her position at KJCT, Diane also helped with publicity about Partners. She was the hostess for an annual TV auction that raised money for the cause.

In Michigan, King served on the board of directors of the Salvation Army. An advisory committee recommended her as a board member, and Major John Homer asked her if she had an interest in helping. "She said yes immediately. No hesitation. She wanted to get involved in the community and meet the needs of the people. She was extremely outgoing, friendly, caring, and very willing to help. Anytime we needed anybody, she was quick and eager to help," Homer said. The Salvation Army had tapped King to be their Christmas chairperson for 1991. It would be her distinguished responsibility to line up the bell-ringers for the kettle collections, which would buy toys for needy children, food and shelter for the homeless, clothing for the poor, and medical help for addicts and alcoholics.

Diane also became active in the Food Bank of Southwest Michigan after she had done a story about hunger and children. Battle Creek, the birthplace of the breakfast-food industry, is the home of Kellogg Company, the Post cereal division of General Foods Corporation, and the Ralston-Purina Company. Diane was in charge of the task force to raise food from these corporate giants and distribute it to the needy. Her campaign to help kids had the theme, "You can be there when a child is hungry." It was printed on posters and grocery bags all around town. Also, Diane organized a campaign to collect canned goods for a program called Second Harvest, which distributed food in rural areas through the church pantries and small towns in the eight counties around Battle

Creek. She helped anyway she could, whether it was doing public service announcements on WUHQ or showing up in a sweat shirt and jeans to bag food. Brad sometimes helped her with pickups and deliveries. "She could organize and orchestrate a campaign, but she was very unpretentious. She was incredibly exuberant and cheerful," said the food bank director Robert Randels. "She was so full of life."

CHAPTER 3

The call seemed so harmless that nobody remembers precisely when it came in. It was camouflaged as a compliment, arriving among the news tips, story ideas, complaints from viewers, and the routine weeds TV reporters hack through daily in the pursuit of stories.

A few days after the Fourth of July in 1990, the telephone jangled at WUHQ-TV, Channel 41. On the line was a star-struck stranger calling for Diane Newton King.

"News room," said Diane.

"Hi, Diane. I watch you on the news and I admire your work. I've always wanted to be in TV news, and I'd really appreciate any advice you have about getting started," the caller said.

The male voice was unfamiliar, but it struck two receptive chords. First, like most people who make a living in front of the camera, Diane enjoyed being watched and appreciated. There's nothing like a little outside validation to massage the ego, and Diane's needed stroking from time to time. And second, having a newcomer approach *her* for career advice, well, that was delicious irony.

She told the caller to enroll in some courses at a community college, watch some newscasts for pointers, polish his writing, and be willing to work hard. After a pleasant enough chat with someone she didn't know, Diane hung up and went back to work.

Then the guy called back, within minutes, asking the same questions. Boy, this was odd, she thought. And she made a quick transition from being willing to help to being annoyed.

Over the next few weeks, the anonymous fan pestered Diane with more phone calls—two or three times a week. He'd always say the same things. The mystery man also said he wanted to have lunch with Diane because he thought she was pretty. This was too much. Diane had mastered the art of giving someone the brush-off, and this guy was about to get it.

"There's no reason to have lunch with you. I've helped you all I can. There's nothing more I can do. I am very busy. I can't accept these calls at work. Please don't call me anymore," Diane said, hanging up.

Diane also told station management some creep was bothering her. She didn't recognize the voice, but his speech was slow, as if he were on some drug or trying to disguise it somehow. Larry Neinhaus, the news director whose desk was next to King's, began screening phone calls. It was not so much out of a sense of alarm but to keep some crackpot from bothering a busy worker. And in August, the calls seemed to stop.

"We never saw them as a serious problem," Neinhaus said. "They were more of an annoyance. She wasn't afraid, and we weren't afraid for her that there was any imminent threat. The guy wanted to have some kind of relationship. He wanted to meet with her and get to know her better. She was uncomfortable with that. It started to bug her."

Neinhaus intercepted some of the calls, and when he asked to take a message, the caller said things like, "I'd rather speak to Diane." He never left a name or address. Neinhaus also noticed a halting feature in the voice, as if the man were insecure or something. Family and friends tried to defuse Diane's fears by joking that maybe it was the janitor, or her boss checking up on her. Diane tried to shrug it off but got more flustered with each call. At one point, she even confronted her husband and asked, "Are you trying to play a sick joke on me?"

Brad pleaded innocent. And Diane dismissed the notion that the person closest to her in life would be responsible for something that was upsetting her.

In the instant world of TV news, things become ancient history in a hurry. The calls stopped coming because of the informal screen at the station, and everyone forgot about them. Then one day in October, the nuisance returned in a terrifying way.

It was Tuesday, October 30. After work that day, eight months into her pregnancy, Diane stopped to pick up Marler at the Child Development Center on Territorial Road. Marler stayed in day care because Brad had a part-time job teaching classes at Western Michigan University in Kalamazoo. And during this semester, Brad was away on Tuesdays and Thursdays.

Before going to the farmhouse, Diane stopped in Marshall to visit Cindy Acosta, a friend and colleague who had worked at WUHQ before Diane was hired. Acosta still did the morning cut-ins if Diane was off and she also worked on some special projects.

After a friendly visit, Diane left at about four-thirty for the brief drive out to the farmhouse. When the Kings first moved to Michigan, they rented a townhouse apartment at 200 Rambling Road in Battle Creek. But since April, they had moved to Division Drive south of Marshall to the idyllic spot that seemed immune to the world's ugly dangers. The entire 500-acre estate is known as the old Schaefer farm. Much of the land is leased out to farmers who grow wheat and corn; about two hundred acres is a stand of Michigan hardwoods. The property has two large ponds—Crystal Lake and Zinn Lake—plus a stream called Talmadge Creek running through the property. Because the owner prohibited hunting on his land, the population of white-tailed deer had exploded. Herds of seventy-five or more have been counted in the open fields. It was almost like living on a nature preserve.

The house where the Kings lived included an old horse barn and several outbuildings, including a silo. What used to be the dairy barn had collapsed on itself in a pile of rubble. The house was in a state of disrepair and required some fixing up, and the Kings exchanged some home improvements for breaks on the rent. That helped a budget that always seemed to be strained. Marler loved the open space. He already had a sandbox, a toy tractor, and toy lawn mower. Diane had plans for planting a garden in the spring, and she talked about getting a lamb, a horse, and some chickens for Marler. The farm was a way of getting back in touch with the land. She had lived on a farm as a young child, and it almost seemed as if she were re-creating an idealized slice of her own life.

The last thing Diane expected to find in the black mailbox at the end of her unpaved driveway was a threat.

A hand-delivered note comprised of letters cut out of a magazine and pasted onto a sheet of paper read, "You should have gone to lunch with me."

Diane was too frightened to go into the house, so she dashed back to Cindy Acosta's house. This guy knew where she lived. She wondered if he had been tailing her and for how long.

Crying hysterically, Diane gave the handmade note to her friend. Acosta showed the letter to her husband, Juan, before calling the Calhoun County Sheriff's Department. Then Diane called Brad at Western Michigan University, where he was teaching part-time while he pursued his doctorate. This fall, he had classes on Tuesday and Thursday nights she knew, so he would be at the campus in Kalamazoo at this particular time. Diane left a message because Brad wasn't in his office, and she also called to leave a message on the answering machine at home in case he failed to get the word at work.

Sergeant Al Lemkuehle arrived at the Acosta home at six-fourteen P.M. to examine the note. He put on gloves to keep his fingerprints off—although Diane, Cindy, and Juan had handled it already—and placed it in a plastic bag. Lemkuehle also accompanied a sobbing Diane back to the farmhouse to make sure no intruders were there. He searched for evidence of a break-in and checked all the rooms in the house. When he returned to the station to write a report so the detectives could get working on the case, Diane went back to Cindy's house. Brad got there at about nine-thirty P.M.

It was an emotional time. Cindy left the couple alone so Diane could tell her husband everything that had happened. When they emerged from their private talk, Cindy thought Brad's reaction was a bit peculiar. He wasn't the kind to express much outward feeling. But it seemed odd that he showed no shock, anger, or outrage at the threatening note his wife had just received. The only thing he said was, "I wonder how the station's going to handle this."

The Kings worked out a detailed security plan. They purchased a movement-sensitive security light for the farm. It was the kind that would click on if somebody was walking around, so if a stranger approached the house, it would be under the glare of the light. Diane's sister, Darlene, gave her a guard dog, a brown Doberman pinscher puppy named Penny. Brad balked because he was allergic to dogs. They had a black French poodle when they moved into their Battle Creek apartment, but it had died suddenly. Brad theorized it had swallowed a poisonous tree frog. But he relented and accepted the Doberman, sometimes tethering it to a tree in the yard but mostly keeping it penned in the barn. Diane stationed the dog nearer the house when Brad was away.

Most importantly, the Kings had a strict ritual. Whenever Diane returned home, she honked the horn and sat in the car until Brad appeared and gave the all-clear sign. And if Brad wasn't home, she stayed in the car and waited for him. Sometimes, she asked friends to come over or went to stay with Cindy Acosta or other friends. When she returned home, she circled the lawn around the house in her Jeep, visually inspecting windows and doors to make sure no one had broken in. She felt like a prisoner in her own house. At dusk, she peeked out from behind drawn shades to make sure no strangers were lurking about. She asked sheriff's deputies to check the grounds periodically. The Kings even mulled over putting up a fence.

"She was afraid, and I was afraid for her," said her mother, Freida Newton.

Diane was so upset the morning after finding the note that she couldn't do the news. WUHQ went to its own lengths to make sure this obsessed fan didn't pester her anymore. Receptionist Rita Gillson was instructed to screen all phone calls going into the newsroom. She was told to send any calls for Diane through to Larry Neinhaus. If he wasn't available, the calls were directed to Mark Crawford, the station's vice president. Once a man called and asked for "Diana." Rita put the call through to Neinhaus, who told her, "I think that's the guy."

But when the guy talked to Neinhaus, he offered nothing about who he was or what he wanted. When Neinhaus asked if he wanted to leave a message, the caller refused and said, "I'd rather talk to Diane." Then he hung up.

"He only called one or two times after that. I recognized his voice. He asked for Diana. After thirteen years as a receptionist, I got to know my voices," she said. "I knew Brad's voice. He'd call often, sometimes right after Diane had finished the news. She'd be walking by my desk and I'd say it's your husband. And she'd say, 'Oh, he's my best critic.' "

Nobody could say for sure if this was the same caller who started this madness in July. He never left his name, number, or a message.

And because Diane arrived at five o'clock each morning for work, WUHQ installed extra security lights in the parking lot and made sure no one was lurking there in the mornings. In addition, Mark Crawford adjusted his schedule to come in earlier so Diane wasn't there alone.

Just like athletes or movie stars or pop singers who

attract the public spotlight, media personalities are often targets of infatuated fans. Nobody talks about it much for fear it will encourage copycats, but it comes with the territory. On one hand, popularity means higher ratings and more money. On the other, it can be a major annoyance—or worse—if some captivated fool gets carried away. In Diane's case, she entered thousands of homes each morning via the airwaves and total strangers were acquainted with a version of her. Maybe there was a warped soul out there who thought he actually knew her. But being stalked seemed as implausible as a Hollywood plot line, like a twisted version of *Play Misty For Me.*

David Letterman has been stalked. So has Johnny Carson, Michael J. Fox, Janet Jackson, and lots of celebrities. But stalking is more than a nuisance, it has become the crime of the technological age. More than thirty states have laws against stalking, including California, which in 1990 became the first state to outlaw the practice of following, harassing, or posing a threat of bodily harm to someone. The problem for police is whether to intervene if no crime has been committed. The Los Angeles Police Department, charged with protecting Hollywood's Tinsel Town stars, even created a special squad to deal with stalkers. They learned a painful lesson in the case of actress Rebecca Schaeffer, killed by a stalker on the doorstep of her Hollywood apartment on July 18, 1989. Schaeffer, star of the TV series *My Sister Sam,* was murdered by a 357 slug fired at point-blank range into her chest by Robert John Bardo. A nineteen-year-old high school dropout who had never lost his virginity, Bardo dogged Schaeffer for two years. He became infatuated when Schaeffer answered one of his fan letters and signed it "Love, Rebecca." The smitten fan once traveled from his home in Arizona to a

Burbank film studio carrying a bouquet of flowers and a five-foot-tall teddy bear for Schaeffer, but a security guard turned him away. Bardo claimed he worshipped the actress. Eventually his uncontrollable obsession turned violent. He formed his plan of attack after reading a *People* magazine article about how stalker Arthur Jackson used a private detective to track actress Theresa Saldana, who was brutally stabbed and slashed on the face by her infatuated admirer. Bardo paid the detective $300 to locate Schaeffer through the California department that handles driver's licenses. Because he was too young at nineteen to buy a gun in Arizona, Bardo had his older brother purchase a 357 Magnum for him. Then the killer took a bus from his home in Tucson to Los Angeles, wandered around for a time, and went to Schaeffer's apartment. He rang the buzzer, handed her a note, and left. An hour later, after ordering onion rings and cheesecake at a diner, Bardo returned, carrying a red-and-white plastic bag that included the gun, extra bullets, a compact disk of U2's "The Joshua Tree" and a copy of J. D. Salinger's novel *The Catcher in the Rye.* The book, published in 1951, tells the story of a prep school dropout's search for self-understanding and meaning in his life. A copy of the book was also carried by Mark David Chapman, the man who shot and killed John Lennon in 1980. Chapman got Lennon's autograph on an album cover hours before he gunned him down outside his Dakota apartment building. When Schaeffer appeared again, Bardo fired the pistol into her chest. A hollow-point cartridge engineered to do maximum damage tore through her body. After Bardo killed Schaeffer, he hopped the bus back to Arizona, where police tracked him down. He was convicted of first-degree murder in 1991 and sentenced to life in prison without parole.

* * *

Diane King was filled with unanswered questions. Was some guy following her? Had he been slinking around the house? Had she met this guy in public? Would he threaten her son? Every time she made a move, she wondered if a stranger's eyes were on her. The feeling hounded her when she drove to the bank, or went to the market, or browsed at the mall, or sat down at a restaurant. When driving, she glanced furtively into the rear-view mirror in case she was being tailed.

And all this was happening in the late stages of her pregnancy, which only made her more hyper. She was an excitable person under normal circumstances, and the hormonal changes heightened her fears. Plus, like any expectant mother, she worried that harm might come to the child if a stalker confronted her.

Diane also had a dark and nagging suspicion. Maybe it was Brad.

A small station like WUHQ tends to operate as a family. People get to know each other really well and develop relationships. And Diane found a mother figure in Nancy Gwynne, the sixty-year-old woman who worked in the accounting department. Nancy's father was the chief of military police at Fort Custer in World War II; as a child, she had played with the German POWs. Diane was so outgoing and so much fun to be around, Nancy felt naturally drawn to her. Most mornings, after Diane's last cut-in at eight-thirty, she'd grab a cup of coffee and migrate to Nancy's office, where the two women shared their most intimate secrets.

After the October 30 letter arrived, Diane sat down with Nancy and cried.

"It could be Brad just pulling another of his tricks to keep me in line. Why would he want to hurt me this way?" Diane sobbed. She pointed out the letter was neither stamped nor postmarked, which meant the federal authorities couldn't be called in.

She shared her fears with other close associates, including Stella Pamp, a Chippewa Native American whom Diane had met at a weekend powwow in Burlington, Michigan. They had developed something close to a mother-daughter relationship. It seemed that every time Diane had a problem, she was on the phone to Stella. And soon after the letter arrived, Stella got a call from Diane at the station.

"You want to come have supper with me?" Diane asked.

Stella detected the quiver in her friend's voice. "Diane, what's wrong?"

"I need somebody to talk with. I need to have somebody stay with me. I really need to talk to you," Diane said. She was crying, and this was one of the days Brad was teaching.

Stella drove from her home in Battle Creek out to Marshall. She found Diane with Kameron Knowlton, a neighbor girl who Diane had called over because she didn't want to go into her house alone. Diane took the neighbor home, then sat down with her friend. She talked of how disgusted she was that the person who sent the letter and made the calls had forced her to alter her life.

"It just makes me mad to think somebody can control your life like that," Diane said. "To be always looking over your shoulder, to think somebody's following you."

"It's probably nothing really," Stella said, trying to reassure her. "But if you are concerned, I'll come and stay with you until Brad comes home."

Then Diane blurted out, "I just think this is a bad joke

Brad's playing on me. It sounded like his voice on the phone."

Stella didn't quite know what to say. Brad wasn't the type to be a practical jokester.

But once again, Diane shoved aside her misgivings and went on with her protective plan. It was almost as if she couldn't bring herself to believe her husband would do something like this. And she wasn't going to take any chances.

A short time later, on a Thursday night when Brad again was teaching, Diane called Stella from the station and asked her to come out to Marshall. Stella found her sitting in the driveway in her car. The two of them drove around the house to make sure the windows weren't disturbed. Only when she was convinced that things looked okay did Diane venture into the house.

"She would never get out of the car if Brad wasn't home. She would either sit in the driveway or go stay with one of her friends. She was really scared," Stella said.

Someone even closer to Diane than Nancy and Stella was Regina Zapinski, the person she called her best friend. Regina drove out from the Detroit area to spend some time so Diane wouldn't be alone. "Every time a car drove past, we'd both look out the window," Regina recalled.

Almost everybody who knew Diane witnessed how upset she was and how seriously she took the threat. On November 9, ten days after the letter appeared in her mailbox, Diane noticed a car following her after she left work to pick up Marler at the Child Development Center. Glancing nervously in the rearview mirror, she noticed a 1980 Ford Thunderbird with two youths inside. The car seemed to be right on her tail. And what really spooked her was it followed her when she turned onto Territorial Road, where the day-care center was located. When Diane went inside to pick up Marler, she called the Battle Creek Police Department. She told Elizabeth Way, who worked at the Child Development Center, that it may have just been two kids playing a game with her, but she was calling the police just in case. Officer Jennifer Joyner responded to the call, and she discovered that the Thunderbird belonged to Dawn Campo, who lived at 1915 West Territorial Road. Her son and a friend had taken the car, and it was just a coincidence that they had followed Diane to the same street. Even though there was nothing to the incident, Joyner filed a report because Diane told her of the phone calls and the letter.

All of this was happening when Diane was pregnant. She did her last news show on a Friday, announcing to her viewers she was going to deliver a baby and would be on leave. Four days later, she gave birth to Kateri.

But even while she was on a sixty-day maternity leave from WUHQ, King couldn't drop her guard, not even on getaway weekends. On December 11, she visited her sister, Denise Verrier, to show off her new daughter. She stayed overnight, but she didn't come home the next day as she had planned. Brad called at 8:37 A.M. to say that someone had tried to pry open the door to the house. He found pry marks on the door jamb.

"Don't come home," he told his wife. "Someone tried to break in last night. I've been up all night walking around with a gun."

Then at 9:15 A.M., Brad called the Calhoun County Sheriff's Department to report an attempted break-in. Deputy Jim Gieske drove out to 16240 Division Drive to investigate. Brad said his wife was very nervous after receiving threats over the phone and via a letter, so he was in the habit of often checking the house for possible indications of trouble. In checking his rear door, Brad discovered some pry marks on the dead-bolt lock. Gieske checked out the scratches, but noticed there were no indentations in the wood trim around the door or on the wood of the door itself.

Brad pointed out that he had just installed the wood trim four days earlier and the marks must have been made the previous day because he and Diane weren't home that day.

But something else was troubling Gieske. The top half of the door was comprised of small glass panes. If someone wanted to break in, all he had to do was knock out one of the glass panes, reach in, and open the bolt. Also, most times people break into houses by kicking in the door.

Brad figured whoever did this was trying to enter the house on the sly—without being detected. It could be someone planning to lay in wait for Diane.

Gieske didn't think so. The deputy noted that Brad's compound hunting bow and arrows were hanging on a nail near the door. If someone had broken in, he would have taken the bow and arrows. Brad didn't have an explanation. Gieske told him that he didn't think the scratches came from someone trying to break in, but if it would make Brad feel better, Gieske would make a report.

The one-page report noted

> It appears that an object similar to a small screw driver was pushed between the door jamb and door and used in an attempt to push the dead bolt back.

Under the heading of suspects, it read

> None at this time; however, Mr. King's wife has been the receiver of threatening mail and this may be related.

He passed the report on to Jack Schoder, one of the county's two detectives.

Diane returned with her two children on December 13, the day of WUHQ's Christmas party. She was on maternity leave, but she came to the station to visit with Nancy Gwynne. Diane cried when she told her about the break-in, but Nancy was startled at the reason.

"Brad called me and told me somebody tried to break in. He told me not to come home and he was patrolling with a gun. Nobody broke in. I think Brad was trying to scare me again. Why would he call me up and frighten me?" Diane said.

"Well, it does seem strange he'd stay up all night with a gun. If somebody did try to break in, they wouldn't come back that same night," Nancy answered.

"I can't live with these lies anymore, Nancy."

But once again, Diane dismissed her own thoughts about her husband. Every time somebody came over to visit, Brad showed them the scratches on the door jamb. He pointed it out to neighbors and his in-laws. He figured this was a legitimate attempt at a break-in. Brad also gave the police a copy of a letter a fan had sent Diane back in July asking her for an autographed picture. The station had a policy not to fill such requests, but maybe the fan was connected to the calls or the letter somehow. The sheriff's department said it would check it out. It hadn't made much progress on the letter yet; it still hadn't obtained fingerprints from Juan Acosta so it could eliminate background prints.

Meanwhile, whenever Diane called her old friends to

tell them about her new daughter, she also mentioned the star-struck stranger. Debbie Rich, her old colleague at KJCT, remembered such a conversation.

"She's a pretty strong person, but that's pretty freaky. She was nervous about it. You hear too many things about freaky people. Being in the public eye, you never know," Rich said.

In mid-January, King also called her old KJCT boss, Jan Hammer, to discuss some career matters. Toward the end of the conversation, Hammer learned of the anonymous suitor who had been a pain for the past six months.

"Well, you're all right then?" he asked.

"Yeah, but I've had this nut calling me."

"Oh?"

"Yes, this guy's been calling the office and he left a note in my mailbox saying that I'll be sorry because I didn't have lunch with him."

Hammer was not really alarmed, he says now. "This is not uncommon in our business. People get infatuated with news reporters. Some even send love letters. I didn't really pursue it with Diane. I assumed it had just started recently."

A neighbor also was aware of King's anxiety. Joanne Karaba lived on Division Drive, although her home was separated from Diane's by Interstate 69, a north-south four-lane highway. The two women became acquainted at the market in the summer and discovered some things they had in common: both were interested in Native-American culture and both had done some modeling.

Karaba's son, River, was a year younger than Diane's son, Marler, but the two boys made good playmates. All of them attended an Indian powwow—a celebration of Indian customs, culture and cuisine—at Burlington in

August, and they had been to each other's homes several times. Shortly after Christmas, the mothers took their sons to a *Disney On Ice* skating show in Kalamazoo, about 35 miles from Marshall. In her position at WUHQ, King was host for the show and did the driving that night, leaving Kateri with a baby-sitter. Along the way, when they weren't listening to a cassette tape of Dr. Martin Luther King Jr.'s favorite spiritual "We Shall Overcome," the conversation turned to the strange calls and the letter King had received. The caller's voice was slow and deliberate, and every word was precise.

"I thought it was Brad playing a sick joke," King told her companion. Both of them laughed when she said it.

When the kids got tired, the women left the world of Disney make-believe at eight-thirty P.M. for the drive home. King stopped at the baby-sitter's to pick up Kateri, then drove to her house to drop off her kids. When Karaba started to get out of the car in the darkened driveway, King stopped her.

"Don't go," King said.

She sounded the horn, and Brad appeared from the house to take the kids.

"She did not want me to get out because she was scared," Karaba said.

A similar episode occurred February 3. The two women went to the food auction in Battle Creek, arriving back at the King residence at dusk.

"I started to get out again, and she said to just wait. She waited until the light came on and Brad appeared and came out," Karaba said. "I never saw anybody that scared."

Four days later, Diane left for Sterling Heights with her son and daughter after she did the Thursday morning news. She had requested Friday off from the station so she could attend a speech given by General Eva Burrows, the international leader of the Salvation Army who had come from London, England, to dedicate a new headquarters in the Detroit area. But the kids weren't feeling well, and she never made the February 8 dedication. Besides, she seemed preoccupied.

Diane's older brother, Gordon Marler, was getting married in a month. And Diane spent February 8 shopping with her future sister-in-law, Mary Kozak. She helped Mary pick out Gordon's gold wedding band from the Service Merchandise store. At Winkleman's, where women's clothes were on sale, Diane must have tried on thirty dresses before she settled on a red dress with a white lapel to wear to her brother's wedding. She also bought a similar dress in green for the upcoming christening of her newborn daughter, Kateri. Diane hadn't gotten her figure back yet, so she had to buy a size 9 instead of the size 7 she wore before her pregnancy. She made Mary swear not to tell anyone she had to buy the larger size.

This was an all-day shopping trip, lasting from ten A.M. to four P.M., and Diane also looked in Sears for a down coat for Brad.

"She tried on tons of dresses. We were laughing so much. The store must have thought we were crazy. She had my hand, and she had me running through the mall," Mary said.

But at times, the two women talked about serious matters. Her future sister-in-law inquired about the man who had called her at the station and sent that letter.

"Whatever happened to that guy? Have you heard anything more?" Mary asked.

"I just have to go on with my life. I can't worry about it. Brad and I have worked out this security system, and it seems to be working. I haven't heard anything further," Diane said.

On Saturday, Diane made baskets with her cousin, Elaine Wash. Diane had three baskets to show off—one for her daughter, Kateri, a black-and-white one for her mother, Freida, and a green-and-white one in the colors of Michigan State University. This one was for Diane's stepdaughter, Alissa King, who was a child of Brad's first marriage and was a student at MSU.

While working on the crafts, Elaine also mentioned the anonymous troublemaker.

"Why don't you just load a gun and keep it on top of the refrigerator?" Elaine asked.

"I can't live my life looking over my shoulder. I've just got to go on," Diane said.

She was supposed to visit her sister Denise in nearby Mount Clemens that afternoon. But she spent so much time with her cousin that she put off the trip. Diane and Elaine left Freida's house at the same time that Saturday, but Diane never reached her own door.

CHAPTER 4

"Trouble" calls always seem to come at the most inconvenient times for the police. They always seem to happen on holidays, days off, or family moments. No wonder cops have such high divorce rates. Jack Schoder, one of the two detectives on the force of the Calhoun County Sheriff's Department, hadn't been out for an evening with his wife in two years, so he was looking forward to the Valentine's Dance on Saturday, February 9, sponsored by the Fraternal Order of Police. Lots of his colleagues from Battle Creek and other jurisdictions in the county were gathering at the George Armstrong Custer American Legion Post No. 56 on Columbia Avenue in Battle Creek. Arriving shortly after eight P.M., he had ordered a Seagram's and Coke and had downed about a third of it when he was called to the phone. "I didn't even get to sit down," he said. He should have been used to it. His dad, Paul Schoder, was a lifetime cop and former Calhoun County sheriff.

It was headquarters. A woman had been shot and

killed at 16240 Division Drive. She was Diane Newton King, the TV reporter from WUHQ. Schoder left word for Jim Statfeld, his detective partner, who was also due at the FOP dance. Then Schoder headed home to get his squad car before heading to Marshall. It would be twenty-eight hours before he saw a bed. Just five weeks earlier, he had been called out to investigate the death of Carolyn Holdridge, age fifty-four, of Albion. She was found in the burnt rubble of her home, but an autopsy showed she had been shot multiple times. The fire was set to cover up the murder, and Schoder had spent the past weeks sifting the ashes through a screen in a search for clues. None were ever found.

When Statfeld got the messages at the American Legion, his first thought was that somebody was playing a practical joke to get him to leave the party. But he called the station to discover he wouldn't be sleeping for a while.

Time is critical in a murder investigation. If a suspect can be identified and located within the first seventy-two hours, the better the chances are of making an arrest and getting a conviction. Diane King had already been taken away by the ambulance, so there was no corpse to glimpse. But every arriving cop wanted to view the spot where the body was found. This woman was a celebrity, a TV news reporter. And this was rural Calhoun County, not some homicide-by-the-hour killing zone like Detroit.

The facts known at this time were as follows. The children were in the car at the time of the shooting, but their view of things was limited because they were strapped in their car seats and they were too young to realize what was going on. Their father had left them tethered to their seats when he called the police, and in all the activity, they had remained there untended until well past the time the ambulance left. All this time, Brad made no move to retrieve them, even when it became apparent Diane had been shot. Finally, three hours after their mother had placed them in their seats for the drive home, Brad emerged from the house to bring them inside and change their soiled underclothes. Brad sat them on the couch as Sergeant Harold Badger began the delicate chore of questioning a bereaved husband about the shooting death of his wife.

There didn't appear to be any witnesses that could provide any helpful information. Brad King said he went out for a walk at about six o'clock on the farm grounds. He heard some gunshots, which he didn't think was unusual because despite the hunting ban the area was frequented by rabbit hunters and deer poachers. When he returned home forty-five minutes later, he found his wife in the driveway and dialed the operator to get help. There was nothing suspicious in what King said, but the way he behaved struck Badger wrong. "He seemed kind of distant to what was taking place. It just didn't seem right to me," said Badger.

Robbery wasn't a motive. Diane's wallet was found in the driveway with cash and cards inside. Nothing was missing from the house. There didn't seem to be any signs of a struggle. From all indications, the dead woman never saw this coming.

So the cops began to look for signs that could tell them what happened, or at least pieces of what happened. It's true of every crime scene: whoever was there left something behind and took something away. That's why there are no perfect crimes. But it's also true that every cop on the scene can bring something with him to contaminate the picture or take something away that could be a critical piece of evidence. That's why there are no perfect investigations either.

Deputy Guy Picketts, the first person on the scene, remembered the open door in the barn and went to investigate. Accompanied by Sergeant Bagder and Deputy William Lindsay, he moved passed a tack room in the barn and shined a flashlight on Penny the Doberman, who had been quiet and unnoticed. In the second-story loft, Picketts noted the twelve-inch opening on the sliding white door. The way Diane's Wagoneer was parked, the gap provided a perfect line of fire for a sniper. With the help of a flashlight, Picketts found a spent casing for a .22 caliber bullet. It was barely visible because the brass blended in with the straw strewn about the place. Without disturbing the casing, Picketts borrowed a ballpoint pen from Badger and lay it near the casing so he could find it again. Somebody had left something behind.

At 7:55 P.M., well past dark, Trooper Gary Lisle of the Michigan State Police arrived with his tracking dog, a black-and-tan German shepherd named Travis. The oldest working canine team at the Battle Creek post, Lisle and Travis were more than partners. The dog lived with his handler and traveled everywhere with him. They were like family and had been together for ten years, ever since Travis was six months old and the two trained at Fort Custer, the old Army base where WUHQ was located. The trooper and dog had worked about 1,000 tracks in those years, and Travis had never failed a yearly recertification from the state police. On this night, Lisle got Travis out of the pen in the back of his station wagon and put the dog in a harness with a twenty-foot lead. They were directed to the barn where the bullet was found. Lisle let the dog cast about for human scents. When Travis found one, he put his nose down and wagged his tail. The higher a tracking dog's tail goes, the fresher the scent is. So when Travis's tail jumped up smartly, Lisle figured the person they were looking for had been there not much longer than an hour ago. A German shepherd works differently from a bloodhound, which gets a scent from a piece of clothing and then follows one specific person. The shepherd locates a trail and follows it without knowing specifically whom he is tracking. This trail started to the left of the casing, which is the way a spent bullet would eject from a bolt-action rifle fired by a right-handed shooter. With Lisle carrying a flashlight in blackness, Travis took off down a steep pair of steps to the first floor of the barn. If Penny the Doberman hadn't barked as the team made its way out of the barn, Lisle would never have known she was there. Travis ignored the bark and stayed hard at work. Picketts, who knew the grounds, accompanied Lisle and Travis for a time before he was called back to the house.

When Travis emerged from the barn, he turned left in a southerly direction along an old farm lane, or two-track, that was once the route of plow horses and tractors from the barn to the fields. It went past some outbuildings, a silo with a shaky roof, and an old dairy barn that had collapsed into its foundation. Man and dog came to a flimsy bridge made of a telephone pole and a two-by-six spanning Talmadge Creek, the stream that runs north and west through the property. The creek is only about two feet wide at this point, so it's easy to step across. The trooper noted a frozen impression of a boot heel on the pole.

Across the creek, the underbrush got thicker. Travis followed the trail along a fence line, where Lisle spotted two more boot prints—one facing south and one facing north. It was as if the person they were tracking was indecisive about which way to go. Dogs are natural hunters, so they always follow a scent in the freshest direction. Soon, the trail turned sharply to the east and into a marshy area. The underbrush was so thick a man would have to stoop down to duck under branches. And this ground was black Michigan peat, so if you stepped in a soft spot, you could sink up to your knees. Somebody coming this way must have known where he was going. The track followed a path worn down by deer, which, like humans, are creatures of habit and tend to walk over familiar ground. Lisle found another boot impression in the freezing mud and snow. It looked similar to the earlier ones he had seen.

Now the track had circled around again to Talmadge Creek, and when he got to the water, Travis exhibited a higher level of excitement. Lisle let go of the leash to let the dog cross back to the other side, and he went farther down the bank to jump across. He figured something worth checking out was nearby, but it was dark and he was still on a trail. So he took a roll of toilet paper from his jacket and wrapped half of it around a bush; he carries the paper for just such a purpose. Using his portable radio, he contacted the deputies back at the house and told them about the spot he marked.

"Be sure to check this area out real good when you get down this way."

Travis kept going east across a mowed field, then he headed north back toward Division Drive. He emerged from the field and crossed to the north side of the road, where he proceeded west back in the direction of the Kings' farmhouse. The trail was coming full circle. Then the dog crossed to the south side of the road and went into the driveway where Diane had been shot. It was at this point, about fifty feet from the barn where the track started, that Travis lost the scent. The entire track was about 380 yards. Dogs track best in tall grass and shrubs, which hold human scent. The toughest surfaces are roads and drives. And all sorts of ambulances, rescue vehicles, and police cars had been on the King property.

Lisle tried to reestablish the track, taking Travis back across Division Drive and areas around the house and the fields, but the dog had no luck.

While all this was going on, Jack Schoder started his end of the investigation. A twenty-one-year veteran of the sheriff's department, Schoder was present with Sergeant Badger when Deputy Lindsay relayed the grim news from the hospital that Diane was dead. Bradford King promptly broke down and cried.

Schoder made three phone calls on King's behalf. The first was to Randy Wright, a lawyer in Birmingham, Michigan, and a brother with Brad in the Tau Kappa Epsilon fraternity when the two were undergraduate students at Western Michigan University. It was Wright who had introduced Diane and Brad in 1983, a year before they were married. The second call went to Brad's minister, Rev. David Robertson of the First Presbyterian Church in Battle Creek. Robertson wasn't home, so Schoder called the assistant pastor. Brad did not ask Schoder to call his in-laws.

The cops asked Brad to come into the station so they could get a statement. But who would stay with the kids? King looked up the number for Barb Elgutaa—a Native-American friend of Diane's. Told there had been a horrible accident, Elgutaa raced to the King house with her husband to find the place crawling with police. Inside, she found Marler and Kateri on the couch. The baby was crying. Brad was in the kitchen fixing a bottle when he looked up.

"Oh, Barb," he said. Then he broke into tears.

Elgutaa gathered up the baby. Brad carried Marler and an overnight bag to her car, and she and her husband drove to their home.

Brad rode into Marshall with Sergeant Badger in his squad car. At about nine-fifteen, he sat down in the squad room of the Calhoun County Sheriff's Department. Jack Schoder produced a microcasette recorder to take down Brad's statement; it's standard procedure for all statements to be recorded in a homicide investigation.

"I guess we just need to talk to you, Brad, here about anything we can that might help us shed some light on it. I guess in terms of what you heard or what you saw, or how you came upon this. I know it's going to be difficult to go through it so, so damn soon, but why don't we just start from there, Brad."

"Okay. Well, I went out for a walk. I don't know what time. Maybe six o'clock or a little after. I was home alone. My wife and kids were on their way home from Detroit."

"What were they doing?"

"Visiting Grandma."

"When did they leave, Brad?"

"They left Thursday, in the morning, after I went to the university. I think when I talked to her she said she left the house about ten-thirty."

"How long had she been planning on it?"

"Maybe two weeks."

"Who all knew she was going?"

"Ah, family in Detroit knew. As far as at work, I would guess probably everybody she works with knew she was gone."

"Her plans on when she was arriving back home, was that set when she left?"

"Well, it was set that she was coming home today. But the time wasn't set. In fact, I didn't know when she was coming home. She called me today, I don't know what time it was. Maybe noon. I don't know. Somewhere in there. She called me twice. She called me this morning sometime. Said she'd be leaving after she talked to her cousin, who was—she hadn't seen her in a while—who was coming over to her mother's. Then she called me later and said she was leaving later than she had planned because her cousin—she wanted to spend more time talking to her cousin. Anyway, she was gonna go to her sister's, cause her sister's kids wanted to see our kids. And then she was gonna come home. And I said, well, just let me know when you're coming home, when you leave, so I can kinda have an idea of when you'll get here."

"Sure."

"So her mother called me, and I think that was about four-thirty. And, ah, said Diane had just, and the kids had just left. I had been takin' a nap at that time."

"When the mom called there?"

"Yeah. I laid back down for a little while. Then I decided to take a walk, just kinda wake myself up. I usually take one back through the property whenever it's a nice day."

"How many acres you got back there, Brad?"

"Well, there's five hundred. It's not mine."

"When you went for your walk, ah, I guess I'm tryin' to think of, in terms of maybe hearin' somethin', or, how, where'd you go on your walk?"

"Ah, across the creek. Ahm, just straight down the lane, on the other side of the brush. It's a deer trail out in back there."

"Do you remember, as far as putting a time on this

thing, 'cause I don't have all the facts, you know. Just got called in on this. You remember what time it was you took off on your walk? Roughly."

"Around six o'clock. It was around then. I walked back a ways, and just kinda sat on one of the old bales of hay for a while. Decided it was startin' to get dark, probably be close to the time for them to come back, so I started walkin' back."

"So you're kinda just out there, catchin' a little peace and quiet, I guess, while you were out there. How far are you from the house? Quarter mile, half mile?"

"At least a half mile, if not more. Closer to a mile. I walked quite a ways. Hard to judge."

"Yeah, yeah, I don't know either. So you went back and just kinda sat, and then you figured it's about time for them to get gettin' back home."

"Yeah, it was, you know, dusk. Just startin' to darken up. You could still see good. I don't know what time it was. I didn't have a watch with me or anything. I just walked back. By the time I got back to the house, it had gotten a lot darker than when I started walkin' back."

"Yeah."

"Saw her layin' there, by the car. I ran over, grabbed her, called to her, shook her, and she was just motionless."

"Let me ask you, and it's an obvious question, I'm sure you would've mentioned it, but did you hear anything at all in the solitude of being out there?"

"No. I could hear the traffic from the expressway."

"That's it, huh?"

"I thought I heard what was a gunshot, but it sounded like it came from way at the other end of the property."

"That's not unusual out in the country."

"No, I didn't pay any attention to it. I mean I was

hearin' them off and on all day today. People were, I don't know, rabbit huntin' or poachin' deer."

"Okay, you thought you heard one gunshot?"

"Yeah, but I didn't pay any attention to it. I didn't think anything about it. It sounded so far away. It sounded like it was from . . . away from the house."

"How many did you hear?"

"Just one."

"Didn't hear or see nothin' as far as walkin' up towards the house? Damn car door slam, or two doors slam? Tires peal out? Engines run?"

"Nope."

"Not a goddamn thing?"

"Nothin'. Totally quiet around there. Totally quiet, like it always is. My car was sittin' there. I walked up."

"So you went up, shook her, and she was kind of motionless. What'd you do then?"

"I cried. I knew something was wrong with her, called to her. I have the sheriff's department on speed dial. I could never remember what the number was, so I just pushed zero for the operator. I told them I wanted, needed the police, and then I don't remember much of the conversation. She gave me the Marshall Police Department. Seemed like it took forever."

"You got that speed dial thing, and forgot which one it was?"

"It's sittin' right by the phone, too. I guess I just wanted the police. Or somebody."

"Let me ask you, over the last few days, or few weeks, if there's been any strange activity at all in the neighborhood, anybody driving by that you've noticed, or that you and Diane have talked about?"

"No."

"Has she received any of these calls?"

"No."

"She's not received any of them for quite a while actually."

"No, true. But there was the letter."

"That goes back several months."

"Yeah, then there was the letter."

"Okay. Let's go around surrounding this trip and her getting home. She went to see her mom and dad and cousins and some relatives."

"She was gonna go to a conference. She's on the Salvation Army board in Battle Creek, and the head honcho was giving a talk at a conference, so she was going to listen to it. That was one of the reasons she was goin' to Detroit. I don't think anybody even on the board knew she was gonna go listen. Just something she decided on her own."

"Yeah."

"And it would be an opportunity to take the kids to see Grandma and Grandpa. She didn't talk to anybody other than me about it. And she just said, 'I'll be coming home Saturday,' and we hadn't settled on a time."

"I guess she didn't even know for sure what time she was coming."

"No. Called in the morning. Said she was coming after she had spent some time with her cousin. She called me back and she was going to be leaving later than she had thought originally."

"She was gonna let you know when she left?"

"Her mother called me."

"Yeah, okay. As far as, and I know we just spoke about it briefly, but as far as this threat from work. I guess it was actually last summer?"

"It was fall. Yeah. I was at the university when she called me when she found it. Maybe in October."

"And she's not brought that up or had any more problems though in the last few weeks?"

"No. Would've been on the phone with you if we had."

"Yeah, I talked to her not too long ago, you know."

"We always tried to be careful."

"You guys have a pet dog?"

"More like a lover than a dog. Still a puppy. She doesn't bark."

"Doesn't bark?"

"Only at animals. If you walk up she won't bark. She'll just jump up on you if she's loose."

"Was the dog loose when you went for your walk?"

"No, I didn't take her. I rarely, very rarely take her 'cause I'm afraid she'll chase down deer."

"So the dog was up in the barn?"

"She's chained up there by the barn. I only keep her loose when I'm there and outside. Keep an eye on her."

"I guess as far as Diane's daily routine, as far as she's been back to work for a few weeks now anyway."

"The first of the year. Well, the second day of the year."

"So what's her workday hours?"

"Leaves the house between four-thirty and five o'clock in the morning. Usually home by quarter to two."

"Who takes care of your children?"

"I do. Except on Thursday. They go to day care, because I have to leave for the university, and I drop them off."

"What do you do, Brad?"

"I teach at Western Michigan University."

"What, are you a professor?"

"I'm an instructor. I don't have my Ph.D. yet."

"How many classes do you teach over there?"

"I'm teaching one right now."

"So you only work one day a week?"

"Yeah. Last semester I had three."

"And that's your source of income?"

"Mm hm."

"So then you're around the house all the time?"

"Except Thursday. At least this semester. And I was only gone two days a week last semester. Tuesdays and Thursdays. The rest of the time I was around the house."

"And you got your own car and she's got a car?"

"Yeah."

"And if you're there, your car is parked . . ."

"Parked in the yard somewhere."

"You don't park in the barns?"

"No. Put her car in the barn at night. So it's not snow-covered in the morning."

"I guess I'm trying to think, if I was kind of watching the house and picking up on the routine—you know what I'm saying."

"Yeah, we're pretty routine, to tell you the truth. We tried not to be. There for a while we were doing a lot of varying things, and I think over time just kind of lapsed back into doing stuff."

"Yeah."

"I don't know what I'm gonna do." Brad was crying now.

"Yeah, it's a real difficult situation. To say the least."

"God, I loved livin' out there, but I don't know."

"Be pretty tough."

"I don't want to take the kids away from there. They love it. Well my son loves it so much." Brad sobbed heavier now.

"How old's your son?"

"He's three in March."

"Then you have the infant. Your mother-in-law's coming to get them?"

"Yeah, she's gonna watch them. That's gonna be a problem. I don't want them to go with her."

"Let me ask you, Brad. Can you just think of anything at all that might help us have an idea as to what the hell happened there? Any indication or any feelings you've been getting from Diane that . . ."

"No, in fact, last time we even discussed this problem was when she was home on maternity leave. Hadn't heard from this guy. We know if there's anybody strange around here. Kinda hard for us not to know if somethin's outta place. I would've had to notice it. If there was a lotta traffic . . . But as far as if there were someone trying to watch the place, you would know it."

"Yeah, there's no place to watch."

"No, there isn't. You would just know it. And I was outside almost all day."

"Were you?"

"Yeah, I was working on the porch. I was in and out of the house, in and out of the barn. The dog was loose today, all over the place."

"Okay, do you remember what time you laid down? Talking about taking a nap."

"What time did I say my mother-in-law called?"

"About four-thirty."

"I probably had been down a half hour, maybe an hour, I don't know, somewhere in there. I really didn't pay any attention to the clock."

"Right. You're not wearing a watch, I see."

"No, I carry a pocket watch in my jeans."

"Just so I know what's going on around the house. What time did you get up and go out and start dillydallying on the porch?"

"I was up before ten o'clock. I started workin' about ten o'clock. I got up at eight o'clock. That's pretty standard for me."

"Then you're outside, probably in and out."

"I went and got a McDonald's for lunch. Right after she called I went and got it."

"And then you're back outside working?"

"I ate it inside, then back outside working. Went over to the barn and let the dog loose again. I tied her up while I was gone."

"So your dog's loose, runnin' around. You're home. You're back out. You lay down."

"And then I went out and went for my walk. I took her over and hooked her back up on her chain."

"Tryin' to pin times down again. What caused you to think it was four-thirty when you got that phone call?"

"I looked at the clock on the VCR, to see what time it was, so that I would estimate when she was gonna get home."

"How long does that trip take?"

"Oh, about two hours and fifteen minutes, give or take."

"What I guess I'm tryin' to figure out is how long you were around that house. So if somebody's drivin' by there, seein' activity . . ."

"And I was around the house until around 6 o'clock. I went for my walk. I did not look at the clock. I just kinda looked outside and said well, if I'm going to go for a walk, I better do it now, it'll wake me up. By the time I get back, Diane and the kids will be coming home and we'll go get a pizza and have dinner."

"I'm thinkin' of somebody being around, you know, maybe window-peeking to find out what's going on."

"Before I left the house, I closed the blinds and turned

on the light in the living room. 'Cause it would be gettin' close to dark when I got back. I knew I wouldn't stay out after dark."

"What makes you think it's about six o'clock?"

"I'm just saying it was around six o'clock based on how light it was out. It was starting to get a little dark, but it was still pretty light out. I thought, well, a little twenty-minute walk and I'll be back in time."

"In time for Diane to . . ."

"Yeah. She won't have been home more than a minute, couple minutes, ten minutes or five minutes, and the truth is I figured I'd be back before she was."

"Yeah."

"I really didn't even think that she'd get home before me."

"Your house when you left, was it locked?"

"Just the bottom lock."

"Are there any guns in the house?"

"A shotgun."

"That's it?"

"Taken apart. It's a breakdown. Use it to hunt deer with."

"Okay. Let's see. You're in and around. Hell, you're in layin' down, in the house, the car's there. You got up at four-thirty, laid back down, watched TV for a few, out around six, still movin' around. Well, why don't we just end this here for now, okay?"

"All right."

Nobody in Sterling Heights had a clue as to what was going on. Diane always called her mother when she got home, just to let everyone know she and the kids were okay. As Freida Newton waited for a phone call from her daughter, she watched TV. She even dozed off for a time. But when she woke up at about 8:15, which was two hours past the time Diane should have been home, she figured she'd better call Marshall.

Brad answered with some frightful news. "There's been an accident. Diane's in the hospital."

"What kind of accident? Where are the kids? How badly is she hurt? What's going on?"

Her first thought was Diane had wrecked the car on the way home. Only a mother who has just been told her child was injured can know the terror that overcame Freida. It only made things worse when there were no answers to her questions.

Then she demanded, "Why aren't you with her?" Brad said the police wouldn't let him accompany Diane to the hospital and he had to watch the kids. But beyond that, he wasn't volunteering any information. The moment was a sad commentary on how strained the relationship was between Brad and his mother-in-law. A mutual dislike had festered for years. Freida, frustrated in the past at getting Brad to explain things, felt she wasn't getting anywhere with him now. "I'm coming out there," she said as she hung up the phone.

The shock and confusion of the moment caused paralysis of action. Freida roused her husband, Royal, who began calling hospitals and the police without learning much. He convinced Freida to sit tight until they had firm information. There was no use driving blindly into the night if nobody knew what was going on. It would be agonizing long hours before anyone learned anything, so in the gathering nightmare, Freida did what she routinely did in times of crisis. She gathered her family around her.

One of the first people Freida called was her oldest daughter, Darlene, who lived seven miles away in Utica.

"We raced over there. My mom just couldn't sit there by herself. She wanted us to be there," Darlene said. "She said Diane was hurt and was in the hospital. I just knew something more was wrong. We waited for hours and hours, calling the police station and the hospital. Nobody could tell us anything."

Eventually, the family discovered Diane had been taken to Oaklawn Hospital in Marshall. But nobody would release any information. Instead the family was instructed to call the sheriff's department. What would the sheriff's department have to do with this, they wondered. But the only people who knew anything were out at the farmhouse, so no information was available for the family. Finally, around eleven o'clock, they called the sheriff's department and got patched through to the squad room where Detective Schoder was questioning Brad. Schoder handed the phone to Brad, who simply said, "Diane's dead." Then he gave the phone back to Schoder.

Now the rest of the family had to be told. Donald and Denise Verrier had already tucked their four kids in for the night when Royal Newton called.

"Donald, you got to do something bad," Royal said.

Puzzled, Don had no idea what he was trying to say.

"You have to tell Denise that Diane's dead."

"What?"

"Diane's dead."

"How?"

"Don't know. All we know is she's dead."

Denise couldn't believe what Royal was saying and grabbed the phone.

"Where was Brad?" Denise asked.

"Out for a walk."

"A walk? Where's he at now?"

"The police are taking him to the station."

It was routine procedure for the police to question Brad. He was the first one on the scene after the shooting, the closest thing to an eyewitness the police had. But Denise's stomach churned. Maybe it was this nut who had been calling her and sent that letter, but a lot of things about this stalker weren't adding up. How would the stalker know when Diane was coming home? Why wasn't Brad home when Diane arrived?

Denise tried to dismiss her suspicions. "No. Get that out of your mind. That can't be. He loved Diane and the kids. Wait till we know something for sure. Don't jump to conclusions," she told herself.

Darlene, the oldest sister, felt the same thing. "The second it happened, as soon as I heard she was dead, I thought it was Brad. I don't know what it was. I wanted to believe it wasn't. I wanted it not to be him real bad. It would have been a lot easier to take if it was a stalker. It wouldn't have been so awful."

Over the next few hours and days, lots of other people thought the same things. And they tried the same denials.

The family gathered around Freida, just as they had when their father died so suddenly and when other crises hit them. Gordon Marler, the oldest of Freida's five children, was home with two of his daughters cutting a birthday cake. He was going to be forty-one the next day. The early birthday celebration was cut short by a phone call. "Diane's dead," Gordie told his family. He was hysterical. The uneaten cake was left where it was, and everyone headed to Freida's house.

Allen Marler, Diane's younger brother, had been out with his girlfriend, Nancy Rapo. When he got to her house, he had a message to call Freida. "Someone murdered my sister," he told Nancy when he got off the phone. They joined everyone else in a fitful vigil.

Nobody in the family was getting straight answers, and being 120 miles away didn't help. So rather than sit and do nothing, Allen Marler and Donald Verrier volunteered to drive to Marshall to talk to Brad in person. Plus, they wanted to check on the kids. No one knew where they were. It was an awful drive, and in the silence, Don ruminated on the circumstances.

"It was just odd. All the precautions Diane had made. We knew she drove around the house to see if anyone had tried to break in. We knew about her laying on horn until Brad showed himself, and the sheriff would drive her home if Brad was at school. And he's out for a walk? I wonder," Don said.

At home, Freida was in shock. She did things to take her mind off what happened, even if they seemed inappropriate. She scooped up her dog, a white French poodle named Pierre, and took him into the bathroom because he needed washing. Nancy Rapo found her scrubbing and scrubbing and scrubbing the dog.

"Freida, are you all right?" Nancy asked as she touched her shoulder.

Freida was so startled she almost jumped out of her skin.

"She had fallen apart. It's what any mother would do. She spent a lot of time in the bedroom by herself. She didn't want to be seen in a moment of weakness," Nancy said.

"It was a very rough night. Everybody just sat around and waited for news. We didn't know what to do. Nobody wanted to say, 'My God, he did it.' Everybody was afraid to admit it, but I think we all felt that way. He was such an odd person. There was something about him.

Every time the man hugged me I felt strange vibrations. The family accepted Brad because he was Diane's husband. They didn't ignore him and weren't rude to him. But you could tell there was a strain. He was so different. He never participated in anything. There was such a contrast between him and Diane. She was so bubbly, so full of life and love. He drained the life from her."

Before the police let Brad King go for the night, they asked for his boots. They were size 10 Thermolites, a brand favored by outdoorsmen because they insulate feet from the cold. King's pair had leather tops and rubber bottoms, with a distinctive grooved sole. The pattern resembled the footprints found on the farm grounds, which was hardly surprising since King lived there and said he had been out walking. King voluntarily surrendered his footwear in exchange for some rubber flip-flops issued to inmates at the county jail. He couldn't face the thought of going back to the farmhouse, so wearing his sandals, he checked into the Arborgate Inn, a motel west of Marshall. His lawyer friend, Randy Wright, had come to the police station, and the two men shared a room. The assistant pastor of the church was also at the police station to console Brad.

Because crime doesn't abide by the calendar, the day seemed to never end. It was already past midnight and Saturday had merged into Sunday when Detective Jim Statfeld arrived for the second time at 16240 Division Drive. A twenty-three-year veteran of the Calhoun County Sheriff's Department, he had been there at about 8:20 P.M. to get briefed on what happened. Statfeld stayed for at most thirty minutes, then left to obtain a search warrant signed by the district judge on duty. Again, it was standard procedure. There had been a shooting death and probable cause that a crime had occurred. The police needed to gather evidence and search the grounds for clues.

By this time, Schoder had finished questioning Brad and returned to the farm. The county's two detectives went to the barn loft and seized the spent cartridge, sealing it in a plastic bag. It was made by CCI-Speer of Lewiston, Idaho. Also bagged were the car keys, hair barrette and wallet that lay in the driveway near the Wagoneer.

Moving into the house, Statfeld was shown the sixteen-gauge shotgun, broken down into two pieces and sitting near a water softener in a first-floor utility room. The shotgun wasn't seized because the cartridge casing in the barn was a .22 caliber, and Diane apparently was hit by small-caliber bullets, not a shotgun blast.

But up in the attic, in a box marked "Camping Equipment and Tools," police found two boxes of Remington and Winchester .22 caliber ammunition, which were confiscated. Also found was a cleaning rod in a cabinet for a small-caliber rifle, like a .22. Odd, didn't Brad say he owned only a shotgun? What was the ammunition and cleaning rod for?

The three-bedroom farmhouse had a living room, dining room, kitchen, and bathroom downstairs. It also had a Michigan basement, which meant a dirt floor with rock sides.

On the door leading to the back porch, Schoder checked the lock where Brad had found pry marks on December 12. The detective ordered it removed from the door and seized for evidence.

In the meantime, Allen Marler and Don Verrier had arrived from Sterling Heights. They went straight to the sheriff's department, where there was only one deputy on duty, and he didn't know anything. The two men drove to 16240 Division Drive, but they never got past the police car in the driveway. They pleaded for some information, and Schoder came. They talked with him in the detective's car.

The police didn't know much more than that Diane had been shot twice, Brad had found her in the driveway when he returned from a walk, and the two kids had been in the back seat. The children were now staying with Barb Elgutaa in Battle Creek. Schoder asked Allen if he knew anything about the alleged breaking and entering on December 12.

"Brad showed me that lock, but it looked like someone scratched it with a fingernail file. It didn't look like a break-in to me," Allen said.

"That's what I thought," Schoder said.

Schoder also asked about the security ritual. Wasn't Brad supposed to be home when Diane arrived? If that was your wife, would you have gone for a walk? Did anyone know what time Diane was due home?

The two men wanted to talk to Brad, but Schoder wouldn't let them until he had called Brad to make sure it was all right to send some visitors. Brad said it was okay, so Schoder directed them to the Arborgate Inn, where he and Randy Wright were spending the night.

Brad was lying on one of the beds in the motel room, wearing some sweat pants. He started wailing when Allen and Don entered, and he got up to give Allen a hug.

"Brad, what happened? Did you hear anything? Did you see anything?" Allen asked him.

"No," Brad answered. "It's so wide open back there you couldn't hear anything."

There were dozens more questions. But every time they posed one to Brad, Randy Wright answered it. And the lawyer wasn't being too specific. Finally, after no more than a thirty-minute session, the two men headed back to Sterling Heights with what little information they had gleaned. They left about 4:00 A.M. for home, where family members slouched on chairs, the sofa, or the floor, waiting to hear something.

That was about the same time the last police cruiser pulled away from 16240 Division Drive, nine hours after Deputy Picketts arrived. Not that all the police business had been finished. Nobody photographed or made plaster casts of the boot prints found by Trooper Lisle and Travis. And there was a missed opportunity with the canine team. If Travis finds the person he is tracking, he is trained to sit and wag his tail because he expects a reward. By the time Travis finished tracking, Brad King was already downtown being questioned and wasn't on the property for Travis to check. Nobody sealed off the property because Schoder figured his deputies had completed their initial search. No yellow tape or barricades were set up to warn anyone to keep out. No guard was posted before everyone drove off into the wee hours of the Michigan morning.

Diane Newton King lay in the cold morgue of a funeral home. Her bewildered and now motherless children were at a friend's house. Her husband was in a motel. Her mother and immediate family huddled in shock. The day may have finally ended, but the trauma was just beginning.

CHAPTER 5

Up to the day she was murdered, Diane King was on a lifelong search to find out who she was. Many forces shaped her life, but two of them were seismic. She was half-white and half-Indian, which meant she had one foot in each world and sometimes wondered which one she belonged to. As a child, she had endured cruel taunts about the color of her skin. If color was so hurtful, who could blame a child for coming home from school and trying to scrub it off in the bathtub. On the other hand, she developed a deep sense of pride in her culture and wanted to learn as much of it as she could. A lot of it had been lost because whites had literally beaten it out of her forebears, who were forced to live the white way. Her ultimate dream was to be a role model for Native Americans and to bridge the two worlds. Second, an unfillable void lodged in her spirit when she was ten. Her father died in a botched hospital operation. He was strong, handsome, and perfect, and life with him seemed ideal. After he died and left her brokenhearted, life was painful and puzzling. She developed an armor of toughness and self-reliance.

Both of Diane's parents were from the Montreal area of Canada. Her mother's family tree was rooted on the Kahnawake Reserve for Mohawk Indians, a 10,200-acre expanse established by the French Jesuits in 1676. Located on the St. Lawrence River just south of the island city of Montreal, the reserve is home to 6,000 Mohawks. *Kahnawake* means "village by the river," and it has special meaning to Mohawk Catholics. It's the burial place of Kateri Tekakwitha, whose bones are interred at St. Francis Xavier Church. Part of the reservation has a Kateri Hospital and a Tekakwitha Island.

Diane's maternal grandmother, Cecilia Leaf, was born and raised on the reserve. But her lifestyle and culture were completely different from what prevailed before the Europeans stumbled onto the continent. The winners write history, and in the white world, the history of the Americas starts in 1492 when an Italian sailor employed by Spain chanced upon a New World while he was trying to find India. Other explorers followed Christopher Columbus, claiming the lands they found for Spain, Portugal, France, England, and Holland. The native inhabitants were rolled over by a tide they never understood. Nobody consulted with them when their lands were given to kings and queens and then doled out to settlement companies. It was as if they were background props whose culture was irrelevant.

At first, the new settlers made deals and signed treaties with the natives. Then it became official government policy to place them on reservations in a forced segregation. That policy gave way to "assimilation," which meant taking the Indian out of the Indian by forcing him to think white, act white, and be white. Thomas J. Morgan, the U.S. Commissioner of Indian affairs, said in 1899 that Indians "must conform to the white culture or be crushed by it." It was only in the 1960s and 1970s that policy changed to "self-determination," meaning that Native Americans could decide for themselves how they should live.

Cecilia Leaf was sent to boarding school, away from her family. If she spoke Mohawk, she was beaten. Anyone holding the feather of an eagle—the Mohawks' symbol of vision and communication between this world and the spirit world—was punished. Anyone who dressed like an Indian was berated. It was as if someone hung a sign at a cultural barrier that said "No Mohawk-Speaking Red Bastards Permitted Beyond This Point." When Cecilia married John Canadyan and bore eight children, she could pass on very little about the way things were before the whites came.

The Mohawks, who called themselves "the people of flint" or "real human beings," inhabited a territory that is now western New York and lower Quebec in the lower Great Lakes region. They constructed palisaded villages along the banks of rivers that sprang to life in the middle of the continent and flowed toward the Atlantic Ocean. Families lived in long houses that resembled giant overturned canoes and were made of wooden beams and shingles of elm bark. According to Mohawk legend, the earth was created by a woman who fell from the sky. And it was the women who nominated members of the tribal council and removed them from office if they misbehaved. While the men hunted game and defended their lands from warring tribes, women cultivated the fields in the eastern woodlands. The crops they planted and harvested had female identities: Bean Sister, Corn Maiden, and Squash Sister.

The people had a sophisticated system of self-government built on the Great Law of Peace, which enunciated such concepts as individual rights, female independence, freedom of speech, and separate branches of government held together by checks and balances. The Iroquois Confederacy—the oldest league of nations in the world—was made up of six separate tribes linked by a single government across a great expanse of land. It included the Mohawks, Senecas, Cayugas, Onondagas, Oneidas, and later the Tuscaroras. It served as a model for the Founding Fathers when they were writing the U.S. Constitution. These were the people of Hiawatha, who teamed with a peacemaker sent by the Creator to settle fights between warring nations. Hiawatha and the peacemaker persuaded the Mohawks to abandon war and cannibalism to advance peace, civil authority, righteousness, and the Great Law.

The Mohawks had a life expectancy that was greater than the Europeans in the sixteenth century. But their world changed forever in 1534 when Jacques Cartier explored the lands on each side of the St. Lawrence River. He claimed it all as New France in the name of the king. The natives naturally questioned how these strange men could take their land and give it to a king who had no right to accept it. This led to war—the Indians were willing to die for what was theirs, and the French were willing to kill them so they could exploit their riches. To fight the French, the Mohawks became allies of the British, who had their own claims to the land. The alliance worked for a time, until the Mohawks got caught in the middle of another white man's struggle, the American War for Independence. Again the Mohawks sided with the British, but when the war was lost, they were placed on reservations in New York and Canada. They never lost their feistiness, though. At the beginning of World War II, when the U.S. and Canadian governments went to war, the Iroquois League independently declared war on Germany! And in the fight for self-determination in the 1960s, the Mohawks erected a sign at Kahnawake that said, "In Washington, They Call It Assimilation. In Ottawa, Indian Progress. We Who Are The Victims Call It Genocide!"

George Herbert Marler was an Englishman from Montreal. He was tall and charming, with red hair, and everyone called him Bert. He was an ironworker employed at a cannery outside Kahnawake. In the industrial age, Mohawk men developed great reputations as ironworkers. They were admired for their balance and bravery, working long and hard, high above the ground, putting the iron beams on metal skeletons. One of Freida's brothers was just such an ironworker, who introduced her to Bert. Freida and Bert courted and married, but unlike Indians, Bert wasn't entitled to the quarter-acre of reservation land that Mohawks get when they turn eighteen. So with job prospects rather grim, he moved with his wife to Michigan to find work and seek a better life. At first, the family lived an idyllic life on a farm off 14 Mile Road, one of the neat grid of roads the area was sectioned off into, while Bert also worked as an ironworker for the Ford Motor Company.

In the early sixties, they moved to a two-story frame house on St. Joseph's Drive in Sterling Heights, a town north of Detroit in Macomb County. It was more rural than suburban back then. The Marlers' street wasn't even paved, and there were only four houses on the whole block. But the subdivisions grew and grew, and Macomb County became something of a national social symbol. This was where white families of European ethnic heritage moved to escape the increasingly black neighborhoods of inner-city Detroit. The place is ninety-seven percent white, heavily Catholic, and dominated by blue-collar workers who toil in the auto plants and factories. It was once heavily Democratic, voting huge margins for John F. Kennedy and Lyndon Johnson in presidential elections. But things started to change in the late sixties. Macomb County was the place of the original swing vote, Democrats who started to prefer the more conservative candidates of the opposing party. They piled up such huge margins for the Republicans in 1980 they became forever known as Reagan Democrats. It was in Macomb County, at a Chrysler plant in the town of Warren, that Democrat Michael Dukakis took his ill-fated ride in an M-1 Army tank in 1988. That was the year Republican George Bush won 65 percent of the vote.

But before Macomb County became a bellwether of presidential politics, it was home for George and Freida Marler and their five kids. Diane, the middle child, was the darkest and chubbiest of the lot. Diane's skin was so bronze, especially in the summer, some people in this white bastion mistakenly thought she was black. When her brothers and sisters teased her, they called her "chunk of chocolate" or "Chubby Checker." Or they told her she was so different she must have been adopted. These were just kids at play, but the barbs made her self-conscious. "She never felt pretty. She was always chunky," said Denise, her baby sister.

On the inside, Diane took after her father. Bert bounced her on his knee and called her "my little papoose." And he planted positive seeds in a young mind. "This is my Diane," he'd say. "She's so smart. She's going to go to college someday." Indeed, Diane was the first in her family to attend college, something she was fiercely proud of. It was her way of telling her taunters: "I'll show you." And, as little girls are wont to do, she wanted badly to please her father. She wanted to be a success, to be somebody that others would have to take seriously, to do something important with her life. Sadly, she never had the chance to show her father her accomplishments.

Trouble started for Bert when his back started to hurt. His family doctor sent him to the hospital for tests. In the meantime, his oldest daughter, fifteen-year-old Darlene, got an infection when she had her ears pierced. So when Bert took Darlene to the hospital to get the ear lanced, he decided to check on the tests the doctors had run. What they told him was startling. He had to be admitted right away and undergo immediate surgery. An X ray showed that something was blocking the bile from exiting his gallbladder. On March 4, 1966, he was taken to the operating room at eleven A.M. Although his family doctor was supposed to do the surgery, another doctor filled in. Part of the procedure involved scraping Bert's pancreas. After surgery, Bert was carted back to his room to recuperate, but he seemed to be getting worse, not better, over the next several days. He was unable to eat and kept losing weight while puzzled doctors fed him placebos. Then after weeks of deterioration, Bert died in the hospital at eight-thirty P.M. on March 25. He was thirty-five and left five kids, ages sixteen to seven.

Freida was crushed. She wasn't the pushy type and trusted that doctors and hospitals knew what they were doing. When she was told her husband was being taken to the OR, she didn't even know that meant operating room. She ignored a cousin's plea to get a second opinion, assuring herself that all Bert needed was a little more time and things would be fine. Now it would take legal wrangling to try to get some justice.

It turned out that the X rays showed Bert's gallbladder had been functioning all along, and the surgery wasn't necessary. The family also argued that he never gave consent to have an operation but was wheeled down while he was medicated. The fill-in doctor who, as the X rays revealed, had ruptured Bert's pancreas, wasn't even licensed. And then afterward, Bert was given the wrong medication during his recovery. Because of all the errors, the family sued the doctor and the hospital. It took twenty months, but just before Christmas in 1967, a Macomb County court awarded the family $230,523 in wrongful-death damages. Throwing in legal fees increased the award to $300,000. But because of the doctor's appeals, the Marlers didn't get any money until July of 1968. It wasn't much satisfaction for the loss of a husband and father. It was so hard for Freida to let him go that she kept Bert's woolen cap. She still has it.

As for Diane, "she was very angry when her father died," said Freida. "She could hear me crying at night. It was hard for her to accept." Diane was so devastated that she blocked out memories of her father. It was just too painful to remember.

Diane's sister Denise recalls, "Diane's whole life was, 'who am I?' It started with what happened to my father. She wanted a dad but didn't have a dad. So she was always searching. She blocked a lot of things out. She never talked about him. She said she couldn't remember anything, and it bugged her. She was always seeking counsel about the past." Later on in life, Diane dated older men, and even she wondered if there were psychological undercurrents. "Am I looking for a father figure?" she asked her sister. When she did get married, she chose a man eleven years her senior.

Elaine Wash, Diane's cousin and Bert's niece, said Diane had memory lapses whenever family conversations involved Bert.

"She had a total blackout. She couldn't or wouldn't put a face on him. It was very traumatic. That's why she searched for her identity. She was always searching. She was always grasping for roots and permanence," Wash said.

Regina Zapinski, who knew Diane ever since junior high school and roomed with her for a semester in college, also picked up on Diane's yearning.

"Losing her dad was a very big deal. He was handsome, strong, big, and perfect, and he wasn't there. She missed him a lot. There was something missing in her life. She was always trying to fill that void. Diane needed a lot of attention, a lot of acceptance, a lot of love. That's why she did so much. She wanted her family to appreciate her. Her life would have been different if he had lived. She was never really happy with herself. She always wondered if she was thin enough, if she was attractive enough, if she made enough friends, if she made good enough grades," Zapinski said.

By 1969 Freida had remarried. She and a girlfriend walked into a bar called The Hitching Post looking for work. The bartender was Royal Newton, brother of the owner. Royal was also a veteran of the Canadian Army and a former court bailiff in Hamilton, Ontario. The new marriage, however, didn't bring instant stability to the family situation. Denise described those days as being punctuated with "lots of drinking, lots of violence, lots of police." It took a long time for things to settle down. So when Diane decided to use her stepfather's last name,

Newton, as part of her own, it was a symbolic gesture of acceptance to Royal.

The family lived a middle-class life in their four-bedroom house. They even had a foster child for a time. At Christmas the kids had more presents than the neighbors, but they didn't make a big show of it. They had two horses, one named King and another named Tumac, a brown quarterhorse. It belonged to everybody, but Diane tried to claim it as hers and gave it special attention. The family never really went on a vacation together, except for summer visits to the Kahnawake Reserve to see their grandmother, aunts, uncles, and cousins. And the kids were learning they weren't fully accepted in either of the two worlds they lived in. The Mohawks thought of them as whites; many whites thought of them as Indians. On the reservation, Diane heard the word "half-breed" a lot. She and Denise used to sing the song "Half-Breed" by Cher that included the line, "Both sides been against me since the day I was born." It was just as bad in the white world. Once, when she had a Mazda, Diane broke down on the side of the road near Detroit. A passing motorist yelled at her: "Nigger!" Her crime was having dark skin and driving a Japanese car in the birthplace of the American auto industry. And when she got to college, she lamented that the only guys who asked her out were the black football players.

In high school, though, Diane gained the all-around popularity she sought. After attending North Elementary School and Grissom Junior High, she made her mark at Sterling Heights High School, where she was a member of the student senate, the French Club, and the Modern Dance Club, sang in the chorus, and for all three years was a Stallionette, a performing unit that marched with the band and wore western-style outfits and cowboy hats.

One of the guys she dated was the captain of the football team and the basketball team.

"She was always involved in something. Always on the go. Had lots of friends. Lots of boyfriends. We were in a real popular clique and traveled with the 'in' crowd, although we had to work at it. It was a predominantly white, middle- to upper-class school. That wasn't our backgrounds," said Regina Zapinski, who was a cheerleader and member of the homecoming court.

They were a self-reliant, headstrong pair of strong-willed women. And like Diane, Regina was half-Indian.

"We never thought we'd get married and have kids. We were very individualistic. There were people to meet, places to go. And we were always moving. I mean, we dated a lot of guys. But we never discussed children or home life. Marriage and settling down was something we never thought we'd do," Regina said.

After graduation in 1974, Diane became the first person in her family to go to college. She and Regina were roommates the first semester at Western Michigan University in Kalamazoo. They both kept up their extracurricular activities: Diane was a cheerleader, Regina a ball girl with the football team. But Diane dropped out after that first semester and went home to regroup.

After taking some time off, Diane searched through her college catalogs and picked out a two-year college she liked—Mount Ida in Newton Centre, just outside Boston. She enrolled in September of 1975 and earned an associate degree in physical education. Her grade-point average was 3.5, good enough to qualify her for the junior college honor society Phi Theta Kappa. But here education didn't stop in the classroom, especially in this bastion of eastern Establishment people. One of the customs at Mount Ida is to have one of the students live with the family of the chancellor, which is a way of keeping up with student concerns and problems. And partly because she was one of the first Native Americans to attend Mount Ida, Diane was selected to live in the home of Dr. F. Roy Carlson. To her, he was like a father figure.

"I liked her immediately. She had a very pleasant disposition. She got along well with everybody. She loved life. With her personality, she should have gone far. She was a good kid, and there are very few of them around," Carlson said.

Diane was introduced to a society she never knew. She ate in her first fancy restaurant, went to symphonies and art shows. She polished her social skills. It was perhaps the best growth experience of her young life.

Love was also abloom in New England. Diane fell for a pharmacy student named Marcel Bess. They lived together for a time and there was talk of marriage, but Marcel left the area for a job in New York, and that was that. Whenever Diane fell for someone, she fell hard. And whenever she lost a boyfriend, as she had lost her father, the breakup was painful.

Another telling episode in New England involved going to a party accompanied by Marcel. Diane was dressed in a fancy gown. She overheard another woman comment, "That's the flattest chested woman I've ever seen." The remark cut so deeply into Diane's psyche, she decided to get saline breast implants to improve her figure and her image of herself. Within weeks, she had the cosmetic surgery done, paying for it with money she earned from her part-time job.

After getting her associate degree, Diane remained in the Boston area for about a year. She had a job at Filene's Department Store and worked until June of

1978 at the Brookline Savings Bank in Brookline, Massachusetts. Her sister Denise came to live with her for a time. Denise had also been accepted at Mount Ida, but she never attended classes. Both of them moved back to Michigan in 1978.

That fall, Diane enrolled at Wayne State University near Detroit and began work on her degree in communications. Her family joked that she was continuing her career of being a professional student. But now she had a new interest. She enlisted in the Michigan National Guard on October 23, 1978. In time, she converted her military time to joining the Reserve Officer Training Corps at Wayne State. And just like everything else in her life, if she was going to be a soldier, she was going to be a good one. She was a distinguished cadet and later a cadet commander, earning a sword and scabbard engraved with her name—Diane Marler. The Army recognized her accomplishments in 1981, sending her to Fort Riley, Kansas, for an advanced course. And on June 30 1983, she was selected for a regular Army appointment and commissioned as a second lieutenant. Freida was so proud she rewarded her with solid-gold ornamental lieutenant's bars.

Now the Army looked like a career opportunity. In July 1983, she was assigned to the basic course of the U.S. Army Signal Corps at Fort Gordon, Georgia. But she never completed the training. Love got in the way. By this time, she had fallen for an ex-cop named Bradford King, who had moved from Michigan to Colorado. Diane wangled her way into a transfer to Fort Carson, near Denver, to be near him. And she was discharged from the Army on February 27, 1984. What she hoped at one time would be a career lasted seven months and twenty-eight days on active duty.

* * *

It was in Colorado that Diane uncovered so much about Native-American culture. Tribes were much more visible in the West; bigotry against them less so. Native Americans embraced their heritage more out here. Diane met Ben Nighthorse Campbell, who became the first Native American elected to the U.S. Senate, representing Colorado. And she met Russell Means, president of the American Indian Movement at an event called the March Pow Wow in Denver. The ember she carried in her heart about Indian life soon became a raging fire, because, as she always told friends, "You can't know where you're going until you know where you have been."

Powwows are get-togethers that celebrate Native-American culture and customs. They can last a day or a week, but most are held on weekends. They are part religious service, part rally, part celebration and a whole lot of fun. They are chances for individuals, families, and tribes to gather for food, dancing and storytelling. There are Indians in full regalia—feathers, beads, buckskins, and moccasins—and tourists in cutoff jeans and sleeveless T-shirts. Vendors sell Indian soup made of maize alongside booths peddling Pepsi-Cola and Coors beer. Diane and Brad used to make batches of corn soup and Mohawk meat pies to sell at weekend events. At a powwow, the main attraction is the dance to drum music. The drum, symbolic of the heartbeat of Mother Earth, sends out pulses of rhythms to concentric circles of participants and spectators. There is a gourd dance to simulate warriors riding into battle against an enemy. Another dance depicts warriors who would stake themselves to the ground during battle, a signaling their determination to fight to the death. There are men's dances, women's shawl dances, children's dances, and intertribal dances—even a veteran's dance for all Indians who served in the military. Non-Indians are invited and encouraged to join the dancing if it does not involve a sacred ritual. Cash prizes are awarded to the best dancers and best dress.

In time, after she had worked in television for a few years, Diane hit on an idea to bridge her two worlds of Native-American and mainstream culture. She wanted to produce educational videos that would tell the real story of Native Americans, not the cowboy and cavalry versions. She planned to call this endeavor Two Worlds Productions, and she fancied using the trade name Thunder Spirit, which was about as apt a description as you could find for an independent, self-reliant entrepreneur such as herself. But she needed some heavy financial backing, and she had put together a proposal to some corporate and philanthropic foundations to see if there was any interest.

It was at a powwow sponsored by Western Michigan University that Kristina Mony, the intern at WUHQ, interviewed Diane for a paper she wrote for her first-year journalism class at Kalamazoo College in 1990. She got an A for writing about Diane, the TV reporter, and Diane, the Indian activist:

> Diane's main focus in life is her Native-American heritage. The first of five children to graduate from high school and the only child to graduate from college, Diane has always felt strong ties with the Indian culture. Originating from the Mohawk tribe in Quebec, Canada, she can remember the signs of racism, such as the separate restrooms and separate eating areas. Three generations of Diane's family

> assimilated, or married non-Indians to weaken the blood line. Diane remembers, "The goal in my family was to become as non-Indian as possible. I was never encouraged to have pride in Native-American heritage."

Diane was deeply honored to be the focus of such a school paper. One of her heroes was Dr. Martin Luther King, Jr. Coincidentally, Brad had the same surname and birthday (January 15) as the black leader. Diane routinely scheduled some type of observance of Martin Luther King day. Just as he tried to bridge the black and white worlds, Diane tried to connect the Indian and white worlds. A month before she was murdered, she organized a T-shirt fashion event within the family. Hers read, "World Harmony, World Peace." Most of the social problems Native Americans endure today are a conflict of the two worlds, and Diane learned first-hand about it when she tried to hold her family's first-ever reunion the summer before she died.

The reunion was planned on the Kahnawake Reservation where her mother was born and raised and where Kateri Tekakwitha was buried. She had sent out one hundred invitations to aunts, uncles, and cousins, and she planned to hire a band. But something ruined the idea: an Indian uprising involving a land dispute over a golf course expansion. It became known as the "golf crisis" or the "golf course war," and the residents, 111 in number, were smack in the middle of it, along with a Mohawk reservation to the west of them. Like their ancestors, the Native Americans decided to fight for their land. Two worlds were colliding once again.

The battle erupted March 11, 1990. Just as in the old days, Indians covered their faces with war paint and took up weapons. The battle lasted seven months and required the intercession of Canadian Army troops, tanks, helicopter gunships, and armored personnel carriers. A Canadian policeman was killed in action, and the Native Americans seized a major bridge adjacent to the Kahnawake Reservation that leads into Montreal.

The land in question was part of a 240-square-mile area of wilderness that King Louis XIV granted in 1717 to the Seminary of St. Sulpice for the use and benefit of the Indians. Most of it, however, was sold off between 1800 and 1940 for the benefit of the seminary. One chunk of it became The Golf Course at Oka, a town eighteen miles west of Montreal and just outside the 2,000-acre Kahnesatake Reservation of Mohawks. The nine-hole course was built despite Mohawk objections in 1961. And now the Oka town council wanted to expand it to eighteen holes by clearing fifty-five acres of white pine forest that was once Mohawk common land. The Indians said the land included ancient burial grounds, and they didn't want the bones of their ancestors trod on by the spiked shoes of golfers chasing a little white ball. They tacked homemade signs on the trees: "Mohawk Territory—Keep Out."

At first, they fought the golf course the modern way, with a lawsuit. But when the courts allowed the expansion, the Mohawks put up barricades to stop construction bulldozers. They vowed to defend their land by any means necessary, even if they had to take up AK-47s, M-16s, and pump-action shotguns. The Mohawk Warrior Society, a militant group dedicated to protecting Indian lands, got into the action. Police say this self-styled security force buys its guns with profits from gambling and selling tax-free cigarettes. Because of its fights against the Canadian and American governments, the Warrior

Society has received money from such sources as Libyan leader Colonel Moammar Gadhafi.

The Mohawks and the provincial police stared each other down for four months. Then on July 11, the Sûreté du Québec made an ill-fated decision to enforce the court order against the Indians. Officers wearing helmets and fatigues and armed with automatic weapons and stun guns stormed the barricades. But tear gas fired by the police was blown back into their faces by the wind. In the cross fire, Marcel Lemay, a thirty-one-year-old corporal in a police tactical unit, was killed. The Native Americans insisted he was shot by an errant police bullet, but a coroner's report later said the fatal shot was probably fired by one of the Mohawks. The weapon was never found and no charges were filed. The police were forced to retreat, and the Mohawks used the wrecks of police cruisers to reinforce their barricade at the edge of town.

When the gunfight erupted at Oka, sympathetic Mohawks on the Kahnawake Reserve—where Diane's reunion was supposed to be held—blocked the Mercier Bridge that connects Montreal with its suburbs south of the St. Lawrence River. About 55,000 cars used the bridge daily, and what was normally a thirty-minute drive could take as long as three hours because of the detours. Angry commuters vented their wrath at the Native Americans who had the audacity to block their bridge. A racial war of nerves followed. In the city of Chateauguay near the reservation, Mohawks were burned in effigy from lampposts. Posters appeared of caricatures of Native Americans with a slanted line drawn across their faces. Phrases involving "savages" and "a different color of nigger" were heard. In response, signs were at

Mercier Bridge that said, "Stop Canadian Apartheid and Amer-Indian Genocide."

At the height of the dispute, Freida Newton packed up a car with food and supplies and joined a convoy. Her sister, Edith Cupples, lived at Kahnawake with a number of nieces, nephews, other relatives, and friends. It took two days for Freida to get from Sterling Heights to Kahnawake, but she made it.

Meanwhile, the Canadian government attempted to settle the dispute in Oka by buying the fifty-five acres of land in question and giving it to the Mohawks. Saying that too many of their ancestors had died because they trusted a white government, the Mohawks refused to give in. They made this a larger war over land claims and demanded their own separate nation on land straddling the Canadian and New York borders. Other tribes made their own demands. More than 200 chiefs came from across Canada for a three-day gathering at Kahnawake, where they endorsed the Mohawk demands and added their own. Finally, Quebec Premier Robert Bourassa sent 4,400 Canadian Army troops to Kahnawake and Kahnesatake to restore civil order. Tanks were poised to roll at the Mercier Bridge and helicopters hovered overhead when the Kahnawake Indians abandoned their positions on August 28. The Mohawks' request for political negotiations was denied. The bridge reopened September 6 for the first time in eight weeks. During a raid on a longhouse on Tekakwitha Island, police seized .50 caliber machine guns and armor-piercing bullets. Also confiscated were Israeli-made submachine guns and assault rifles.

Meanwhile, the conflict continued at Oka. About twenty Mohawk warriors and their families holed up in a drug-and-alcohol treatment center—a not-too-subtle symbol of what reservation life had come to. They erected concrete bunkers and barricades made of pine logs around the rehab center, a white clapboard structure on a bluff overlooking the Lake of Two Mountains. The Canadian Army circled the place with coils of razor wire and armored personnel carriers. Finally, on September 26, 300 troops with bayonet-tipped weapons routed the Native Americans. Soldiers had beamed lights into the building from 110-foot towers and had cut all phone lines. The Mohawk warriors in turn aimed loudspeakers at troops and played Mohawk songs. During the last stand at Oka, about four hundred Kahnawake Indians again rushed the Mercier Bridge with baseball bats, lead pipes, and rocks in hand. Troops dispersed them at gunpoint.

One of the casualties of this Indian war was Diane's reunion. But she was determined that Two Worlds Productions was more necessary than ever if centuries of racial tension were to be erased.

CHAPTER 6

Everyone who knew Bradford J. King described him as quiet or "laid back." He is the older of two boys of a conservative, heartland, WASPish family dominated by a proud and strong-willed mother. Emotions, especially negative ones, were things to be controlled in this family, not shared.

His father, Willis King, was a native Texan tempered by the forces of his generation. He came of age in the Great Depression, an experience that cut bone-deep in him the value of a job and the value of a buck. Perseverance and self-sacrifice were admirable qualities to Willis. And like so many young men of his time, he went off to Europe with the U.S. Army to defeat fascism and save the world for democracy. It was while he was fighting the Nazis in France that Willis got hit with a German shell. Shards of shrapnel tore up his left leg, and despite all kinds of medical attention, he was never completely free of those tiny, irregular pieces of metal that earned him a ticket back home to a military hospital. But his war wound had one fortuitous circumstance; it brought him together with his future bride, Marjorie.

She was born and raised in Cadillac, Michigan, a small town in the north central part of the Lower Peninsula where the winters were as bleak as the economic prospects in the 1930s. Her father, president of the town bank, was a frugal man who practiced thrift in matters of money and emotion. Marjorie became a nutritionist, and when America was forced into World War II, she did her part on the homefront by working in the hospitals where wounded GIs were brought for recuperation. It was in a hospital that she met Willis King; and this dietician found the way to this particular man's heart was indeed through his stomach. Marjorie helped nurse him back to health, then made him her lifelong partner. Eventually Willis became president of the State Bank of Croswell in Port Huron, Michigan, and earned a good living for his family—Marjorie and two sons.

Willis underwent dozens of operations to repair tissue and take out more shrapnel from his wounded left leg. Much later in life, it was amputated, and complications from the operation hastened his death. At home, Marjorie had some years ago stepped forward to take care of things Willis was physically unable to do. Circumstances made her a forceful, self-reliant woman and head of the household.

Bradford King was born January 15, 1947. He was part of the baby boom—the great statistical bulge of births to servicemen who returned home from war to start families. A brother, Scott, was born four years later.

Brad's mother taught him how to cook and sew. She provided order and structure, plus discipline. But he was closer to his father. People who knew Brad earlier said his mother pushed and prodded, but Brad never seemed to develop the self-motivation to order his own life. Marjorie King wouldn't be the last woman in his life to hold power over him. The object of doting grandparents, Brad craved attention and the outside validation it gave him. When Scott was born, he was jealous of this sibling intruder who took attention away from him. But Brad didn't let his jealousy show much. He didn't show much of anything, in fact. One of the key features of his personality was his lack of emotional display. Brad kept his feelings, especially any hurt ones, tucked away in a locked box. He learned to project an image and personality that kept others from prying. He was something of an enigma to people.

Growing up in the Middle American town of Croswell, Michigan, north of the great industrial factories of Detroit, Brad was a well-rounded student when he graduated from high school in 1965, just as the Vietnam War was heating up into a heavy commitment for the U.S. military. He learned to play golf when he was eleven, and the game became one of his great passions. He was on the golf team for four years at Croswell-Lexington High School; he was also on the football and wrestling teams, a member of the Ski Club, an actor in the junior and senior class plays, and a member of the Spanish Club and the Booster Club. Elected to the student council as a freshman, Brad also was one of several students selected from around the state of Michigan go to Lansing for a week to elect a mock governor and state legislature. As a senior, he served on the yearbook staff that produced *Pioneer Memories.*

A clean-cut image and academic success earned him the nickname "Mister America" at Western Michigan University in Kalamazoo. He was active in the social scene, pledging with the Tau Kappa Epsilon fraternity.

And when he was a sophomore, he met Gail Elaine Goins, a sister in the Phi Mu sorority and the daughter of a police captain from Pontiac, Michigan.

They met in February of 1967. Both of them were majoring in education, and their friendship evolved into a serious relationship. Brad was an introvert, not given to outward displays of emotion. But a year after he met Gail, Brad sent a dozen Valentine's Day roses, one for each month he had known her. And if he couldn't find voice for his feelings, he substituted one that could, borrowing the eloquence of Shakespeare in his love letters. They were married on December 21, 1968, the day Gail graduated. Her father had made a rule that she had to be finished with her studies before she could marry. Brad graduated the following semester with a degree in speech communication and a minor in history.

Brad did student teaching at Pontiac Central High School, helping his kids produce the school play in the spring. He liked to teach, and his students liked him. But teachers didn't make much money, certainly not as much as cops. And serendipity played a role in Brad launching a career in law enforcement. One of his TKE fraternity brothers had joined the Pontiac police force, which was looking for recruits in 1969. He enthusiastically talked Brad into applying. There were things about a police career that appealed to Brad. The regimentation was one thing. The force offered structure and order. There was also a camaraderie similar to what he knew at the TKE fraternity; the police union is a brotherhood.

Although his new bride's father was a police captain, Brad never used his father-in-law's influence to land the job or rise through the ranks. He was on the job for two years before some officers knew of his relationship with Captain Fred Goins's daughter. Actually, Fred had some real reservations about whether this was a good job for a young man to get into and tried to talk him out of it. These were the violent sixties. Race riots had turned parts of Detroit into smoldering rubble, and police were literally under the gun. Also, it was a time of civil unrest over Vietnam. It just wasn't the most popular time to be wearing a uniform, including a blue one. Then there were the occupational hazards—high stress, strain on marriages, late-night calls to duty, working holidays, crappy hours, and burnout. But Brad signed on as a clerk/dispatcher on July 1, 1969, and then became a full-fledged cadet. He got his silver badge and .38 caliber police revolver in December.

"He was a good policeman," said Sergeant Gordon Bovee of the Pontiac Police Department. "Brad was kind of the laid-back type. It took a lot to get him excited."

Over a fourteen-year career, Brad worked as a training officer, as a school liaison in the youth section, on the road patrol, and undercover with the surveillance unit. He earned several letters of commendation for meritorious arrests during that time.

"We didn't talk business when we were around each other," said Fred Goins, who was in charge of the vice squad and worked mostly nights when Brad was hired. "I didn't want him to think I was pushy. He didn't discuss police work. He was introverted. He was not outgoing. Lots of times, he was just silent. Not talkative. I never saw him violent or anything. We never had a complaint as far as I know of him using excessive force or being brutal. I thought he did a good job as a policeman. His record indicates that."

One of the people Brad rode with was Brian Fisher, a veteran on the force who helped break in rookies. He and Brad were partners later on.

"He was just a good fellow. He was very intelligent, had a good rapport with the citizens. He was never a heavy-handed person. He didn't go out of his way to put somebody in jail. He was laid back and easygoing. He had potential to aspire to higher things. He got the most from the job he could. Brad was almost handpicked for a job in training officer section of the department. He would research schools and training seminars and classes and things like that for the detectives and vice guys to attend. He did a hell of a job. He was somebody you could rely on. You never had to worry about looking over your shoulder and not seeing him. He'd be there. He didn't pry into your life, or bore you with his problems."

In the meantime, Gail taught English and history at Waterford High School, and they lived quite comfortably on two incomes.

"I handled our finances. We were squeaky clean. Our credit rating was clean as a whistle. Everything was paid for except the mortgage," Gail said. Like his mother, Brad's wife provided order and structure to his life.

There were adjustments, of course. Gail had three sisters and an open, outgoing family. It took a while for people to accept Brad's moods and introspection, but everyone learned to accept him.

"He was unusually quiet. He just wasn't very talkative. Some people mistook that for cockiness or being superior. Actually, he was an introvert," said Carolyn Van Bibber, Gail's oldest sister. "One time he came over to my house and he just sat there and watched a movie. I gave him a soft drink and he left. He said, 'It was nice visiting with you.' But that was just Brad. He'd just sit there and twirl his moustache."

"He was not the life of the party, generally speaking," said Jan Goins, the second oldest sister. Sometimes he would go sit in another room for a little peace and quiet. That was just Brad. He was used to a more tranquil environment. His way of showing of that was withdrawal. You could tell when he really liked you. He would open up a little bit. But he was somewhat remote ninety-nine percent of time."

The youngest sister, Melba Goins, knew Brad since she was fourteen. She attended Pontiac Central High School when Brad did his student teaching. She even dated Brad's brother, Scott, for a time.

"We're a pretty outgoing bunch. And at Christmas time when we'd open presents, Brad might be sitting there rubbing his chin and then just get up and leave. People that didn't know him very well might have been turned off by that. Really, some people thought he was rude or aloof. If he wanted to be off by himself, he went off by himself. We just accepted his moodiness. He didn't know how to express emotions, especially hurtful ones. I just consider him my big brother. I can't say one bad thing about him."

Gail and Brad's marriage seemed like a fairy tale for the first four years. The sisters remember Brad for being a good cook, the gourmet stuff like French dishes, quiche lorraine, bouillabaisse, chocolate mousse, and omelettes. He was his mother-in-law's favorite.

"If I ever had a son, I would have wanted him to be like Brad," Alice Lucille Goins used to say.

And it was when Alice came down with cancer that the family really appreciated Brad. He worked the afternoon shift, and before he went to work, Brad would come over to sit with her. He didn't talk much; sometimes he'd just sit in the same room reading a magazine. But he was there for her.

"I would come home, and Brad would be there sitting

with my mother. He just sat there just to be with her. I feel that was pretty compassionate. I felt he went out of his way to be there," Melba said.

Alice died in 1976, and Brad had a difficult time with the death. Although he could sit for hours with her when she was alive, Brad couldn't visit the funeral home when she was laid out.

Things started to change in the marriage when Gail and Brad gave birth to a daughter, Alissa Jean King, on March 30, 1972. The baby wasn't planned, and fatherhood wasn't something Brad was ready for. Within a year, there was a trial separation.

"Maybe it was the responsibility of being a new father. I felt he was having an adjustment period. A child hadn't been in our plans, and I was giving most of my attention to her. Maybe he was a little overwhelmed," Gail said. It wouldn't be the last time he had an intense reaction to the birth of a child either.

Gail's sisters noted Brad's reaction and had their own theories. "It was like he was jealous. Brad didn't want to share Gail. He wanted to be number one. He needed the attention and wanted it," Carolyn Van Bibber said.

His father-in-law noted something, too. "I don't think he was loving enough. He was kind of withdrawn. He wasn't normal when it come to showing affection."

The separation lasted about three weeks. Gail went to Texas and Arkansas to visit her sister and father. Then Brad sought a reconciliation, and they went into marriage counseling. Gail agreed to get back together, but she laid down the law. If this kind of thing ever happens again, that would be it. She wasn't going to be married to someone who kept having second thoughts or wavered about a commitment.

Brad and Gail tried to make the relationship work.

During one discussion, the subject of household chores came up.

"What job do you hate the most?" Brad asked.

"Ironing," his wife said.

"Okay, I'll do the ironing for you." And he did.

In the meantime, Brad was having a personal crisis of his own—a receding hair line. Actually, his hair started to thin when he was in college. It got thinner in the seventies—the decade of disco, wide-collared shirts, platform shoes, and frizzy hairstyles. And at one point Brad got a perm. But he had much more hair on the sides and the back than he did on top. His fellow cops dished out some good-natured ribbing and gave him the nickname Bozo, because he looked like the clown with the curly hair sticking out on the sides and back. Brad finally made a three-hundred-dollar concession to his vanity in 1975, buying a hairpiece. He wore the toupee for about a year. Most people figured he looked better without it.

Brad had an offbeat sense of humor. Gail remembered that in college he got a kick out of a trick played on the fraternity pledges where, after tacks were placed on the floor, the fire alarm was sounded and the barefoot brothers had to run across them. It was like something out of "The Three Stooges," and Brad thought it was hilarious. Another time, there was a discussion about oral sex, which one of his conservative sisters-in-law thought was disgusting. She shuddered when somebody joked that she should think of the male orgasm as salty-tasting apple sauce. That Christmas, as a gift from Brad, she received a can of apple sauce wrapped in holiday paper and adorned with a bow.

It's hard to pinpoint what exactly sets off a male mid-life crisis, but Brad went through his right around 1980.

All the threads of his life were unraveling. He questioned his job and what he wanted to do with the rest of his life. He wondered about staying married and being stuck in that commitment for another couple of decades. There were lots of doubts and no answers.

"He was at a stage in his life. He did not like being a police officer at all. He didn't want to be a cop anymore. He hated it too much. He made good money, but there was so much stress with the job. And he didn't want to be married anymore. He didn't want the responsibility," Gail said.

True to her earlier warning when there had been a trial separation, Gail didn't hesitate when doubts crept into the relationship again. If Brad was uncertain, he should end it. And she made him file for the divorce. She didn't want him coming back a couple of years later saying he had reconsidered.

"He filed on me. It was his decision. It was weird. We had a lot of fun together, and we always cared about each other. We didn't argue that much. There was never any violence," Gail said.

It was a civil if not amicable breakup. But Brad lost everything. He moved out of their home and into an apartment in Union Lake, Michigan, in February of 1981. He formally filed papers for divorce on April 29. In the stilted, stiff language of the legal briefs, he asked "that the marriage bonds be dissolved and a divorce from the bonds of matrimony be adjudged in accordance with the statutes in such case made and provided."

The divorce became final on May 11, 1982, when Judge Alice Gilbert signed an order that said, "There has been a breakdown in the marriage relationship to the extent that the objects of matrimony have been destroyed, and there remains no reasonable likelihood that the marriage can be preserved."

Joint custody of Alissa was awarded. The child lived with Gail, with Brad having custody on alternate weekends, alternate holidays and Father's Day. He also got her on alternate birthdays. Brad was ordered to pay child support of sixty dollars per week, based on twenty percent of his annual salary. Also, he was to pay necessary and reasonable hospital, medical, and dental expenses until Alissa reached eighteen or graduated from high school. Both parents paid one-half the cost of tuition at Our Lady of the Lakes parochial school.

Gail got to keep a 1978 Oldsmobile Cutlass; Brad took ownership of a 1979 Dodge pickup truck. Both vehicles were paid off. The tax refunds from 1981 were supposed to be split fifty-fifty, and each got to keep any furniture, furnishings, appliances, ornaments, money, personal effects, clothing, paper, and jewelry currently in their possession.

Brad also paid Gail $6,350, which was half of the interest in his retirement benefits with the Pontiac police. Gail continued to live at their home at 6858 Wellsely Terrace in Waterford, although she had to pay him half of its value if it were sold.

Mitchell Ribitwer, once the assistant prosecutor in Oakland County, represented Brad during the divorce. They had worked together on a couple of criminal cases that Brad investigated. "He was a good guy, a hell of a good guy. I never saw him angry. I saw him upset during the divorce, but I never saw him angry," Ribitwer said.

It never came up during the divorce, but rumors surfaced later about Brad having an affair while he was married. Gail confronted him about it, but he denied it. "It's possible. It's very possible," Gail said.

Funny thing, though. Brad invested a lot of psychological energy getting out of his marriage, but he attempted to get back into it within about three years. At the time of the divorce he was burned out, and he thought he wanted to do something different. But the years he was married to Gail and worked on the police force were the most stable in his life. After Gail, he dated other women, including a new love interest named Diane Marie Marler. They had made marriage plans, but he canceled them as he tried to patch things up one more time with Gail. His new pastures weren't any greener than the old ones.

"We had been divorced for about three years, and he asked me to remarry him. I said no. I felt it wasn't going to work out. He had just broken up with Diane. We needed to get on with our lives. I wasn't even in love anymore," Gail said.

In the meantime, Brad did some part-time teaching at Henry Ford Community College after he obtained his master's degree in criminal justice at Michigan State University. While working nights at the police station, he taught a juvenile justice class from 1977 to 1983 as part of an internship program. "He was not the most communicating person in the world," said Henry Schroeder, director of the criminal justice program at Henry Ford CC. "He would just come here, teach class, and then leave."

Brad left there in January of 1983, and it was the last time Schroeder saw him. On August 13 of that year, he resigned from the Pontiac police force.

"He was at a time in his life when he wanted to move on. He needed more than this agency could offer him. He was still in the process of growing," said Ray Gottschall, a detective who was a senior at Pontiac Central when Brad was a student-teacher. Brad and Ray used to play handball together, and they worked in the same office. Ray was in charge of the budget, and Brad lined up classes for officers to attend. "He had lots of irons in the fire. He was a brains over brawn kind of a guy. He was more intellectual. I don't think I ever saw the man lose his temper. He wasn't a time bomb waiting to go off or anything. I've never known him to be violent in any way, shape, or form."

When Brad decided to do something different, he picked something really different. He got involved in the assertiveness-training group called est, and he was packing away his police revolver and badge to spread the word of Werner Erhard.

"He tried to recruit several people here. I don't think anybody took him up on it," said Pontiac police sergeant Gordon Bovee.

CHAPTER 7

Every relationship begins with some common ground—the spark of a physical attraction, liking the way someone thinks or acts, a mutual desire to fill a need and share things. In Bradford King, Diane Marie Marler thought she had found quite a catch. She was always looking to better herself, and she wanted somebody with upward mobility. She thought she had found it in a man who had been a police officer for fourteen years and had a master's degree in criminology. He was an older man, someone she felt secure with. And in Diane, Brad found an attractive, high-spirited, take-charge personality who could bring order to his life.

Diane and Brad met at an est seminar in 1983. Although they came from entirely different backgrounds, they were drawn individually to the self-fulfillment movement and what they thought was a foundation for the future. Diane was trying to fill the void over the loss of her father while searching out her identity in her Indian and white roots; Brad was seeking a different path following his failed marriage and fourteen-year stint as a cop. At one of the seminars in Detroit, Diane met Randy Wright, a lawyer who attended Western Michigan University and belonged to Tau Kappa Epsilon fraternity with Bradford King. It was Wright who introduced Diane and Brad, and a romance blossomed.

They were hardly the only people of the time seeking to tap their full potential. So much had happened in the seventies: the war in Vietnam was lost and America had lost face in the world; there was a sense of diminished expectations from things like the Arab oil embargoes; President Jimmy Carter wailed about a national malaise; and tens of thousands of people flocked to the guru of self-awareness, Werner Erhard. He had founded Erhard Seminars Training in 1971 and told salvation-seekers to take charge of their own lives. He had a seductive message: you are responsible for your own life, you have a right to do what you want, you can transform the world and you can make it a better place to live.

For tens of thousands of people, est was a way to organize their lives, improve their communication skills, manage their time better, and get rid of unneeded emotional baggage. At its best, it was just a kick in the pants to get people going in the direction they wanted to go anyway. For some, like Diane and Brad, it became a way of life. Those devoted to it dressed alike and talked alike. Some acquaintances jokingly called them the pod people. Others feared they had been brainwashed by a cult-like organization.

Werner Erhard was born Jack Rosenberg in a Philadelphia suburb. He changed his name to a combination derived from space scientist Wernher Von Braun and former German Chancellor Ludwig Erhard. A one-time used car salesman, Werner Erhard moved to California, where he was a personnel-motivation expert. In San Francisco, he studied Zen, Yoga, the martial arts, transactional analysis, sensitivity training, and encounter therapy. During a mystical experience while driving on a California freeway, Erhard became a positive-thought evangelist. In a blinding flash, he "got it"—the key to a more satisfying life is to accept yourself for who you are and define the world in your own terms. Just exactly what was "it"? Well, those who took est said it can't be explained, only experienced. In the Tao, "it" is the way it is. In Zen, "it" is the suchness. In est, Erhard called "it" riding the horse in the direction it is going. What he offered was enlightenment for sale, packaging Eastern religion and Western philosophy for mass consumption. One of the movement's cardinal principles was, "I am the cause of my own world." There wasn't anything terribly controversial about teaching people to be honest about their lives and taking control of their destinies. But there was plenty of criticism about the method.

Everything was geared for quick consumption, so recruits were given a sixty-hour package on successive weekends. For the first eighteen hours, they sat on hard-backed chairs in hotel ballrooms with only one break to eat and go to the bathroom. During the sessions, est trainers harangued the crowd with drill sergeant–style epithets. Students were called "turkeys" or "assholes" and screamed at to "wipe that silly smile off your face." The verbal abuse and physical deprivations were a transforming experience. The idea was to discard the clutter of the past so they could "get it together." The program challenged people to question the way they lived and to see themselves as products of their parents' programming. Then you could put yourself back together in a better package. Sessions included mind and body exercises, such as staring at someone for hours at a time. Late in the fourth session was when you were supposed to "get it." Those who got it said est improved their marriages, helped with diet and discipline, cured headaches, led to better grades and improved work performances. The stuff became part of the popular culture. In the movie *Manhattan,* Woody Allen whined that his neurotic wife had left him to join est. By 1985 Erhard even had come up with a yuppified version—without the yelling and swearing. He called it The Forum, and if est was about getting it together, The Forum was about making it happen. He even exported some of his teachings to the Soviet Union, which earned him the nickname Guru of the Gulag. Eventually, est became Werner Erhard and Associates, reporting U.S. revenues of $45 million in 1989. Then it became an employee-owned company called Transnational Education Corporation, which later became Landmark Education Corporation.

Erhard dropped from sight when problems surfaced. Some of his disciples charged that Erhard—who was called the Source and revered as a god—enforced obedience through violence, intimidation, and abuse. Some of his trainers complained of emotional and psychological problems from overwork. The organization was sued by people taking the sessions; one family sought damages because a man had a fatal heart attack. Another man allegedly suffered a manic episode during an est session. It got worse. The IRS claimed Erhard owed millions in back taxes, and his ex-wife sued him for half of everything.

But Diane got a lot from est. Here was something that told her she was perfect the way she was, that she was able to see the world through the prism of her own consciousness. What you want is what was okay. There is no right or wrong. It was a liberating experience for someone who thought of herself as too chubby, unattractive, and too dark. And like a stump preacher chasing sin, she wanted her friends and family to see the light the way she had. She nagged them about taking the seminars until she became a pain.

"Anytime she called, it was almost a drag," said her sister, Denise Verrier. "That's all she talked about. She kept trying to get us to sign up for it. I didn't want her in it. Those people are very much into self, like they are their own gods. They played a lot of mind games. It seemed to be a lot of brainwashing."

The family was turned off by est's authoritarian methods, the way trainers degraded and swore at people. But when Diane finished her training, she coaxed her mother, brother Allen, sister Denise, and Denise's husband, Donald, to come down to Cobo Hall in Detroit for the final ceremonies. She said it was a graduation, but it turned out to be a sales pitch for new converts.

"She had a way of making you do things, even if you didn't want to do them. She'd call up and say, 'Nobody cares about me.' So me and my husband went," Denise said. "It just seemed like a lot of propaganda. People got up and said what est did for them. They gave us name tags with different colors and tried to separate us, to herd us into different rooms. They were trying to intimidate us so we would join. It just wasn't for us."

Diane also tried the hard-sell with Regina Zapinski, and it almost wrecked a friendship that dated back to junior high school. When Diane asked her to attend a seminar, Regina wanted to know more about it. What exactly was this stuff? Diane said it could only be experienced, not explained. But Regina didn't want any part of something she didn't understand.

"It got to be a real sore point between us. It was not a good time," Regina said. "I read everything about it I could, but I didn't understand what it was. I was leery of it, and she couldn't explain it to me. I don't like someone trying to sell me something without being able to explain it. She'd just say, 'Do it. Do it. Do it.' And if I didn't have the money, she said she'd pay for me because it was that important. It got to the point where she would trick me into going to places so I could hear about est. I couldn't trust her anymore."

The issue exploded when the two friends met for lunch at a restaurant called Telly's in Warren. Diane kept hitting one of Regina's hot buttons, telling her that if she took est she could express herself without having to drink so much.

"It was a loud argument. People were staring at us. We were crying as we left the restaurant. I told her I wasn't going to join it, and that I didn't ever want to hear anything about it ever again," Regina said.

Brad promoted est, too. His ex-wife, Gail, and his daughter, Alissa, took a seminar. But people like Ray Gottschall at the police department weren't interested. "He told me a little bit about it. It wasn't my thing," the detective said.

Brad wanted to be a trainer with est. He took a job with the organization in Cincinnati, Ohio. After several months, he moved to Colorado. Diane, who was in the Army at the time, followed him out there. She got a transfer from Georgia to Colorado, then resigned her commission to become a sales representative for Werner Erhard and Associates. Within five months, Diane and Brad were married in Denver on July 21, 1984.

* * *

The first time Brad met Diane's family he made a bad impression, and things went downhill from there. He came over to the house and sat on the two-seater couch in the livingroom. He didn't volunteer much or add much to the conversation. He seemed like he didn't want to be there.

"He never looked me in the eye. I tried to get along with him. I could never get through to him," Freida Newton said.

Perhaps Brad was just being his introverted self, but Diane's family had the distinct impression that he thought he was too good for them. Sure, he wanted Diane, the family overachiever who had gone to college. He just didn't have much in common with anyone else in the family. It was such a large family, too, with all those aunts and uncles and cousins.

It didn't help that the courtship was rocky. Diane and Brad made plans to be married, and then he broke things off and tried to get back together with his ex-wife. Diane was crushed. When she fell for someone, she fell hard. And she had it bad for Brad. Diane even sought advice from Gail about how to deal with Brad and his moods. They talked about his problems with responsibility, and Gail told her that if they ever did get married, she should make sure Brad was emotionally prepared to have a family before they planned any pregnancies.

After Brad did his flip-flop and patched things up with Diane, she decided to scrap her Army career and get married.

"I tried to talk her out of getting married. She was quitting the Army, and I had never seen her so enthused about something like that before," said her older sister, Darlene. "I told her, 'Don't quit. If he really loves you, he'll be there when you get out. It's only two years. If he won't wait for you, he's not worth it.' "

Diane didn't listen. The wedding was held at a nondenominational church because Diane was Catholic and Brad was Presbyterian. With such short notice, there was no time to plan a big wedding. The only ones from Diane's family to attend were her mother and her aunt, Edna Canadyan, of Perris, California. And Diane always felt bad she didn't have a big wedding.

"She said she was never going to get married and have kids," Freida said, reflecting on Diane's previous declarations. But now, "She really wanted me to accept her marriage. I tried. I finally told her, 'You're old enough to know what you're doing. I don't have to live with him. You do.' "

Brad was no longer working at est. He walked out one day in early 1984, and headed back to Texas to spend a week with his mother and figure out what to do next. He was a disillusioned convert, having lost faith in the false prophet of est. It had cost him a lot; after all, he had given up his steady job and his prestige as a policeman to join. He had perceived it as a route to self-esteem. Est is a rather difficult program, but Brad liked it because it offered a quick fix to life's problems. He was attracted to the magical thinking that one could create one's own reality simply by thinking it, not actually working for it. Est gave Brad a sense of power he never had before. But in the end it lacked substance and failed to give him self-fulfillment. Disenchanted, he reverted to form and latched on to a powerful woman who provided him with order and structure, even if she did harp at him a lot. Diane Marler became his answer, and he never again pursued anything with any zeal. He just worked at a series of short-lived jobs.

Diane had a new Mazda when she moved to Colorado, but Freida noted she sold it. Ostensibly it was because they didn't need two cars, but Freida figured she needed the money to pay off Brad's bills. And Freida never again saw the gold lieutenant's bars she had bought for her daughter; she figured either Diane had hocked the jewelry or had it melted down for her wedding rings.

"He didn't have a job. She was always supporting him. And if you can't support your wife and family, you're nothing in my book," Freida said.

Brad's folks, Marjorie and Willis King, came up from their retirement home in Texas for the wedding in Colorado. Marjorie never hid the fact that she was very fond of Brad's first wife. And Diane told family and friends her new mother-in-law was put off by her bronze Indian skin and her family's blue-collar roots. Brad's family seemed to feel his life was going downhill.

One thing was certain, Diane and Brad were never a traditional couple. Each held a variety of jobs. Then Diane assumed the role of breadwinner when she went into television thirteen months after they were married. She had found her career path, and he was going to follow, supporting her in that path, rather than carving one out for himself.

"Diane had a game plan. She was easy to read. He was a little more unknown to me," said Lin Mrachek, who hired Diane at KRMA-TV in Denver. "I don't think Brad was full-time anything. It was never really clear about what he was doing. He wasn't a typical husband with some kind of established career. I felt at the time he was searching, too. When she talked about moving on in her career, she said, 'We don't have any problems along those lines. He's going to follow me whatever I do.' "

When the Kings moved to Grand Junction after Diane

was hired at KJCT, Brad would often come down to the station to pick her up at work. Station manager Jan Hammer got to know Brad well enough to sponsor him in the local Lions Club. When the station ran a public service commercial on behalf of the Lions, Brad dressed up in a Huckleberry Finn outfit.

"In a lot of ways, I don't understand the marriage. They were opposites in terms of personality. Brad was passive. Diane was aggressive. One kind of got the feeling that Diane wore the pants in the family. But then again, they weren't competing with one another," Hammer said. "Brad didn't offer that much in a conversation. He wasn't very forceful. Her career came first. He subjugated himself to her wants. He was always there in a supportive capacity. When people called him Mr. Diane King, it's the kind of description that fits."

Reporters, like cops, get used to working holidays. The news didn't stop on Christmas or New Year's or Thanksgiving. But Hammer tried to soften the blow by inviting the spouses of his reporters over to his house until their shifts were over. It was under this arrangement that Brad met Percy Jackson, whose wife, Carol, worked with Diane at KJCT.

Jackson was a program specialist at Mesa Developmental Services, which worked with disabled adults and children. Brad applied for a job there as a caseworker, but he was rejected. The Jacksons were also involved in the program Partners to help troubled youths, and Brad and Diane volunteered also. The program matched couples with kids who needed a positive role model.

What impressed Jackson the most was how well-dressed the Kings were even though Brad didn't have a full-time job. He always had a stylish trench coat, expensive shoes, and the latest fashions.

"He looked like he was straight out of Gentlemen's Quarterly and she was out of Better Homes and Gardens," Jackson said.

"I asked him once what he wanted to do. He said, 'I've had my career. Now it's Diane's turn.' He was going to see her make it big. He was very supportive of her. He didn't seem to have any goals or ambitions. He was definitely in her shadow," Jackson said. "I can never remember seeing Brad with anyone other than Diane. That's the way he wanted it, it seemed. I tried to get to know the guy. He didn't want anybody to get to know him. He didn't want to get to know anybody. Like, I'd ask him to play racketball, and he'd say sure. Then it would come time to play and he never came along."

Of course, traditional roles have changed between husbands and wives. Women on the career path were no longer a novelty, and roles at home had changed, too. Long gone were the days when a man worked nine to five and came home to a housewife and a brood of kids. Career opportunities were such that women were getting better job offers, and males had to be flexible enough to move with them. That's what Regina Zapinski thought when she visited Colorado and met Brad. Diane had told her she was dating an ex-cop, but Regina had never met him. Her first impression was positive.

"Times are changing. Men can follow women now," Regina said. "She really seemed happy. He seemed pleasant and acted pleasant. My gosh, she had been looking for something like this all her life and she had finally found it. He did so many things to please her. Whatever she wanted him to do, he was backing her. If that meant staying home or not having a job, so be it. He never acted like it was a bother. My first impression was, 'Gee, what a nice guy.' She did all the talking. She spoke for him. Brad just sat there. She never said anything bad about him. And I had no reason not to like him. He liked the notoriety of being married to a TV news reporter. Some friends would say that he looked like he was pussy-whipped, though. I never saw anything but the extra caring, loving, dear husband who doted on his wife. I didn't even think Brad could make a decision without her. Brad always sat in on conversations. He never added to them. He was just there. Whatever I knew about Brad was what Diane said Brad said. Diane talked for him. She was always making excuses for him. They seemed like they were supposed to be together. Brad was right there, supporting her all the way. All she had to do was climb the ladder. He took care of everything else."

The shifting ground of the male role in matrimony was something that Brad discussed with a couple of Colorado friends whose wives had their own careers, Alex Galant and John Van Vleet. John, who has a bachelor's degree in psychology and a master of science degree in clinical psychology from Illinois State University, is vice president of training in a company headed by his wife, Susan Van Vleet Consultants Inc. It was as if none of the old rules applied.

"If you're married to a powerful woman, you live your life differently than an old-fashioned husband who makes all the decisions. It's not the traditional role, so people think you're pussy-whipped or you're a wimp," Alex said. "People say, 'Oh, he must be frustrated.' We discussed how outrageous it is in our society that you can't be in a partnership with your wife without being less of man, that it wasn't macho."

John Van Vleet just figured they were two people with different priorities in life.

"With Diane, her career was so visible. She was much

more career-oriented than Brad. He was happy supporting her. It wasn't that he was wimpy or a Casper Milquetoast. Depending on the time and place in a marriage, one career can take precedence. Her career was the more important at the time. I thought of it as being supportive rather than browbeaten or henpecked," John said. "Brad was laid back. He never really got too excited about anything. He had the ability to adjust to things, go with the flow. He was a big teddy bear. Real friendly. Nice guy. I always thought it was weird that Brad was a cop. I thought he was too nice to be a cop. If Brad had a problem it was that he was too laid back. Working wasn't a big thing for Brad. Money wasn't a big thing for him."

The men went to a few Denver Broncos football games together, but he wasn't a real big sports fan. Brad's big passion seemed to be his interest in Native-American culture because of Diane. He built a ceremonial lodge at an Indian center and was studying the Iroquois language. And his friends teased him about his shaved head, something that Diane insisted that he do now that he was bald. They called him Daddy Warbucks and said he looked a lot more sinister with a hairless head.

"You gotta grow your hair back, Brad. You look like the starting center on the Attica football team," John told him.

Brad did have some holdover responsibilities from his previous marriage to Gail. Alissa was in her teens when Brad remarried, and she came out to Colorado to stay for seven weeks in the summer of 1984. The adjustment to Brad's new living arrangement was awkward, to say the least. Diane worked very hard to establish a relationship with Alissa. Maybe too hard. Also, the easiest way to upset a mother is to differ with her on how to raise a child, and Gail and Diane crossed swords over Alissa. It got to the point where they didn't talk to each other for a year after one falling out that led to an exchange of harsh words and letters.

Then, not too long after Brad and Diane settled in Grand Junction, they started their own family. Diane would have been wise to remember what Gail told her about Brad's reaction to children and responsibility, because there was a telling episode when Marler was born.

Diane had made friends with a Grand Junction couple, Jack and Theresa Nisley, through work. She was doing a news story about hot-air balloons, and she interviewed Jack and Theresa at a Grand Valley Balloon Festival. They got to know each other so well that Diane asked Theresa to be her labor coach during the delivery and to serve as Marler's godmother.

As she recalled, Brad blanched at being a father again.

"He wasn't overjoyed. He said, 'I already have a daughter,' " Theresa said.

As a labor coach, Theresa was supposed to help Diane with her breathing and comfort her as much as she could. She got a call on March 5, 1988, that Diane was going to the hospital. They arrived at seven P.M., but Diane didn't give birth until seven A.M. the next morning by cesarean section. Theresa was honored to help. Yet she was put off that Brad spent the night dozing in a chair and never really got involved.

"I was fit to be tied with him. He wasn't taking an active part in it. He didn't seem to really care that Diane was miserable. He slept through most of it. That's just not my idea of what a husband should be doing. I thought that was pretty crappy, but I held my tongue," Theresa said.

The baby was baptized Marler, after Diane's father, in

the Immaculate Heart of Mary Roman Catholic Church in Grand Junction. Diane's brother, Allen, was supposed to be godfather but was delayed getting there from Michigan. So Theresa's husband, Jack, was a stand-in for the christening.

Theresa also noticed the Kings' marriage was atypical. "She was the dominant person in the relationship. That was real obvious. She was in the limelight. She was a real go-getter. She was going places. From time to time, she really rode him. Mostly it was because he didn't have a job. He was real content to stay home. He didn't have to do anything. He didn't seem to mind at all," she said.

The Kings' circle of friends was growing along with their family. When Lesley Tucker moved to Grand Junction to work for KJCT, the first person she met was Diane, who became like an older sister to her. Lesley thought it was unique to have a husband like Brad fawning all over one.

"I envy you," Lesley told Diane. "I hope I find someone who adores me the way he adores you."

But not very many people got to know Brad. He was like a blank page to Paula Anderson, who once worked at KJCT and was a newspaper reporter with the *Daily Sentinel* in Grand Junction. She and Diane had won an award presented by the town's Human Services Council.

"Diane was outgoing and would seek people out. Brad was to the other extreme. There were no vibes that he had any initiative to connect. He was just there. He was just a sort of shut-down personality. Sometimes couples will offset each other," she said.

There were lots of dinner parties and holiday events to attend. Friends recall seeing Diane and Brad dressed in military attire at Halloween parties. And sometimes when Brad got wound up, he'd put a pair of glasses on backward over his shaved head and clown around.

"They seemed to be a real close couple. They talked a lot," said Debbie Rich, who had gotten a job at the station through Diane. "Brad did play that role of Mr. Diane King or Mr. Mom. She was kind of frustrated with him. She could see his potential and he wasn't using it. I'm sure she nagged him about it. She made the money. She was well known. She was the aggressive one. As a man, how can you take that?"

One of the people Diane met through Debbie Rich was Judith Thomas, a member of the Junior Service League. She had a teaching certificate in English and taught music lessons in her home. Diane sought her out because she wanted to improve her writing and TV presentations. She was told she needed to work on her scripts, and she wasn't going to let a deficiency hold her back. At first, Diane did an hour-long class twice a week, then scaled back to one day a week as she got more proficient.

"She was a wonderful self-starter. She wanted badly to do the best job she could," Judith said. "She was so attractive. She was personable. Yet she was so concerned about any inadequacies. She wanted to be the best person she could be."

They worked on ways of making Diane's scripts more interesting while polishing her basic grammar. Diane tended to use colloquialisms and casual phrases in her speech. Judith taught her to sharpen her phrases and to vary her sentence structure. Oftentimes, she'd bring over tapes of old newscasts and have them critiqued.

"I don't like the way I come across," Diane told her.

"Personalitywise, you're wonderful. All you need to do

is work on some of these other things. There's no way you can't be anywhere you want," Judith replied.

Brad would sometimes pick Diane up after her sessions, and Judith got to know him too. "He looked like he adored her. This big hunk of a fellow just adored this woman. When he came over to pick her up and sat on the couch, he had this fond look in his eye and she in hers."

But Judith also knew that Brad didn't have a full-time job. And Diane was very sensitive to the people who were calling him Mr. Diane King. She thought it was ridiculous and offensive, and she had a heart-to-heart talk about it with her tutor.

"This really annoys me. Why would anybody call him Mr. Diane King?" Diane said.

"Look at opera stars or movie stars. If they have a family member in the public eye, a lot of times people don't know the other person's name. It's common. Don't let that bother you," Judith replied.

"People are insensitive. They can be cruel."

"You've picked your career to be in front of the public. That's part of the price you pay. People think they own you. You have a following. They want to be involved in your life. People will think you're theirs. They think they can do what they want and talk about you."

Judith knew that Diane had sent out audition tapes and résumés to a number of larger stations, including several in Michigan. And she was not the least bit surprised when Diane got the Battle Creek job.

"I would have expected it because she was female, a minority, and so attractive that in eight to ten years she would have worked her way to a larger market or network. She was very good on her feet," Judith said. "The happiest part was that she was going back home. She liked Colorado, but she really felt she needed to be closer to home. And she hoped her husband would find employment he would be happier with. She felt he had not been dealt a good hand."

Funny thing about this Mr. Mom stuff, though. Brad's first wife, Gail, felt he was probably comfortable in that role. "I don't think he minded at all. He wanted her to be successful."

In Colorado Brad had delivered morning papers, worked as a short-order cook, tended the cash register at a twenty-four-hour gas station and peddled men's clothes at a store called The Fashion Bar. His last job in Grand Junction was as a part-time counselor in the psychiatric department at St. Mary's Hospital. He was there from August 5, 1987 to February 8, 1989, and he resigned when he and Diane moved.

In Michigan he found a similar job. He worked as a mental health technician for the Calhoun County Community Mental Health Department. As a client-services manager, he made sure his clients received services appropriate for their condition, such as arranging physical therapy or counseling. During the same period, he worked part-time as a mental health technician at Adventist Hospital in Battle Creek. He left both those jobs to take a job as an intensive probation officer with the Tenth District Court of Calhoun County, but he lasted only a little more than two months before he was fired. County officials refused to discuss publicly the reasons for the January 11, 1990, dismissal. Brad claimed that he had uncovered some wrongdoing against one of the judges and was fired just when he was about to blow the whistle. He hired an attorney and threatened to sue, but the case never went anywhere.

Brad also worked part-time as a census taker for the

U.S. Census Bureau. He was turned down as a manager at Burger King because he was overqualified. Beginning in the fall of 1989, he also taught part-time at Western Michigan University. His classes included the sociology of law enforcement, juvenile delinquency, and criminology. The most he ever taught was three classes in one semester, during the fall of 1990. He was close to completing the requirements for a doctorate, but he didn't seem to feel any particular urgency in getting it.

If you heard Diane tell it, Brad was always on the verge of getting the break required to get his professional life squared away. He was always signing up for a class or applying for a program or lining up an interview that would be his breakthrough. And if things didn't work out or Brad lost his job, it was always somebody else's fault. Diane continually sought acceptance—for her husband as well as herself—and she desperately wanted her family to accept Brad as a worthy husband. But nobody in the family did.

"We thought the guy was a loser. He couldn't hold a job," said Denise Verrier. "Diane was very good at being 'up.' She normally wouldn't tell us if something were wrong. And she was always trying to build the guy up. She'd call and cry over the phone, 'I don't understand why nobody likes Brad.' We'd just roll our eyes. She would never admit that maybe there was something wrong with this man. My mom finally said to her, 'There's got to be something wrong with him. He can't hold a job.' We used to tease her that Brad's first wife got the best years out of him."

On the surface, things looked fine. In fact, Diane and Brad gave the appearance of being the quintessential modern couple with career goals, a family, and a lifestyle that combined the elements of rural tranquility and cosmopolitan sophistication. They even counseled other couples, thanks to a program run by their old friends in Colorado. Susan Van Vleet Consultants Inc. offered advice for married couples juggling the demands created when both spouses work. Contrary to some quaint notions about American households, only fourteen percent had just one breadwinner in 1990. Yet most social institutions and business practices are based on the assumption that the woman stays at home. Van Vleet's program was designed to let couples know they both could work and have an enlivening relationship. Brad and Diane went out to Englewood for a weekend of training, then ran two workshops in Sheboygan. Diane's family wasn't impressed, though.

"That was a joke. We couldn't figure out how he had the authority to talk about dual careers when he didn't work but his wife did," Denise Verrier said.

At family functions, Brad stayed close to Diane's side. He didn't sit and talk with the men much.

"He kind of wears on you. He just followed her around all the time. If the guys were in the room playing cards, he was always in the room with the women. It's like he was a puppy dog. He didn't have a whole lot in common with the men. He didn't have a whole lot in common with anybody. If you asked him a question, Diane would answer for him. The man couldn't speak for himself," Denise said.

From a male perspective, Don Verrier thought Brad was a tough guy to get to know. There was a distance between them because of est, regarded by Don as a cult.

"He was very aloof. I warm up to most anybody. But I could never get anywhere with him. There was a lack of personality with him. I didn't think they had a bad relationship. Each had a definite role. She was dominant. He did take a backseat to her career. He kind of faded into the woodwork. She carried the relationship, practically most conversations. She liked the limelight. It was kind of natural to draw attention to herself. I don't remember him talking about anything. Except when someone talked about cooking. Then he used to come somewhat to life. He would perk up. He was familiar with the kitchen. He kind of had a disdain for the family, an arrogance, like he was better than them," Don said.

With his shaved head, and the way he dressed, Brad also had a somewhat eccentric appearance. He'd wear shirts with blousy sleeves and trousers with baggy legs so he looked like Yul Brynner. And he'd wear his tan trench coat and look like Kojak.

One time, Brad came to WUHQ to deliver his wife's lunch. But on this day, he failed to shave his head and he showed up with some stubble. It looked like five o'clock shadow around the rim of his head. Diane dressed him down in public: "Don't ever come into my workplace looking like that. I would never come to work looking unkempt."

There were other signs of tension between Diane and Brad, but no one knew how deep the divisions ran. One time, Gordon Marler and his future wife, Mary Kozak, stayed at the Kings' apartment in Battle Creek. They talked about going ice skating, and the conversation was upbeat and a bit boisterous. Diane's voice was getting louder.

"These people are in the same room as you are," Brad said.

Sensitive to any criticism, Diane clammed up and fumed. Within a few moments, she proclaimed: "I'm going to bed now." He followed a few moments later. It was only eight P.M. That left Gordie and Mary to do the dishes and fend for themselves the rest of the night.

Mary wondered what these two people had in common. "You got the impression he was totally dedicated to her. Diane would say, 'Iron my pants. Get my makeup out.' And he did it in a heartbeat. He did it all the time. He was the one who sent out all the Christmas cards. It was like, what is she doing with him? She's gorgeous. She had so much personality. He hardly talked. He was nothing."

Every one of Diane's friends had a tough time getting through to Brad. Stella Pamp noted that when Brad and Diane attended a weekend Indian powwow, they camped in their own tent. Diane mixed a lot more freely than Brad. "He was always off in the distance. He was just there, like a shadow. I never saw him talk to the men. I never saw him talk to the elders. He did talk to the young ladies. We noticed he was openly flirting," Stella Pamp said. "I didn't get to know him. He would never sit down and have a conversation with you."

Meanwhile, Diane was still trying to establish some kind of rapport with Brad's daughter Alissa. She and Brad made plans to attend Alissa's high school homecoming, but the connection got botched. When Diane and Brad went to the event and couldn't find Alissa, they figured they had been stood up. But that was a matter of opinion. Alissa said she arrived outside the gate of the football stadium when the game started at seven o'clock. When no one showed by 7:30, she went inside to be with her friends. Diane and Brad got there at 7:45. "They were always late," Alissa said.

Diane kept trying, though. For Christmas in 1989, she and Brad and Marler spent some time with Gail and Alissa. The meeting was civil, but overall it was predictably awkward. "I'll never do that again," Diane said when it was over.

One person who had a close-up view of the dynamics of Diane and Brad's relationship was Kristina Mony, who went to work as an intern at WUHQ in June of 1989. She worked that summer and then part-time during her senior year at Galesburg-Augusta High School. Diane liked her because of her ambition and drive, and the two became more than co-workers or friends. Kristina was like a second daughter. Diane and Brad attended her high school graduation. Brad called her on prom night to wish her good luck. And Kristina was a dependable baby-sitter for Marler. She just thought the world of Diane, and not just on a professional level.

"She was a very devoted mother. Sure, her career meant a lot to her. But her family was the most important thing. She kept a leather-bound diary at home for Marler that read "To My Beautiful Indian Baby." She wrote something in it every day. She was going to give it to him when he got older so he could read it. She was so proud of him. One time, she was going to a black-tie dinner and she brought Marler along. She dressed him in knickers and bow tie," Kristina said.

And she knew how hard Diane tried to please Brad. When Diane was pregnant with Kateri and the center of a lot of attention, she went out and purchased a gift for Brad.

"She bought a ceramic eagle for Brad so he wouldn't feel left out. She said, 'I've had all these baby showers, but nobody ever does anything for the husband.' Now how many women do you know like that?" Kristina said.

But she also noted something of a mismatch in the relationship. She wondered why Diane and Brad were married when they were so dissimilar in personality.

"I often wonder why she picked him. They say opposites attract. It was real obvious she was overpowering him. He was in her shadow," Kristina said. "She used to tell me, 'Make sure you marry a man who looks good on your arm, one who looks good and presents himself in a professional way.' I wanted to ask her why she didn't follow her own advice. I think he weighed her down a lot. He was like a wet blanket over her. She needed someone with life and energy so they could rise together. He just was not like that."

Kristina noticed that Diane was coming to some sober conclusions about Brad's career path. It was great at first that he was so supportive and willing to follow her, but now it appeared that Brad just had no ambition of his own. And like a domineering mother trying to give focus to a child, Diane left lists of things for Brad to do such as sending out job résumés while she was at work. When they weren't taken care of, she got upset.

"She would get so frustrated with him. She felt he had a little bit of a lazy streak. She'd come home from work and he hadn't done anything about finding a job. That would upset her. He was like a child. He seemed to be disorganized," Kristina said.

And there was something to this Mr. Diane King stuff. It was like an old-fashioned marriage in reverse; Brad assumed his wife's identity.

"She was his life preserver. He was totally lost in her. It used to be that women lost their identity to their husbands. They would take their names and be called Mrs. So-and-so. That's changing now. In the generation Brad grew up in, women followed men. He followed her. Some men are threatened by women who succeed. It affects their masculinity, their feelings about themselves.

I think he felt less manly because of Diane's drive," Kristina said.

Nancy Gwynne at WUHQ noted that Brad had perfected his supportive role, being at Diane's beck and call, running for the diaper bag or bottle whenever ordered. But she also said she saw signs of smoldering resentment that Brad did a good job of repressing.

"I think she was too much for Brad. She overwhelmed Brad. He wanted to be in the limelight, too. He wanted to be up front and didn't know how to get there. He was like a child. As long as she had the job, as long as he could have all the candy and eat it too, it was fine. But he'd look at her with those eyes as if to say, 'It's supposed to be me.' Anything she did, she did wholeheartedly. She wanted you to feel what she felt. I told Diane several times, 'I do not understand what you and Brad have in common.' And she'd say, 'I'm beginning to wonder myself.' "

CHAPTER 8

A dead body can tell you things if you know how to listen. There's nothing mystical or spiritual about it. Science is what can coax the facts from a mute corpse. And Diane Newton King had a story to tell.

About eighteen hours after she was murdered, an autopsy began at Blodgett Hospital in Grand Rapids. Diane's body had made the sixty-mile trip from the Craig Kempf Funeral Home in Marshall in a hearse, indelicately called the "meat wagon" by cops. Robert Kiessling drove the wagon after he removed the body from the morgue, and he was accompanied by a deputy sheriff who brought along evidence bags with the Desert Storm sweat shirt, jeans, and undergarments Diane was wearing. Her clothing would have something to say, too.

Like each of Michigan's eighty-three counties, Calhoun County has a medical examiner. But he does not do forensic pathology exclusively. Places like Blodgett Hospital handle a high volume of autopsies and do a first-rate job on criminal cases. About six hundred autopsies a year are done here, and Dr. Stephen Cohle, a forensic pathologist, personally does about three hundred. It's his job to determine the cause and manner of death for homicides, suicides, accidents and unexpected natural deaths.

His work is done under an elaborate security system because a body, like any piece of evidence, can present facts only if it has not been tampered with. Only authorized persons can enter the Blodgett morgue. A special card must be inserted into a lock—the kind that hotels use in place of keys these days. A central computer logs who goes in and who leaves. It discourages outsiders from trying to sneak in and steal valuables—rings, necklaces, car keys, personal papers, or even weapons—from the dead.

A body bag was wheeled in on a stretcher into a room with two operating tables. The bag was unzipped, and a nude female body was lifted onto the table. The bag itself was checked for fibers, hairs, spent slugs, or other evidence that may have come off the body. Likewise, it's standard procedure for police to go through all the pockets in the clothing looking for anything that may assist them.

A forensic pathologist approaches his work like a clinical doctor. There is a proscribed process designed to learn as much as possible so a conclusion can be drawn. Instead of a diagnosis for a living patient, however, it's a finding on the how and why of a death.

First Cohle checked the medical history. He read the hospital reports on when, where, and how the woman died. He also wanted background information. In Diane's case, she had given birth twice by cesarean section, as attested to by the five-inch scar in her pubic region. And she had a one-inch scar on each breast from the saline implants she received in Boston. Cohle also wanted to know exactly what medical treatment was rendered. He routinely asks that hospitals keep intravenous and air tubes in so he can account for every mark on the body. Her fingernails were checked and scraped to see if there were any signs of struggle. Swabbings were taken of her mouth and nose.

Cohle's second step was a complete external visual examination of the body. On the table before him was a five-foot-two, 137-pound woman whose body was tagged with her name. She had a ring on the fourth finger of her right hand and two rings on the fourth finger of her left hand—the wedding and engagement bands. The body was photographed and checked for markings, tatoos, and other physical things. Cohle measured and recorded the entry wounds of the two bullets; there were no exit wounds, so the bullets had to still be inside. The wounds were cleaned of any dried blood and photographed up close. X rays were taken to give Cohle a general idea of the bullets' paths through the body and a preliminary indication of what organs were damaged.

Now came the internal exam. Starting at the right shoulder, Cohle cut on a diagonal line to the bottom tip of the breast plate. Then, from the left shoulder, the scalpel cut to the same point, completing a V on the upper chest. Where the two incisions intersected, Cohle cut down the abdomen to a point just above the pubic line. This way, he could peel back the flaps of skin like peeling away a wrapping. Next, Cohle's scalpel sliced through the ribs—a certain point to the side usually has the softest cartilage and tissue—to expose the heart and lungs. When the body was opened, samples were taken of blood, urine, eye fluid, and bile from the gallbladder. These were screened for the presence of drugs, alcohol, medication, or poison. Organs were weighed and examined for damage.

When all of this was finished, Cohle made his conclusion. And obviously, this was a homicide.

"There's a lot of things a dead body can tell you, but you have to know what to ask," said Cohle. The first thing Diane Newton King told him was she never saw this coming. There were no gunpowder marks or burns on her clothing or her skin. Gunpowder follows the same path as a bullet, but it dissipates quickly once it leaves the gun barrel. If the distance between the shooter and the victim is four feet or less, there should be traces of gunpowder. The absence of burns told Cohle she was shot at some distance. There were also no signs of a struggle.

Another thing he learned was the gunman was either damn good or damn lucky. The bullets from a small-caliber gun—probably a .22, but the crime lab would ascertain that—did irreparable damage.

Bullet number one entered the right upper chest, two inches above the nipple line. Cohle also found the corresponding hole in the sweat shirt. The slug entered between the third and fourth rib, leaving a hole one-eighth of an inch in diameter in the skin. It pierced the upper part of the right lung, struck the heart, punctured the aorta, grazed the spinal column, and came to rest in the soft tissue of the woman's back. Cohle calculated it traveled downward at an angle of ten degrees and moved through her body on a right-to-left path. There was blood in the sac around the heart and the lung. Even if the shooting had occurred in a hospital, no power on earth could have saved her. The shot to the heart and aorta—the artery that carries blood from the heart's left ventricle to the body's major organs—was not survivable. She truly was a defenseless victim.

Bullet number two made a hole three-sixteenths of an inch in diameter. It entered just above the pubic line to the left midline of the body. It went twice through the small intestine, punctured the left side of the diaphragm, through the left lung, and into the upper chest before it stopped. This one moved upward at an angle of seventy-five degrees, which told Cohle she was probably flat on her back when she was shot. The only other way a bullet would have traveled that path would be if she were standing on a ladder and had been shot from below. The second shot was also an insurance shot, because the first one was lethal. This was no surprise shooting.

Generally, a .22 caliber is one of the least lethal guns. Weapons such as a nine-millimeter, a 357, or a .44 pack a lot more wallop. The two variables on how much damage a gunshot causes are its size and the velocity which the bullet travels. Of those two variables, the speed is the more critical one because of the energy it disperses. It's like the old math formula from physics class, energy equals mass times velocity squared. A .22 is small and relatively slow, so to kill at a distance, it has to hit in the right spot.

A .22 also has a tendency to lose its form when it hits something solid—like a human body. That makes it more difficult for police to trace it to a particular weapon. A slug that remains intact can be traced to the gun that fired it. One of the reasons professional hit men prefer .22 caliber bullets is that the slug will be deformed, and the altered bullet will be almost impossible to trace. The first bullet to hit King was mangled because it struck the spinal column; the second was less damaged but still deformed.

Among those at the autopsy were Calhoun County's two detectives, Jack Schoder and Jim Statfeld, who had been on duty since being called out of the Valentine's Dance. Statfeld carried the spent .22 casing that Guy Picketts had found in the straw of the barn loft. Statfeld took the two slugs that had been plucked from Diane's body and took the packages to the Michigan State Police crime lab.

On the ride back to Marshall, Schoder started mulling over why a stalker would get into the barn if he didn't know when Diane was returning. He also wondered about Brad. Why did he go for a walk when his wife was coming home? And if all he owned was a shotgun, why had deputies found .22 caliber bullets and a cleaning rod in the house?

"We gotta go back out to the scene. We gotta search again, even if it means searching every foot on that farm," Schoder told his partner. But it was Sunday. It would take the rest of the day just to get enough men lined up so they could go over the grounds at the crime scene with a more careful eye.

In Marshall, Brad emerged from the Arborgate Inn with his lawyer friend, Randy Wright. The grim task of calling family and friends about the shooting had already started. Brad's younger brother, Scott, was on his way up from Texas. So were his mother and stepfather. Brad and Randy had breakfast at Big Boy's, and after checking with the sheriff's department to see if it was okay to return to the farmhouse, they drove out to Division Drive. They changed clothes and picked up some diapers and clothes for Kateri.

Sometime before noon they returned a movie Brad had rented from the Neighborhood Video Store the afternoon of Diane's murder. It was called *Next of Kin,* a shoot-em-up action video starring Patrick Swayze as a hillbilly cop from Kentucky who takes revenge on the Chicago mob for killing his two brothers. There's an eerie coincidence in the movie. One brother is killed after he leaves a diner called Dianna's, which is the name the receptionist at WUHQ said the stalker used when he called Diane.

Marler and Kateri were two bewildered kids. In the span of a few hours, they left their grandma's house, saw their mother fall to the ground in the driveway, watched an ambulance drive her away, witnessed a parade of uniformed men coming into their home, and then spent the night at Barbara Elgutaa's house. When Brad came over with the baby clothes, Barb made brunch for everybody while Brad explained what he knew. He had gone for a walk and thought he heard a gunshot but didn't pay any attention to it. And when he returned, Diane was dead in the driveway.

In Sterling Heights, Sunday was like another bad dream. The family had no information other than Diane was dead. Freida was still in shock. She was stretched across the bed in her room, lying silently and alone, just as she had done twenty-four years ago when her husband died of medical neglect. It was so frustrating not knowing anything that someone suggested driving to Marshall again in an attempt to get some answers. Allen Marler and Donald Verrier hadn't learned much on their first trek, but even a futile drive was a better alternative than doing nothing. This time, Allen went with his sister, Darlene, his girlfriend, Nancy Rapo, and his cousin, Elaine Wash. Just a day earlier, Diane and Elaine sat in Freida's house making baskets. Now Elaine was trying to find out about Diane's murder. During the two-hour drive, Darlene voiced aloud what a lot of people were thinking privately.

"Do you think Brad did it?" Darlene asked.

"I'll know the minute I see him," Nancy replied.

WUHQ-TV had already received calls about Diane's death from a reporter. A deluge of requests for information was about to follow. The media would want to know about the phone calls and letter Diane had received. But on Sunday, the only thing released was a statement by Mark Crawford, the station's vice president and spokesman. "Diane was an important part of our family at Channel 41. Our staff and management are obviously shocked and we would simply express our profound sympathy at this time and our hope that the sheriff's department can resolve this matter quickly," he said.

When the parents of Kristina Mony found out, they drove to Kalamazoo College to bring her home so they could tell her in person. They didn't want their daughter to find out from a stranger.

"I immediately thought it was the stalker. Diane had been so petrified. I said, 'He finally got her.' I also thought, 'Poor Brad. They always suspect the husband. I hope the police don't go after him,' " Kristina said.

In Grand Junction, Colorado, Jan Hammer got a call at home from people working in the newsroom. They had a story that Diane King was dead. Jan's memory immediately flashed back to the phone call he had with Diane just two weeks ago; she was frightened because she felt she was being stalked.

"I thought it was the anonymous suitor. I was stunned by it," Hammer said. "I was deeply saddened and outraged. What a senseless and brutal act. Those two children. A woman with a good career, with the drive, ambition, and talent to get somewhere. To have it cut short like that was just so senseless."

Among those who Brad called was Reynelda Ware Muse, the KCNC anchor in Denver. "Brad was very distraught. He didn't know who could have done it," Muse said. "He seemed lost and in a state of shock. At that point, I didn't discuss any details. It was too painful for me and him. I expressed my condolences and shock, and I asked about the children and plans for the funeral."

At the farmhouse, Randy Wright unpacked the Jeep. It was filled with clothes Diane had taken on her three-day visit to her mom's, plus the new red dress she planned on wearing to her brother's wedding. Also in the back were Brad's boots; the deputies had placed them in the Jeep early Sunday morning. Randy also found the paperwork for the search warrant on the kitchen table. It noted that the shots probably came from the barn loft because a shell casing was found up there.

Later in the afternoon, Brad told Randy about the sizable deer herd that grazed on the back property. Brad suggested they go back and spot whitetails. "There was nothing to do. So we went back to see it," Randy said.

The two men were going to take Penny the dog for a walk—Randy said it was the quietest, most docile Doberman pup he had ever run across. But it was muddy, and Randy had only dress shoes with him. They were headed in the same direction Brad said he went for a walk, and the way Travis the tracking dog had gone, when they decided to turn back. Instead of walking, Brad took the Jeep. He drove west on Division Drive for a few hundred feet, then swung south on an unpaved access road. From there, he turned onto a lane that ran near where he said he had walked to the hay piles. Snowdrifts still dotted the landscape, and Brad got the Jeep stuck in some ruts. He and Randy couldn't free it, so they abandoned it and walked north to the house. They left two sets of footprints on the path Brad said he walked the evening before when he found Diane in the driveway.

About six o'clock that evening, Tom Darling returned with his family from a weekend ski trip in Fairview, Michigan. He and his wife had chaperoned a church group that had left Friday night. Darling, owner of a Marshall hardware store, was unpacking the gear and stowing things away. He hadn't been home five minutes when the phone rang. On the line was his friend and neighbor, Brad King. Brad tried to say something but was too upset to go on. So Darling rushed over to the farmhouse. Brad gave him the unspeakable news: Diane was shot dead in the driveway the night before. Someone had waited in the second story of the barn and shot her twice. "I felt it was wrong to pry, so I didn't press for more details," Darling said. Brad also told him about getting the Jeep stuck and asked Darling if he could free it with his tractor. The neighbor agreed but said it would have to be done on Monday. A chill gripped Darling as he went home and told his wife the news. "Diane's dead. And I think Brad's responsible," he said.

He wasn't the only one.

The group arrived from Sterling Heights and went out to the farmhouse. There was little new to be learned, and plans were made to stay the night. Nancy Rapo made up her mind, just as she thought she would, as soon as she encountered Brad in the kitchen.

"I knew the moment I set eyes on him. This incredible force slammed into me. I thought to myself, 'You bastard. You did it. You killed her.' I felt an incredible presence, an incredible evil. There was like an aura around him. He wasn't solemn. He wasn't grieving. It was like he didn't have a care in the world," Nancy said.

A reporter from the *Battle Creek Enquirer* knocked on doors along Division Drive for reactions. Murders were extremely rare in this area; there hadn't been one inside the Marshall town limits in twenty-one years. Technically, this was outside town, but it was close enough.

One TV crew came into the Kings' driveway. Randy Wright shooed them away, so they did their stand-up shot standing in Division Drive. Many more media crews would be descending on the farm and the town.

Technically, the killing took place in Fredonia Township, just outside the Marshall town limits. And Diane and Brad had lived at the farmhouse for just ten months, so they weren't exactly fixtures on the social and civic scene. But townfolk paid close attention.

If someone wrote a definition of small-town America's ideal of itself, there would be a picture of Marshall next to it. It is a gem of a community, the essence of Middle America, with spacious yards and wide streets adorned with tulip, maple, and pine trees.

The sign welcoming motorists to Marshall touts it as the "Town of Hospitality." Indeed, it has two separate welcoming committees to greet newcomers, providing them with contacts for doctors, dentists, plumbers, lawyers, stores, shops, restaurants and other needs. It is the home of the Michigan Junior Miss scholarship program in January, a huge winter store sale in February, a dulcimer festival the third weekend in June, the world's greatest Fifties party in July and a Christmas parade on the first Monday after Thanksgiving. On a certain day before Christmas, crowds of 10,000 or so—more than the population of the town—line Michigan Avenue to watch

Santa Claus and his elves flip the switch bringing holiday lights to life. But Marshall's biggest claim to fame is an annual house tour every September sponsored by the Marshall Historical Society. A big chunk of the town—about eight hundred structures—are part of a National Historic Landmark District, so designated because of its national importance in representing broad themes and historical movements of the United States. Some people have called it a living textbook of nineteenth- and twentieth-century small-town architecture because of houses adorned with towers, gables, gothic windows, porticoes, columns, lacy woodwork trims, bargeboards and porches on the front, side, and rear. It has been said that a heinous crime in Marshall is a poorly painted house. The dwellings come in a palette of creamy colors with chocolate trim, canary yellow with black shutters, and even royal blue, teal, pink, and red houses are common. Marshall's John Bellars used his hometown as a setting for teen mysteries. In *The House with a Clock in Its Walls,* the narrator says, "Even the ordinary white frame houses had things that made them seem different—a stained-glass window or a bouquet of iron flowers on top of a cupola. And so many of the houses seemed to be hiding secrets."

The main drag of Michigan Avenue is the location for two hardware stores, several antique shops, all manner of gift shops, three cafes, the American Museum of Magic with its 12,000 volumes, a columned post office made from native Marshall sandstone and a Colonial Revival building that serves as a combination town hall, fire, and police station, having once been a livery stable, service station, and taxi stand.

Forty-one historical markers adorn the town. Founded in 1831 at the confluence of Rice Creek and the Kalamazoo River, it was named after John Marshall, the first chief justice of the U.S. Supreme Court, and is the seat of government in Calhoun County. Because of its central location, Marshall was a farming district and trade center in its earliest days. It nearly became Michigan's capital city. In fact, state Senator James Wright Gordon, who introduced legislation to make Marshall the capital, was so sure it would happen that in 1839 he built a house called the Governor's Mansion at 612 South Marshall Avenue. It faces the intended site for the state house, which is now a fairground, and there is a neighborhood still called Capitol Hill. Gordon lived in the mansion with its columned portico when he became acting governor. The state house of representatives approved Marshall as the capital, but it lost by one vote in the state senate in 1847. Instead, the state settled on Lansing, a virtually unknown village with only eight registered voters at the time.

The Reverend John D. Pierce and lawyer Isaac Crary designed the school system for the state of Michigan while sitting under a Marshall oak tree. Pierce later became the first school superintendent in the United States.

Marshall got a second chance at splendor in 1844 when the Michigan Central Railroad opened shop and triggered a thirty-year building boom of Italianate and Gothic Revival homes. The nation's first railroad union was formed here, the Brotherhood of the Footboard, today known as the Brotherhood of Locomotive Engineers. A north-south railroad was supposed to be added in Marshall, but it was never built because the railroad company left for Jackson in 1874. Once again, Marshall never rose to the great heights envisioned by its leaders.

It later developed into a center for patent medicines, a

lucrative enough trade until the Pure Food and Drug Act of 1906 outlawed most of the products. The only one still being produced is Stuart's Dyspepsia Tablets.

But the town owes its historic preservation to Harold C. Brooks, the mayor between 1925 and 1931. He made his fortune from the family-owned Brooks Appliance Company, which makes hernia trusses and supporters for ruptures. The headquarters on Michigan Avenue has a huge sign that reads "Personal Fittings," and the company's motto is "Brooks Supports the World—And Will Never Let It Down." The town patron for over sixty years, Brooks was a man ahead of his time as far as preservation goes. He bought up twelve houses until someone reliable came along to buy them. He maintained trees in a park and gave prizes each year to residents with the best garden, best lawn, and best decorated home. In 1930 he adorned the town's traffic circle with a marble fountain, a reproduction of the Grecian Temple of Love at Versailles. But in a concession to heartland tastes, the fountain was erected without the nude statue of Aphrodite in its center.

Marshall's homes include examples of Federal, Victorian, Queen Anne, Gothic Revival, Greek Revival, Italianate, Carpenter Gothic, Romanesque, Tuscan Villa, Italian Villa, and Bungalow architecture. It is the home of the National House Inn, the oldest operating inn in Michigan. And its most famous building reflects no style other than the eccentricities of its owner. It was built in 1860 for Abner Pratt, former consul to the Sandwich Islands in the South Pacific. The two-story structure has a raised veranda and pagoda-topped tower. A product of money and whim, it is a tropical fantasy painted in red, ivory, and three shades of green. Inside, it has a staircase of imported teak, ebony, and mahogany.

The entire town has a storybook image. Given its designation as an historic district, it appears walled off from sordid deeds like murder. It is not, of course. Oldtimers even recalled a 1948 murder case that was tried in Marshall. A resident named Earl Kent was charged with murdering his sixteen-year-old sweetheart, who was shot through the heart with a .22 rifle. In an eerie parallel to the Diane King shooting, Flavian Watkins was found in the yard of her family's farm south of Marshall. A jury acquitted Kent of the crime.

But now phone lines were buzzing. Joanne Karaba was on the phone with a friend, saying that somebody had been killed on Division Drive. Karaba was shaken, but she remembered that Diane had gone to Detroit to visit her mother.

"Oh good, Diane's away this weekend," Karaba thought. Then she learned it was her friend who was dead. "When I heard, I just started to tremble. It had to be this guy who was calling her."

And over in Kalamazoo, just off the Western Michigan University campus, two female students who were in Brad King's class the previous semester found out separately about the killing.

Julie Cook was watching an *I Love Lucy* special when a bulletin was beamed during a news break stating that news anchor Diane King had been killed.

"Oh my God. He killed his wife," Julie said. But when the word flashed that she had been hounded by a stalker, she sighed, "Thank God. It wasn't him after all."

And a friend called Ann Hill, another ex-student of Brad's, about eleven o'clock.

"What was Brad's wife's name?" the friend asked.

"I don't remember," Hill said.

"Was it Diane?"

"Yes."

"Was she a newscaster?"

"Yeah, why?"

"She's dead."

CHAPTER 9

By any measure, 1991 was going to be a watershed year for Diane. She had already come to grips with the biggest change in her life. She had decided to leave her job at WUHQ so she could spend more time raising her children. She had some ideas about going into business for herself, which would allow her to work at home and pursue a different kind of career. But the change meant upheaval for Brad, too. If she quit work, the responsibility of being the breadwinner would fall back on his shoulders.

At age thirty-four, she was nursing a newborn daughter and caring for a son about to reach his third birthday. Like a lot of working mothers, she liked the sense of accomplishment her career offered while she also loved the time with her family. The demands of being a hotshot TV journalist had to be balanced against those involving dirty diapers, day care, laundry, shopping, housework, and being a lover and a wife. She felt like the juggler on the old television variety shows who balanced spinning plates on sticks. Life was constant motion, getting a new plate spinning and then running back to spin the others so they wouldn't fall and break. Tend to Kateri. Tend to Marler. Take care of Brad. Go to work. Do volunteer work for the Food Bank and the Salvation Army. Have a social life. Pursue Indian studies. Back to the kids. She had to run faster and faster just to keep from losing ground, no matter how energetic and organized she was. Lots of career women in the 1990s faced the same challenges. There was more pressure on Diane because she had been the breadwinner for so long.

Her top priority was to spend more time at home with her kids. And this decision was such an about-face for a woman who was so focused on her career that it startled her family and friends. No one was more surprised than her younger sister, Denise Verrier.

Three years apart, the sisters looked alike and sounded alike, but they thought very differently. Diane took off to find herself in college and ROTC and est and TV. Denise was much less venturesome. She didn't even enroll in Mount Ida College after being accepted. And after living for a time in Boston, she returned to Michigan for good. She married Donald Verrier in 1981 and settled just a few miles from the house she was raised in. She had the first of her four children in 1985, and she also took in a foster child. Her husband would have rather worked two or three jobs than see Denise get a job, not because he was against working wives, but because both of them felt it important that a mother be home with her children. Diane, on the other hand, "was a real feminist," said Denise. "At one point, she was very much anti-family and anti-marriage. She despised everything I represented."

The younger sister noticed a change when Diane had

Marler in 1988. "She wrote me a letter apologizing for degrading marriage. After she had Marler, she understood how important motherhood is."

After Kateri had arrived, the pressures on Diane increased. Because she got up so early to get to work, she was never home when her kids awoke in the morning. And because she was breastfeeding the baby, she would have to get up extra early to pump milk from her breasts for Kateri to have in the morning. She did the same thing at work sometimes if she knew she had to work late; she'd duck into the women's room and pump breast milk so Brad could pick it up. But there was more to it than that. She wanted her children to have the perfect childhood. So she set about re-creating the farm that she enjoyed before her father died. Her mother was buying a lamb for Marler. Diane wanted to buy laying hens. Her sister Darlene had arranged for her to take a horse from a friend. And Diane was eager to plant a garden and wildflowers on her farm.

"She wasn't being fulfilled. She thought she was missing out on some things in her life. It was just real evident that after Kateri was born, she became more at peace with herself. She was going to accept who she was. Someone remarked to her that she wasn't what she used to be. I can remember her saying, 'I don't even know who I was.' Maybe she realized it wasn't that important to try to impress everybody, and it used to be that she wanted you to know how important she was. She also told me, 'My job's not that big a deal. Anybody can do it. It's not that big a challenge anymore.' She wanted to be home more with the kids. She wanted to be a full-time mom," Denise said.

People who knew Diane in Colorado can't believe she would ever feel that way. Susan Van Vleet, the hard-charging woman who founded her own consulting business, knew Diane as a careerist. The only way she could envision Diane staying home with the kids on a farm was if "she had a frontal lobotomy."

Some of her old colleagues were also amazed at Diane's U-turn. Debbie Rich had taken over the morning news slot at KJCT, doing the 7:25 and 8:25 A.M. cut-ins to *Good Morning America,* the same as King was doing in Battle Creek. But the station wanted Debbie to come in earlier to do a 6:45 A.M. segment, which would have meant leaving her home at five o'clock. It also would have meant going to sleep at eight P.M., which would have left little time for her husband and two sons. "Working at a five-dollar-an-hour job while your family rots? No way," Rich said. She decided family came first and left the business. "When I quit the morning news, Diane was upset with me. She said I was too good not to be in TV. But I had to make a decision about what my priorities were. My family came first. Diane talked a lot about career priorities." Now Rich was observing Diane wrestle with the same desire to spend more time with her children.

Returning to a more traditional home life was something that Diane mentioned to a number of friends. One of them was Christine Babic, who sometimes did Diane's hair and makeup before TV tapings. The women had met at the International Hot Air Balloon Festival, which naturally in Battle Creek—the cereal capital—included a splashy balloon shaped like Tony the Tiger of Frosted Flakes fame. Babic recognized Diane from TV and struck up a conversation. Both of them had their kids with them. And Babic, who owned a local modeling agency called Exposure Talent Management, remarked that Marler was cute enough to model kids' clothes.

Babic thought Diane had a future as a model, which would give her an alternate career and allow her to spend more time with her kids. So Diane had some portfolio pictures taken. The two women talked about taking their kids in the summer to the swimming pool at Beadle Lake Park and doing lots of motherly things.

"We wanted to be old-fashioned moms. She was ready to be a kid again with her kids," Babic said. "She was really happy to have a little girl. I never saw her look better. She wanted to leave her full-time job on television and be a full-time mommy and a part-time model. She really expressed an interest in that. It was hard for her not seeing the baby get up in the morning. She just wanted to stay home and be a good mother. She wanted to be there when they scratched their knees and to see them get on the school bus in the morning."

The officers at the Salvation Army heard the same story. At a board meeting in early February of 1991, Diane proudly showed the pictures of Kateri for the first time. "She was very excited about her newest baby and being a mother. She was thinking about giving up her work just so she could be home with the kids. That's how much she enjoyed being a mother," said Major John Homer.

Diane even had a tentative timetable for leaving WUHQ. The place was in the process of being sold. Diane said she wanted to be gone in June.

Some people at work were aware of her feelings, if not her specific plans. "I know she loved being a mom. Her two kids were the most important thing in the world. She would express regrets she wasn't able to be home more with the kids," said Larry Neinhaus, her immediate supervisor at WUHQ.

But such a major decision would cause upheaval at

home, too. Brad would have to get a job and perhaps postpone getting his doctorate. Denise asked how Brad felt about Diane leaving the TV world.

"He's not too happy about it. He likes being a celebrity," Diane said, alluding to the perks Brad enjoyed because his wife often got invitations to ice shows, festivals, openings, parties and social events. He also asked her, "Can we afford you not working."

None of this suggested, however, that Diane planned to be a one-dimensional person. She would become a self-employed businesswoman who could work out of her home. It was a project that would combine her TV experience and her pride in Native-American culture with her desire to stay home with the kids—and make some money. The concept was Two Worlds Productions, which would make educational videotapes about Native Americans and their families, history, culture, customs, religion, and philosophy of living in harmony with the land. Diane dreamed that her documentary tapes, designed to be shown in schools and civic clubs, would tear down the stereotypes of Indians as warring savages put in their place by U.S. cavalry and cowboys. Diane wanted to bridge the two cultures that she was part of.

The mission statement of her venture read as follows:

> Two Worlds Productions will produce educational videotapes on contemporary Native Americans, so Indians have role models, professionals whom they can look up to and aspire to be like. There are many prominent Native Americans who have maintained their cultural identities while gaining professional acceptance and success in mainstream society. Cultural diversity will not only allow native people to strengthen their self-images but will also educate

non-Indians as to what value these indigenous people serve in society. . . . Our education system is homogenized with a severe slant to the historical impact Europeans have made. There is virtually no in-depth look at the contributions Native Americans have made in making the United States what it is today. This contemporary Native American series is a vehicle by which Indians can become clear about their roots and their futures."

Diane wanted people to know that the Iroquois Confederacy's Great Law of Peace enunciated such concepts as individual rights, female independence, freedom of speech, and separate branches of government held together by checks and balances. It had served as a model for the U.S. Constitution.

Such a venture would take Diane off-camera and into a position as president and chief executive officer. She remembered some advice from her mentor in Denver, Reynelda Muse, who said there were lots of women in front of the camera but not many behind it. A woman who could produce and direct would be a powerful pioneering force.

And she didn't think small. She figured there are 84,000 public school districts and 15,000 private schools. In the first year of production, she planned to have two complete six-part series on Native Americans. The projected start-up and first-year costs were estimated at $470,000, including $130,000 for hiring a business manager, executive producer, producer, editor, writer, and secretary. If this worked out right, Brad could work for her.

To get money for the idea, Diane planned to contact the Adolph Coors Company, Upjohn, the National Endowment for the Arts, the National Education Association, and National Geographic. But her strongest hope was the Kellogg Foundation, a philanthropic organization from the corporation that made Battle Creek the Cereal City and the Best Known Town of Its Size in the World.

In 1894 Dr. John Harvey Kellogg, a Seventh Day Adventist dedicated to the philosophy "you are what you eat," accidentally discovered a way to bake wheat flakes while he was trying to create a tastier bread product. A dry cereal made of wholesome grain made a perfect breakfast food when mixed with milk. Kellogg's younger brother, William Keith Kellogg, a one-time salesman of brooms made from corn stalks, later developed the first cornflakes and was the genius who had a feeling the masses would love the stuff. Breakfast cereal was precooked, which meant no more slaving over a hot stove in the morning. And the crinkly flakes added much appreciated variety to the monotonous and heavy diet of the time. In 1906 William Keith (W. K.) Kellogg founded the Battle Creek Toasted Corn Flake Company, forerunner of Kellogg Company, whose Corn Flakes, All-Bran, and Rice Krispies created one of the great fortunes in American history. The money enabled W. K. to establish the Kellogg Foundation, dedicated to helping people help themselves by funding projects in health, education, agriculture, and leadership. Diane's hopes of obtaining a grant were buoyed every time she went to the Kellogg Foundation. There in the lobby was one of her favorite sculptures, a bronze statue called "Courage to Lead." A work by Denny Haskew, it tells the story of the Society of the Sacred Arrow, which existed among many Plains Indians. Society members would shoot arrows straight up into the air, then stand still as the arrows fell among them. They believed they were protected from harm by their own bravery and the spirits of their ancestors. The theme is that courage in the face of a personal threat adds to potential for leadership. Every time Diane passed the statue, when she was filling out applications for grants for Two Worlds Productions, she got tears in her eyes.

That her Indian dream might be fulfilled in Battle Creek was not without irony. According to local legend, this spot in south central Michigan was the ancient site of a day-long battle between two Indian tribes. They fought so ferociously that a stream ran red with blood, and was called Waupokisco, which means "River of Battle." A more probable version involves a ruckus on a much smaller scale between Native Americans and whites. In 1825, when Calhoun County was the frontier, two Native Americans sought food and supplies from two white surveyors plotting the land for settlement. The tribe was already in a bit of a snit because the surveyors marked the land with stakes or by cutting notches in maple trees, disrupting the harvest of maple syrup. At any rate, tribe members and surveyors tangled on March 25 near the site of an unassuming stream—known to the whites only as a number—that flowed into the Kalamazoo River. Although some rifle shots were fired, no one was badly hurt, and the place and stream became known as Battle Creek. The Native Americans were removed, and the surveyors' work opened the area to settlement.

There were all kinds of pressures building in the King household, and Diane was pursuing alternatives that seemed ambiguous if not downright contradictory. At the same time she wanted to quit her TV job and be a full-time mom, she was sending audition tapes to the

Detroit stations and asking about TV openings back in Colorado. However, it wasn't too surprising that she might look back over her shoulder. She had found herself once in the Rocky Mountains. It was human nature to think of perhaps duplicating her feat there. She inquired about job prospects at KREX in Grand Junction, which had a noon, evening, and nightly news program.

"I just got a sense she was bored. She wasn't working in a full-fledged news operation. She wanted hard news. Diane didn't want to be a reader of the news. She wanted to report. I think she missed the daily action," said Jan Hammer, her old boss at KJCT.

In a 1990 Christmas card sent to Lesley Tucker, Diane wrote, "Looking forward to being back in Colorado. Have a glorious holiday." It reminded Tucker of a phone conversation they had the previous summer.

"I'll be back some day. Colorado's my real home. I'll probably move back, but I don't know about Brad. He's not interested," Diane said.

"What do you mean? What are you talking about?" Tucker asked.

Diane didn't get very specific, but she indicated things weren't going well in the marriage.

Theresa Nisley, who was godmother to Marler, also noted Diane's interest in returning. "Diane was looking at trying to get back here. She missed her friends. She wasn't happy there. She told me it was time to come home."

Things were changing for Brad too, and he seemed to resent having no control over the changes. The order and structure was being taken from his life, and he was being thrust into a situation he didn't want. Brad had a desire for prestige, which he acquired through Diane.

But he didn't know how or wasn't motivated enough to work for it on his own. The last time he had it was as a cop, when his uniform and badge gave him status as a pillar of the community. At least it did until he burned out and gave it up, along with his first marriage.

Diane was his meal ticket now. As long as she supported the family, he could continue his comfortable life as a part-time instructor on a college campus. Here he was at mid-life, still pursuing his doctorate and not showing any urgency about acquiring it. He didn't want any other job than this part-time position, which did afford some status. Students look up to an instructor.

But Diane was even more than a meal ticket: her celebrity got Brad invited to nice parties and mall openings and free shows. He liked the spotlight which he never seemed able to obtain on his own. He was like a child, who has no thought of earning the toys he desires, but expects someone else to provide them.

Now his wife was that someone. She was like his mother, a woman in power telling him what to do. Diane was the one who told him to shave his head, and she griped if he didn't use the razor diligently enough. Diane grumbled at him to get a job. She left him lists of things to do, then harped at him if they weren't done. But she continued to pay the bills.

However, there was a new baby he hadn't planned on having in the scene now, and the infant was stealing his attention. Diane increasingly barked orders at him: "Brad, get the diaper bag. Brad, get the kids. Brad, get a job. Brad, fix the porch." His rage was apparently growing, like the pressure in a pipe before it bursts. And like always, he kept it locked inside.

Maybe he could find an easier way to fix things.

CHAPTER 10

The two things married couples fight about most often are money and sex. Diane and Brad didn't have an ample supply of either, which meant they had plenty of ammunition for arguments. They hid it well: on the surface, it was hard to tell that anything was wrong, but the truth was, there was a war raging.

"Diane did not like to fail at anything. She wanted to have a perfect marriage, a perfect job, a perfect family. It was real hard for her to admit there were any problems," said Regina Zapinski.

Their lifestyle had put a real strain on the Kings' budget. Both of them liked to dress stylishly and well. They had two cars, a new Jeep Wagoneer for Diane and a 1981 Dodge Reliant K-car that Brad bought for $1,500 from Kristina Mony. And while they lived at the townhouse apartment in Battle Creek, Diane paid for two cleaning women to come over once a week to tidy up the place. She had too many plates spinning to be tied down by housework. They lived from paycheck to paycheck, with nothing left over for unexpected bills.

So when the Internal Revenue Service aggressively pursued them over an unpaid $3,000 tax bill, things really hit the fan. The tax collectors notified WUHQ-TV that the Kings were delinquent in paying their taxes, so they wanted the station to garnishee Diane's wages and send payments directly to the government. Diane was humiliated that the people she worked for might think she was a tax deadbeat. People who are used to filing single returns often underestimate how much money they should withhold when they get married. So newlyweds submitting their first joint return sometimes face a big jolt: they owe the government a chunk of money—and in the Kings' case it was $3,091.42 from their 1986 return. If a couple is unable to pay the tab in one lump sum, and most can't, the Internal Revenue Service allows them to borrow the money or set up a schedule of payments. So on October 1, 1987, the IRS filed a lien against the Kings in Mesa County, Colorado. That meant the Kings couldn't get a refund on future tax returns until the tab was paid, and a payment schedule was arranged. The IRS is a predictable creature. It will give a taxpayer every opportunity to pay up, but the minute there's a default on a payment, it will seize wages or bank accounts. It will get the last 50 cents owed, no matter what that takes. When U.S. Supreme Court Justice John Marshall said, "The power to tax is the power to destroy," he wasn't talking about marriage. But in the Kings' case, he could have been. Because Diane was the one with the steady income, the IRS went after her. And she went ballistic.

The only people at the station who knew were Nancy Gwynne in accounting and Jerry Colvin, the station manager. Deeply upset, Diane said Brad forgot to mail in a form or failed to make some payments, and she promised she'd get this all straightened out. Diane called the IRS and explained everything, so nothing was taken out of her paycheck.

But not more than three months later, the IRS was at the door again when a payment wasn't made. Again, they wanted to garnishee Diane's wages. "Don't take the money out. I can't afford it," Diane told Nancy Gwynne. Once again, she did some fast talking to the IRS.

The state of Colorado also filed a tax lien against Brad for the tax years 1986 and 1987. Tax due was $853.57.

Diane came to Nancy's office for heart-to-heart talks two or three times a week now. Diane would bring in her coffee and grapefruit; Nancy would bake cookies and pastries at home. "They were broke continually. I'd buy her lunch sometimes, and I didn't make piddly-squat at the station. She said they didn't have a dime to spend. And Brad spent money like it was water," Nancy said. "That's why Freida and Brad hated each other so much. Brad took no initiative and Diane did all the work."

Then, in March of 1990, Diane became pregnant with Kateri. She wanted a second child to round out her family, and she was thrilled beyond words when she learned it would be a little girl. But the pregnancy hadn't been planned, and Brad was indignant. Brad was also jealous. Now there would be someone else in the picture to get the attention. And Brad resented the idea of further stretching the family budget. Diane would have to miss some work as well. No, he was dead set against it, according to Diane's friends and family. They said he asked Diane to abort the pregnancy.

"She really wanted the baby. And when Brad wanted an abortion, I think her feelings changed toward him," said Nancy Gwynne, who was privy to the marital dynamics.

Diane talked Brad into seeing a marriage counselor at the Oakridge Center for $85 an hour. Brad went reluctantly. He didn't want to tell his problems to some stranger, and he didn't think it was anybody's business what he did in bed.

It was at the end of March that the Kings moved to the farmhouse on Division Drive in Marshall. It really did need some fixing up, but Diane had big plans to make it into an estate. She'd worry how to pay for it later.

The Kings were always looking for ways to make money. Diane was going all out to raise venture capital for her Two Worlds Productions idea. Among the items in the house was an audiocassette and booklet entitled *101 Ways to Get Cash from the Government.* There were also Bible verses for something called *Discovering God's Plan to Master Your Money.* In addition to the IRS and the Colorado Department of Revenue, the Kings owed money to the Fashion Bar in Grand Junction where Brad used to work and the Grand Valley Co-op Union. They had maxed out on their credit cards, so they contacted American Debt Counseling in Kalamazoo. The service consolidated all their bills into one, and they paid as much as they could each month. They were instructed to cut up the credit cards and pay cash for things they needed. If they couldn't afford it, they couldn't buy it.

There were hints of problems, but nobody knew the whole story. For example, Diane's check-writing habits were legendary. "She bounced more checks. She'd write one of us a check for something and then call and tell us not to cash it, that the checking account is being closed out. She would always say the bank made a mistake.

Diane King as she was known to thousands of viewers.

Bradford King after his arrest.

One of Freida Newton's personal photos of her daughter Diane—with Brad's image cut out.

Diane in a glamorous make-over from a professional photo session.

The former King home visited by jurors during Brad's trial.

Brad at Diane's funeral, holding a feather in a Native American ritual.

Brad at his arraignment with his first attorney, James Brady.

Diane's mother, Freida Newton, on the witness stand.

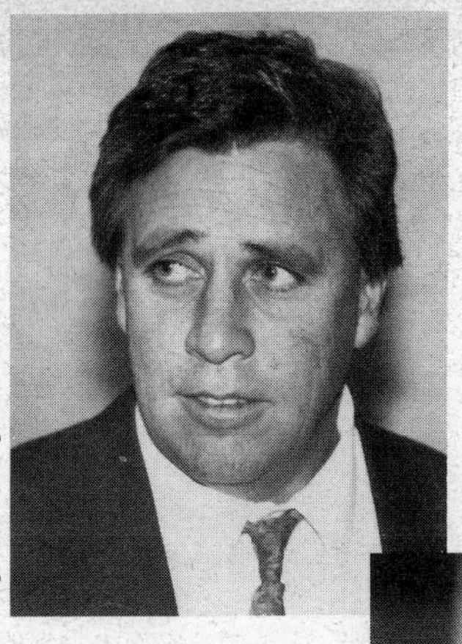

Brad's defense attorney, John Sims.

Prosecutor John Sahli cross-examining a witness.

Detective for the Calhoun County Sheriff's Department, Jack Schoder.

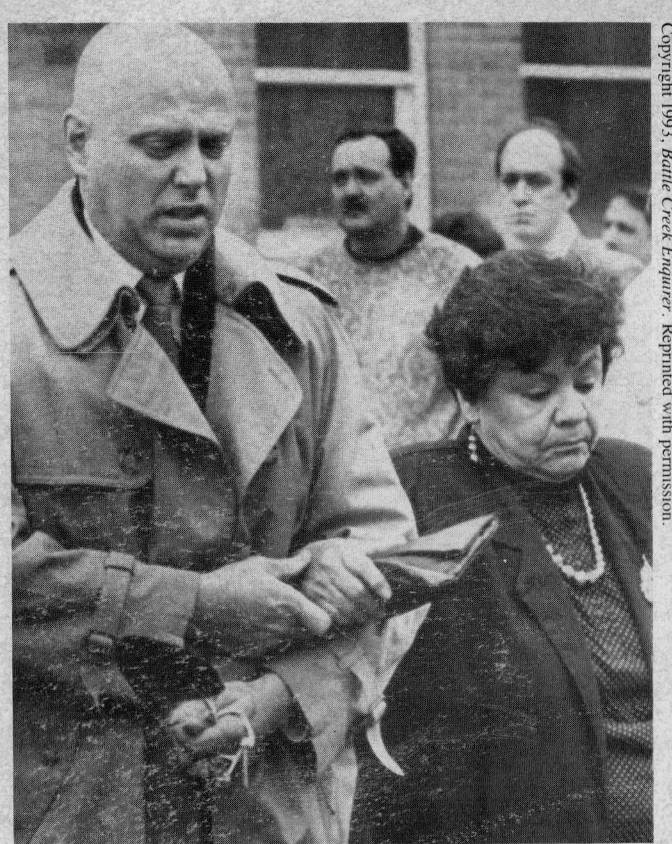

Brad and Freida attend Diane's funeral.

They changed accounts several times, and they were always trying to straighten out their finances. I knew they didn't have money. I knew Diane always lived beyond her means," said her sister Denise.

"She had very expensive tastes. I thought she must make great money. I always thought she did. She was upset when she didn't get that raise," Regina Zapinski said.

On top of the pregnancy and the money woes, Diane's friends and family said she told them Brad lost interest in her sexually. They had an arrangement from their est experiences that if one of them was interested in sex, it was up to him or her to tell the other. Well, Diane was still interested and kept telling Brad. But he rejected her advances, another stab in her sensitive ego. This was the situation when Diane started getting calls at the office from a star-struck stranger, and things fell apart.

Diane shared some of these secrets with Kristina Mony, the intern at WUHQ. Despite the sixteen-year difference in their ages, Kristina and Diane had a good chemistry. They not only worked together, they enjoyed shopping and socializing, too. Kristina also was a preferred baby-sitter. Both women wore size 6 shoes and could fit into some of each other's clothing, and they traded outfits as easily as they swapped intimate details. Although Kristina was a freshman at Kalamazoo College, she had already gained a reputation as a good listener and someone who gave good counsel, especially on women's matters. The girls at Galesburg-Augusta High School called her Ann Landers because she was always giving sound advice.

Kristina and Diane were shopping at the Lakeview Square Mall outside Battle Creek when Diane shared one of her most intimate secrets. She was buying curtains for her unborn baby's nursery. After settling on a country-style calico cloth, dusty blue with tiny maroon prints, she told Kristina about Brad's lack of interest in sex. Tears came with the confession.

"I just don't understand. Things aren't going well. I try so hard. I try to buy pretty lingerie. I try to make myself nice. He just doesn't seem interested in me. What else can I do?"

Diane bought sexy things from Victoria's Secret only to be told by Brad, "Why don't you just wear a T-shirt? It doesn't do anything for me."

Diane also mentioned the problem with the IRS and the back taxes, which Brad blamed on the tax preparers they had hired. And she told other friends about her sexual frustrations.

Nancy Gwynne was joking in the office one day about buying a silk nightgown, something off the shoulder, to attract a male friend.

"Gee, do you think that would work for me? Brad hasn't shown any interest in a long time," Diane said.

Another person who knew Diane and Brad had not been sleeping together as husband and wife was Regina Zapinski.

"There are guys who don't touch their wives when they're pregnant. They weren't having sex, and it was almost like Brad was making up excuses. But she took it personal. She figured it was because she was fat and ugly," Regina said.

There was one more force adding more pressure to the marriage, and it was a whopper. Because Diane got up so early to go to work in the mornings, she was usually in bed by nine o'clock in the evening. Most of the time she was asleep when Brad got home on the nights he taught his class. But she noticed he was keeping longer hours. He seemed even more distant, almost detached. There was a strain that could be read in his eyes and body language. Diane was aware of the claims of an affair during Brad's first marriage, and she thought if he had broken his marriage vows once, why wouldn't he do it again? So one night, she forced herself to stay awake to see what time Brad came home. And she confronted him while he was sneaking up the steps on cat's feet.

"Why are you sneaking upstairs?" she demanded.

"I was trying to be quiet so I wouldn't disturb you," he said.

"Well, why are you coming home so late."

"I had trouble with the car. I ran out of gas."

"Are you sure you're not having an affair?"

"I wouldn't do that to you. You and Marler are my life."

It was a lie, though.

In late August of 1990 Ann Louise Hill registered for a class on sociology of criminal law, Bradford J. King instructing. It was the class that met on Tuesday nights, from six to eight-thirty P.M. She was in her mid-thirties, a single mother with a couple of daughters from a previous marriage. But she had one of those faces that resisted aging, and she could have passed for much younger. She was attractive enough, with a round face and long, brown hair and dark eyes. She also was an approachable personality, with just a bit of a vulnerable side. She was woman enough to get her teacher's attention.

Brad liked to invite students into his office to talk about classroom work, career goals, and outside interests. He met with students in groups and individually. During a one-on-one meeting with Hill sometime in October, Brad asked his student if she wanted to have a beer. She agreed, and they adjourned to Waldo's, a popular watering hole and hangout for WMU students. They were there about ninety minutes, long enough to drink a couple of beers and expand their conversation past schoolwork. Brad found a sympathetic ear for his problems. He was also a single parent, he said, and in the process of getting a divorce. It was a messy breakup, but he had kept custody of his son, Marler. He laid some other things on her, like how he was a veteran of the U.S. Army's 82nd Airborne Division and had developed a tolerance of death because of all the dead bodies he had seen in his army service. That too was a lie; King had never been in the military, let alone as a paratrooper in an elite division. Anyway, he obtained the woman's phone number, and on Saturday, October 27, called to see if she wanted to go out. She was away in Saginaw, with a baby-sitter watching her two children at home. When she returned, she called Brad back. The following week they met in a Kalamazoo park. First kissing, then petting, then a seductive suggestion, and Brad had smooth-talked his way into the woman's apartment, where they had sex.

"I went out with him because I was under the impression that he was separated. We progressed beyond just being friends. It became more of a physical relationship. We became sexually involved," she said.

On October 30, the day Diane got the cut-out letter in her mailbox and waited for hours at Cindy Acosta's house, Brad taught class and spent several hours courting Ann Hill. He saw her again two days later, on Thursday, November 1, but he didn't mention anything about Diane's letter. All he said was Diane was upset with him on Tuesday because he had been late picking up Marler.

Brad and Ann got together two more times in November, both times for sex at her apartment. The tryst seemed to be going nicely. A get-together, sex, some small talk, and then Brad would have to leave to take care of Marler, or so he said. Here he was in his forties, bald, barely scraping by, career track stalled, dependent on a domineering wife, confronted with all kinds of family pressures—and a younger, attractive woman wanted him. He wouldn't be the first college teacher to become involved with a student, and Western Michigan was a target-rich environment for him. There were other women like Ann Hill there.

In November, with Diane in her final month of pregnancy, she and Brad got into a violent argument over suspected affairs. She slapped Brad, and he punched her.

Diane got this off her chest when she called her friend Theresa Nisley in Colorado. They still kept in touch; it was rare for more than two weeks to pass before one called the other.

"How's the marriage going?" Theresa asked, knowing that things had been rocky.

"You're not going to believe this. He hit me. Right in the stomach. That was real dumb," Diane said. Then Diane said they had decided to see a marriage counselor.

"It really upset me that he would do that," Theresa said. "Diane told me she didn't think the marriage was going to last. She didn't need him. She talked about leaving him. She wanted to do those documentaries, but she thought the money might be slow coming in. God forbid he'd have to get a job."

Diane also spilled her guts to Nancy Gwynne at the station.

"She showed me the black and blue marks where he hit her, on the right side under her breast. There were also black and blue marks on her arms as if someone had grabbed her tightly," Nancy said.

"He just lost his temper and I probably said some things," Diane said.

"Why do you let him do this to you?" Nancy asked.

"I don't know what he wants. I'm not attractive like those college girls. I'm not as pretty as they are. I can't take this anymore."

Nancy also was told that Brad was cross with Marler. He'd be working with his tools and he'd just push Marler out of the way. Nancy got the sense that things were disintegrating rapidly.

Diane kept the fight a secret from her family. They disliked Brad already, and she didn't want to give them more reasons. Besides, she was a proud woman. It would have been embarrassing to confess her husband hit her —when pregnant!

What it came down to was a question of control, which is usually what violence or the threat of violence is, a question of maintaining power over a partner. Brad felt very much threatened that he was losing control of his marriage.

Diane confided her marital woes in one other person, her hairdresser, Elise Caporossi, who worked at a shop called Charisma in Portage. Someone at WUHQ had referred Diane to the shop, and she had been going there for two years.

"When I first met her, she was always telling me how wonderful her marriage was. That didn't seem right, because none of us has that good a marriage." Later, though, "she was trying to get pregnant with Kateri because it would make her family complete, but he never wanted to touch her or have sex. She always blamed herself. 'What's wrong with me. Am I ugly? What can I do? What can I do? I can't figure out what it is.' From what she told me, she begged him and nagged him and finally got pregnant. She was real excited when she found out it was going to be a girl. But he didn't want the baby. He was really upset when she got pregnant. The guy always gave me creeps from the minute I met him. He was never sociable. He never smiled. Then she told me they had gotten into a fight. And he tried pushing her into a wall."

Diane was close to a personal meltdown by now. On the one hand, she wanted to do everything she could to save the marriage and make it work. She didn't want to fail as a wife. On the other hand, she was too independent to be a human punching bag or to stay with a loser. When faced with an unpleasant choice, she did what most human beings would do—she postponed it. Maybe the marriage counselor could help her sort out these conflicting feelings.

"She was going to make it last. She told me she'd never get divorced. She was going to make him realize he had to be responsible," Elise said.

Some of Diane's regular TV viewers noticed that the face they saw in the morning reading the news looked haggard and troubled. Kristina Mony was called by her mother at school to hear this report:

"She couldn't hold her lines together. Her timing was off. She looked so bad. She looked like she had been bruised. Her face looked puffy, almost distorted. She looked like she was suffering. I couldn't believe they put her on like that. And I knew it wasn't the pregnancy," Mrs. Mony said.

Nancy Gwynne noticed it, too. But Diane was a professional. It didn't matter if she had the weight of the world on her shoulders, when it was time for her to do the news upstairs, she collected herself and went on.

"She was a different person upstairs on camera. It was

boom, boom, boom. That's a different Diane. All business. She was two different people. It didn't matter if she was crying her eyes out, she'd project what you're supposed to be. She made you feel whatever she was saying was true," Nancy said.

But Nancy told her something was visibly wrong.

"You've been crying again. Your eyes are all puffy. The makeup and the Murine isn't covering it up anymore," Nancy told her.

"It's to the point where I cry more than I smile," Diane said.

On Tuesday morning, November 20, Diane gave birth to a blue-eyed, blond-haired baby girl. Her mother was staying at the farmhouse, taking care of Marler. And Diane got a visit from Barbara Elgutaa, the Native-American woman she had known since the spring of 1990. Barb arrived at Oaklawn Hospital at six-thirty P.M. with a bouquet of congratulatory flowers. She stayed until the hospital staff made her leave three hours later, and no one else visited. It gave Diane a chance to tell her friend that she and Brad had been arguing.

"We just got into the worst fight ever," Diane said. "I could just take Marler and the baby and just leave."

It wasn't the kind of comment Barb expected from a new mother.

The day Diane gave birth, Brad had a class at Western Michigan. He had promised to call Ann Hill but never did. He said he had meant to call, but his wife was pregnant and had delivered that day. This all came as a surprise, because Ann knew nothing about a second child. "I thought that was a fairly large detail not to mention," she said.

Practiced at the art of deception, Brad still insisted he and Diane were separated, but he wasn't sure who would get custody of the baby. He meant to mention the baby, he said, but figured it wasn't all that important. Since his marriage was history anyway, he didn't want to concern Ann with his troubles. This confession—bald-faced lie that it was—was awkward enough; then Brad dropped something else. Although he enjoyed the time he spent with Ann, he figured things were getting too hot too fast. He just wasn't ready for another heavy relationship so soon. This was a lot to digest, and parts of the story were told in Brad's office and parts were told over drinks at Waldo's. Ann felt used, so she began distancing herself from him. It didn't matter to Brad. There were other targets to pursue.

Things weren't exactly going well for Diane in the hospital. On Thanksgiving Day, she got a visit from Kristina Mony and her father, which she thoroughly enjoyed. Brad was at home while Freida watched Marler, and it seemed each would call Diane to inform her how the other was being a pain. They had stopped talking to each other by this point. Diane and Kateri went home from the hospital on Friday, and Regina Zapinski drove from Detroit, planning to stay the weekend.

"All she talked about was Brad and her mom. She always wanted everybody to accept Brad. Brad always sat in on conversations. He never added to them. He was just there. I didn't know anything about Brad. Whatever I knew was what Diane said Brad said. Diane talked for him. They seemed like they were supposed to be together. Brad was right there, supporting her all the way. All she had to do was climb the ladder. He took care of everything else. She was always making excuses for him," Regina said.

After one night, Regina bailed out. She got up early, and after Brad made her breakfast, she headed home.

"It was an uncomfortable feeling. I didn't feel comfortable there," Regina said.

Among the students in Brad's Thursday night class in the fall semester was Julie Cook, a petite brunette with brown eyes. The first day of class, she saw this scary-looking guy with a shaved head who was wearing a flannel shirt, jeans, and boots. "Oh my God. What did we get ourselves into?" she asked herself. But Brad smiled and talked in a gentle voice, putting everyone at ease. Julie noticed he wore a wedding ring the first day of class, but that was the last time she saw it. Brad ran a popular class. He always let the students out at least thirty minutes early, and it was a miracle if they stayed past eight P.M. Brad bragged about his son, Marler, in class. And one time after a quiz, everybody got an A because he said Marler had destroyed the papers when he took them home to grade. His office door was always open, and students would come in to borrow books and munch on lollipops or butterscotch candies that his daughter, Alissa, had sent him. He also always had a soft-drink container from the TCBY restaurant, where another of his students was a waitress. At one point in early December, Julie was in Brad's office to borrow materials for a term paper a friend was working on. Julie and a friend were going to dinner at Pizza Hut, and Brad invited himself along. There were some looks, some casual talk, and some flirting back and forth that day.

"He had intriguing blue eyes. They were like ice. Mysterious. Wolf's eyes. Gorgeous, intoxicating, killer blue eyes. He was a charmer, but it was like there was a big wall. You could only see part of him. He was a chameleon. He put up a facade for whatever fit," Julie said.

On December 11, the day Diane took Marler and Kateri to visit her sister in Mount Clemens, Julie stopped in Brad's office to return a book. It was a Tuesday, one of the two days he taught that semester. Flirtingly, he joked it was a good thing she returned it because she couldn't borrow any more unless she went to lunch with him. Julie caught the come-on and agreed to have lunch at a campus place called Schlotzky's. With the food came conversation about his years of service on the Pontiac police force. He also fed her the line about his Army service and claimed to be one-quarter Indian. After lunch, Brad dropped her off at her residence. He called later and asked if she'd like to go to the movies that night.

"I saw someone who was friendly, charming, open, and easy to talk to. I was dating a man his age, and age is not anything with me. I had dated professors before. I was fascinated. Looking for a little excitement, I guess. He never seemed like a teacher to me. The class was so laid back, I called him by his first name,". Julie said.

Brad arrived about eight-thirty P.M. and asked Julie if he could use the phone. From there, using a credit card, he dialed Mount Clemens and got his brother-in-law. "Tell Diane I'm working late tonight," he was overheard saying. It wasn't a big deal to Julie.

They went to the Crossroads Mall in Kalamazoo to see the movie *Dances With Wolves,* the epoch about the heyday of the Dakota Sioux tribes and their encounters with white settlers. While the couple held hands during the movie, Brad made points by explaining to Julie what certain Indian symbols—like eagle feathers and claws—meant. After the three-hour movie, Brad drove her home and asked if he could come in. Julie had some tests to study for the next day, so they just necked in the car before she went inside.

Brad drove home. And at 8:37 A.M. on Wednesday

morning, just hours after his movie date ended with Julie, he called Diane in Mount Clemens and told her about the attempted break-in he had discovered. Diane was coming home that night.

"Don't come home. Someone tried to break in last night. I've been up all night walking around with a gun," said Brad. Then he called the police to file a report.

Later on Wednesday, at 6:31 P.M., Brad called and left a message on Julie's answering machine. Then he called again at 9:34 P.M. to invite her over to the farmhouse in Marshall. Julie said she wasn't going to drive forty-five minutes to see him, but if he wanted to get together, he could drive to Kalamazoo.

"Aren't you married?" Julie asked him.

"Technically, yes. My wife left me in mid-November. I haven't seen her in three days. So you want some company?" Brad said.

"Sure."

So Brad climbed into the Reliant and headed over to the house in Kalamazoo she shared with several friends. She introduced him to her friends, who had been alerted that a teacher was on his way over. During a tour of the house, Julie and Brad ended up in her room, where they talked for a few moments. He made a sexual advance, and she responded. They had sex in her room. Nothing meaningful. Nothing emotional. Just physical.

"Do you date a lot of students?" Julie asked, noting that he seemed as if he had been doing this for a while.

"You're the first student I ever got close to," Brad replied.

"I don't believe you."

"You don't have to believe me."

"I don't. Just so we have that straight."

He stayed until one A.M., then got up to go back to Marshall.

"Why don't you stay over?" Julie asked.

"I don't have my clothes with me, and I have to go to a Christmas party tomorrow. If you would have come over to my house, I would have told you to bring clothes," he said.

The Christmas party was the one thrown by WUHQ-TV. It was at the Gull Lake Country Club. Advised to stay at her sister's because of the break-in, Diane was rushing around to get home and then get to the party. She dropped Marler and Kateri off at Kristina's, and she got a speeding ticket that night. She and Brad argued so heatedly that night that everybody at the party knew there was a fight.

"Nobody tried to break in. I can't take it anymore. I can't live with the lies anymore. I can't go on this way. I'm getting afraid of him," Diane told Nancy Gwynne.

"If you're scared, why don't you come home with me?" Nancy said. She recognized the signs of a distraught wife. Diane didn't want to believe her marriage was failing. She was in denial, and she still hoped if she didn't confront it everything would get better.

Diane cried and cried and cried.

Even Christmas didn't soothe things. Diane bitched at Brad to buy a tree and get in the spirit of the season. He did purchase a tree, but threw it through the door and said, "Put it up yourself."

Diane was away again on December 19. And Brad saw another chance to get together with one of his students. The phone rang that afternoon in Ann Hill's apartment. Final exams had been taken the day before, and Brad had a proposition. He felt bad that things had broken up like they had, so why didn't she come over to the farmhouse while he graded the tests.

"He didn't want another heavy relationship. I didn't want that either. I just wanted a friend, and we became friends again," Ann said.

She had been at a school function with her children earlier that afternoon. Now she arranged for a baby-sitter and arrived at Division Drive about ten o'clock that night. She had been invited over to the house once before but was unable to make it. This time, she followed the directions to the secluded countryside and parked between the barn and the farmhouse on the dirt driveway. There, chained to the tree in the front yard was Penny, the Doberman guard dog. The animal got up without barking, her eyes locked on the visitor. Brad told her not to worry; the dog wouldn't attack unless the woman acted in a threatening manner. The animal was trained to be docile unless Brad or Marler was in danger, or so he said. Once inside the house, King played the role of the gracious—and horny—host. He gave a tour of the kitchen, the living room and a front room. He didn't take her upstairs, noting that the only quarters up there were bedrooms for him and Marler. The Christmas tree was up and decorated. One thing that caught Ann's attention was the many pictures of Diane, whom she had seen once in the hallway at school. There was Diane in her younger days, Diane in Colorado, Diane in happier times.

"If they're separated, she still has a lot of things here," Ann thought.

In the bathroom were some feminine-looking hairbrushes and some other things that Brad couldn't have any use for. Hill figured Diane hadn't removed them, or maybe they belonged to Brad's daughter from his first marriage. She didn't confront Brad with it. Despite their conversation of a month earlier, and the tale about his wife's pregnancy, the lust that had brought the teacher and student together in the first place began to heat up. They were soon disrobing. Just like old times.

After sex, Brad turned his attention to the exams, and Ann helped him. She read some of the essays, and they watched some television before she returned home to her children.

Brad was still playing the concerned husband at home. A week before Christmas, there was a neighborhood party at the Kings' house. Tom and Sue Darling were there; Brad had done a little hunting with Tom and had shopped at his hardware store. Tim and Lisa Knowlton were there also, with their daughter, Kameron. Tim had helped Brad put down a vinyl floor in the kitchen and had lent him some tools in a neighborly gesture. Brad insisted on showing everybody the lock to the back porch where someone had tried to break in. He commented on how he had taken to patrolling the grounds at night with a shotgun. And on the way home that night, Lisa Knowlton told her husband, "We're not going to take any evening walks in this direction anymore." She didn't want an encounter with an armed guard.

It was January 7 when Ann Hill next visited King at his university office. He told her things were worse on the domestic front. The finances were a mess because Diane had frozen their joint bank accounts. Because he couldn't get access to his money, he was forced to drop a class he needed for his doctorate.

"That meant an interruption in his education. He wished he had the money to pay for his older daughter's education. To show other people they were wrong about him," Hill said.

Brad was in a real funk, and the couple went to a bar, the Knollwood Tavern, for a chat. "He was depressed, sad, and upset more so than I had ever seen him." An attorney told him there was nothing he could do about the money. Diane wanted the divorce, Brad said, and he seemed resigned to things.

"He was unhappy with his life as it was. He felt kind of trapped in a way, although he never said 'trapped.' When he talked about things, it was always 'I have to do this' or 'I have to do that.' He never did anything because he wanted to. He didn't get along with Diane's family. He didn't get along with his mother-in-law. It was not a good relationship."

With things turning so sour, Brad decided to look for another job and maybe take some courses to get his doctorate. Hill helped him. She typed résumés and cover letters for him, and he actively sought the job as community corrections director for Kalamazoo County. If he got the job, he planned to sell his house and move to Kalamazoo, he said—which was a crock because he didn't own the farmhouse in the first place. Whatever, Hill supported him.

At least some of the marital discord spilled over in front of the family. In January, Diane and Brad were visiting her mother before she was supposed to interview rock star Ted Nugent about the opening of his new outdoor shop, Bowhunters World. But Brad had taken the Jeep to get it washed, and he was gone for hours. It took so long that Diane missed her appointed interview with Nugent. People even went to look for Brad, although they never found out where he was. He said water had gotten into the engine and it wouldn't start.

In the meantime, Brad renewed his relationship with Julie Cook, who had received an A in his course after a five-minute, open-book, open-notebook final exam. Since their rendezvous on December 12, Julie and Brad still spoke to each other but acted as if nothing sexual had occurred between them.

After Brad's birthday on January 15, he showed Julie a new pair of Ray-Ban sunglasses his brother had sent him, and talked about how much he hated his beat-up Reliant station wagon. "I look so much better in the Jeep," he said.

"I was very attracted to him, but we had nothing in common. He was into the fraternity scene. There was nothing emotional. There was no relationship. It wasn't a power trip. I didn't feel betrayed. There were no real feelings. What was he after? Sex. Nothing more was expected. He knew that's what I wanted. I wasn't after a relationship. He was pursuing other women. He liked a challenge and liked to chase after someone," Julie said. "He was a very needy person. After the baby was born, it took attention away from him. If he wasn't getting attention, he went other places to find it. He would lie, lie, lie to get his own way."

But she did say the sex was "absolutely incredible" and that Brad had "fantastic legs, like solid rock" because he took walks daily.

On Thursday, February 7, Diane left for a three-day visit to her mother's and to attend the Salvation Army meeting. After doing the news that morning, she came home to pack the car. She had already picked up her $275 check for a clothing allowance from Nancy Gwynne, so she had some shopping money. Diane also spoke about her plans for the weekend. "She said she was going to leave the kids with her mom and go get them on Sunday. I told her I'd watch them if she wanted, but I didn't breast-feed, and we both laughed," Nancy said.

Brad was scheduled for an appointment with the marriage counselor that morning at ten A.M., and then he was off to Western Michigan University, where he had one class in the semester. Julie Cook stopped by his office to drop something off and asked for a ride home. Brad was giving a makeup test to a student, which took fifteen minutes or so. Brad and Julie left about four P.M., and when he got to her house he turned off the car's engine and got out. She invited him in. At least three of her five roommates were home, but Julie asked him if he wanted to go upstairs. He did, and they had sex. There was some concern that one of the roommates might walk in. Brad said his kids would be going to their grandmother's place in March, and he and Julie could have some privacy at his house for the week they would be gone. Brad left about ten minutes after five because he had a class at six.

"He seemed really down, like something was on his mind. He didn't want to go to class," Julie said.

After class was over, Brad and two students went over to a place called the Players Club for drinks. One was Sam Smith, a Chippewa Indian who had also been in Brad's class the previous semester. The other was Kelley Anderson, a student Brad had shown interest in. Brad told his students he was in the U.S. Army Rangers, an elite group of gung-ho warriors. He named the posts and places he had been, including Fort Benning, Georgia. Brad also said he was part Mohawk, and he had a firm enough grasp of the customs to make them think he was being truthful. At some point, someone at the table behind the trio ordered a drink called a Blow Job, made with vodka, kahlua, and whipped cream. The object is to get a woman to drink one without using her hands, which means she has to wrap her lips about the mouth of the glass and usually gets cream dribbling down her lips. It's living testament to the fact that people find countless new ways to act stupidly. Brad thought the concept was hilarious, so he ordered a Blow Job for Kelley Anderson and watched with glee as she drank it with lips only.

Brad wasn't done for the night, though. After a few hours at the Players Club, he left for a party at the Tau Kappa Epsilon House. There, he saw Heather Taylor, the sorority socialite who had been in his class the previous semester. But they didn't leave together.

Brad wasn't one to waste opportunities with his wife gone. So on Friday, February 8, he was on the phone to Ann Hill, just minutes after he got off the phone with Diane. It was just bad timing. Hill had taken her children to visit their father in Illinois, then went to Chicago to visit a friend. So Brad left a message. "Hi Annie. It's Brad. If you get in tonight, give me a call at home. I won't be home tomorrow for the rest of the weekend. So if you get in tonight, give me a call." Friday was open, but Diane would be back home sometime Saturday.

During the shopping trip with Mary Kozak, Diane brought up the subject of money and sex. First, she proclaimed that 1991 was going to be a debt-free year, that she was going to climb out of the red. She also said she wanted to leave the kids at her mother's Saturday night for a quiet night at home. She and Brad hadn't been together in a while. "We just need to spend some time alone. That's why I'm going to leave the kids with mom. We have some things to talk about," Diane said.

That night, Diane and her kids went to visit Regina Zapinski to work on Kateri's buckskin christening outfit. The two friends were sitting at the counter in Regina's kitchen when the phone rang at 7:25 P.M. It was Brad.

The call was a brief one. Then three minutes later, he called again. When Diane got off the phone, she was visibly and audibly upset. She opened up to her friend.

"After the second call, everything started to change. She had just had the baby, and her hormones were all over the place. Diane was a very emotional person. She started to talk, and I just listened," Regina said.

"I could walk out of this marriage, right now," Diane sobbed. "I just had a baby. I have two beautiful children. I have a wonderful job. I should be happy. But I'm not."

Brad still wasn't paying any attention to her, and they weren't having sex. She suspected him of having affairs. Why, she thought, would he want to be with fat and ugly Diane when he had his pick of those pretty college girls. She wanted to stay home with the kids and do things on the farm and she was tired of working to support him. They were up to their ears in debt. They had gotten rid of all their credit cards and everything had to be paid for with cash. Their landlord had been giving them a break on the rent, but the deadline was coming up for them to start paying again.

"She was crying very hard. I said to myself, 'There's really something going on here.' She really meant it when she said she could walk out. And she wasn't one to give up easily. She wanted to work on her marriage. She took everything so seriously. And affairs? I didn't see how anybody else would be interested in him. I didn't see how anyone else would find him appealing. He was bald," Regina said.

There were so many distractions that night. Kids were running around. Kateri was sick. Regina had other guests over, and Diane tried to keep composed in the interim. Regina kicked herself later for not paying more attention.

"We were going to get together again. It was not a smooth evening. We hardly worked on the outfit. I know she kept trying to tell me something. You always figure you have so much time. We had the rest of our lives," Regina said.

Diane went back to Freida's house that night. She lay downstairs on her mom's bed with Marler on her stomach but she didn't say much.

"I had the feeling she wanted to tell me something but couldn't find the words," Freida said. "Marler kept clinging to her, like he had a premonition or something."

During the weekend, she had asked Freida if the kids could stay over Saturday night. And then Brad could come get them on Sunday. She observed that the more kids you have, the less time it seems you have to spend with your husband.

"Brad and I just need time," she said.

Freida said she'd be glad to watch Marler, but how could Kateri stay if she was nursing her? And if only one could stay, it didn't make sense to take just one home. Diane would tell Brad about the change in plans later.

On Saturday, she called home twice to check on things, the last time to say that she was staying later than planned because Elaine Wash had come over to visit. She'd let Brad know what time she'd be home later.

In Kalamazoo that morning, Ann Hill returned to find the light blinking on her answering machine with a message from Brad. She called him in Marshall at 11:47 A.M.

"You just caught me. I'm on my way out the door," Brad told her. He was going out of town and wouldn't be back until late that night or early Sunday.

The truth was, though, Brad was around the house all day, working on the porch, cleaning up the grounds. He took a break to go into Marshall at mid-afternoon, stopping at McDonald's for lunch and heading over to rent the shoot-'em-up cop movie *Next of Kin* from the Neighborhood Video Store. The rental slip said he checked it out at 3:52 P.M.

He was lying on the couch when Freida called him at 4:25 P.M. to say Diane was on her way home. Then at six o'clock, he got up to go for his walk.

CHAPTER 11

Diane was supposed to do the news as usual on Monday, February 11. But there would be no more lively readings or upbeat stories. WUHQ broadcast a brief and somber message lamenting Diane's death. Larry Neinhaus, the news director who had filled in for Diane the previous Friday, asked anyone with information about the slaying to contact the Calhoun County Sheriff's Department. It would be a long time before WUHQ was back in the news business. "It was just impossible for the staff members to treat it as a normal work day," said vice president Mark Crawford.

At the farmhouse, Allen Marler performed a Native-American ritual for his murdered sister. He gathered a supply of wood and in the yard, about thirty feet from the house, he lit a ceremonial fire. It was to light Diane's way to the spirit world, and the rising smoke would carry with it prayers for Diane. It was a centuries-old custom being carried out for a modern woman. Allen had designated himself as the firekeeper. The flames must burn continuously for three days and nights.

Whether those flames shed any light on the case was pure conjecture. But this would be a day of discovery for the sheriff's deputies who were on their way back out to the crime scene. So far, the police knew the murdered woman had received harassing phone calls and a threatening letter from an unknown admirer. She was shot twice with a small-caliber gun, and because of the shell casing found in the barn loft, they could figure that the killer had probably waited for her up there. Except for Brad King, nobody had been seen on or around the property. And Brad had gone for a forty-five-minute walk before the shooting. Travis the tracking dog had found a track that went south in the direction Brad said he went, then circled to left until it came all the way back to the King driveway. The spot at Talmadge Creek where Travis showed unusual interest had been marked with toilet paper in a tree, and that needed to be checked out. Some footprints had been spotted by flashlight on the night of the shooting. And deputies had found some .22 caliber ammunition and a cleaning rod in the King attic, even though Brad said he had only a shotgun in the house.

Deputies who returned to 16240 Division Drive were joined by a volunteer posse put under the direction of Sergeant Harold Badger. The posse fanned out in the fields that had already been cleared by Trooper Gary Lisle and Travis. Interestingly, Lisle couldn't find any footprints at the spot where Brad said he went for a walk. And there was all kinds of snow left over in drifts.

Lisle had stopped by the sheriff's department that morning to tell Detective Jack Schoder of the track Travis had run Saturday night. Schoder also showed him

Brad's boots. The pattern looked similar to the footprints Lisle had seen on the King property.

Out of the blue, Brad showed up in the lobby. He had come into Marshall to begin planning funeral arrangements with the Craig Kempf Funeral Home, and he wanted to see how things were going. Lisle asked Brad about the route he walked, and whether he had gone left or right during his twilight trek back to the haypiles. No, Brad said, he walked straight back. And on a scrap of paper provided by Schoder, he drew a crude sketch showing his walk to the south of the farmhouse. Something didn't make sense.

"Did you ever own a .22?" Schoder asked him.

"I had one once, but I sold it in 1984 when I was in Denver," Brad told him. He couldn't remember the make or model or whom he sold it to. It was just a .22 rifle his dad had given him.

Brad was free to go, but he didn't want to deal with the media horde that had gathered at the station. Schoder escorted Brad through the police garage and out to a quiet street. The detective needed to get out to Division Drive.

At a news conference in his office, Sheriff Jon Olson said his deputies had few leads, although reporters had plenty of questions about a stalker. No suspicious characters had been seen in the area, before, during, or after the shooting. No items had been taken from King's vehicle or home. A volunteer posse was assisting in the search for clues.

The star-struck fan who had been pestering Diane was a possible suspect, but he wasn't the only suspect.

"We have targeted no one and we have eliminated no one. Everyone is a suspect, and no one is more of a suspect than anyone else," the sheriff said.

Olson acknowledged that Diane had received four or five calls at work and a letter had been placed in her mailbox on October 30.

"He was apparently infatuated with Mrs. King. He wanted a relationship with Mrs. King. It's easy to view it now as more of a threat. At the time it was more of a harassment. He was seeking assistance in the media field," Olson said.

Olson said the killer had taken a carefully chosen position east of the murdered woman. "The overall scheme of things would indicate that whoever was the shooter had taken a position that would have given him a clear view of fire. Like a sniper."

The bullet that struck her heart was so well placed that nothing could have saved her, "even if she was standing next to an ambulance," the sheriff said.

The caliber of the weapon wouldn't be known until the autopsy reports were completed. Brad had given an informal statement to police but had not been formally questioned.

In the meantime, deputies were busy at the farm. The spot where Brad and Randy Wright got the Jeep stuck in a snowdrift on Sunday was examined. There were two sets of footprints heading north back to the house. But there were no prints to indicate where Brad had walked on Saturday. Oh, and the prints that were observed by flashlight Saturday were gone. Either the slush had melted or they had been obliterated; one print on a deer trail had been trampled on by a stream of hooves.

At about one o'clock, Michael Shay of the Michigan Department of Natural Resources arrived to help with the search around Talmadge Creek. He worked in tandem with Deputy Guy Picketts, the first officer to arrive at the murder scene. Picketts walked the creek bank in a southeasterly direction while Shay donned hip boots and waded in the water against the current. The creek drains through a marshy area dotted with heavy underbrush and bog grass, but Picketts had the easier time on the stream bank. He was just a few feet ahead of Shay when he shouted: "Here it is!"

About two inches of a rifle butt was sticking out of the meandering creek. Its barrel had been jammed into the muck of the stream bottom. Also visible through the clear, cold water were several shiny shell casings. The spot was right off a trail deer had worn through the brush and where Trooper Lisle had wrapped toilet paper around a bush on Travis's cue.

Jack Schoder rushed down from the farmhouse to supervise the retrieval. Nobody wanted to touch the gun because it had to be checked for fingerprints later. So while Shay delicately unscrewed the butt plate of the rifle, Schoder removed a rawhide bootlace. It was tied under the plate, and the police tried to lift the rifle straight up. But the butt plate broke under the weight. Part of it flew off into the swamp grass and was never found. Shay tried again, sliding slipknots over a screw that went into the rifle butt. This time, the muck surrendered the gun. It was a .22 caliber, bolt-action Remington Model 511 Scoremaster. It was missing a five-round clip, but was otherwise intact. Then Shay recovered the shell casings, inserting a narrow reed into the hollow end. As he fetched each of the casings, Schoder wrapped them in makeshift envelopes of folded yellow paper. Everything was sent off to the Michigan State Police crime lab at Lansing. There was a feeling that the slugs taken from Diane King's body would match the rifle.

Diane's family was still in the dark about what happened. Her sister, Darlene, and cousin, Elaine Wash, had spent a restless night at the farmhouse. In the morning, they assembled the clothes Diane would be dressed in for the viewing of the body, the ones she would take to her grave. They picked out the red dress with the white collar she had bought on her final shopping trip. They also packed makeup, a slip, bra, panties, pantyhose, and shoes.

Brad had spent the night clutching a statue of Kateri Tekakwitha. There was a distinct notion among observers that something wasn't right.

"He didn't do anything or say anything like he was grieving. You just got the feeling in your heart this was not normal," Elaine said. "We knew Diane would have never got out of that car if Brad wasn't there. We didn't just want to blurt out, 'Where were you?' But we'd ask Brad a question and Randy Wright would answer. He was glued to Brad. You couldn't talk to him."

Brad did something else that day. Among the people he called about Diane's murder was Shemane Nugent, the wife of rock star Ted Nugent, a Michigan native and an avid outdoorsman. Diane had met the Nugents twice, once when Ted did a concert and again when he opened Bowhunter's World. Shemane asked Diane about producing videos about her husband, but they were hardly friends.

"We weren't particularly close. I was surprised he was concerned enough to call us. He said she was being stalked and was killed by this obsessed fan who had spent the afternoon in his barn waiting for Diane to come home," Shemane said.

It rankled the family that Brad hadn't had the courtesy to call them on Saturday after Diane was shot. So when Brad went to the florist, the family went to the police station and demanded some answers.

Jack Schoder wanted some answers, too. Even before the gun was found, he had some questions about Brad and his story. The results from the crime lab would take time, but Schoder was convinced it was the murder weapon. Even though he didn't have solid stuff like fingerprints to use as a hammer, Schoder decided it was time to confront Brad. The web of suspicion had strengthened.

By chance, Brad had called the station to see how the investigation was progressing. Schoder suggested that he stop in. "We need to talk," the detective said.

Brad was accompanied by his brother Scott when he arrived at the station. Scott waited in the lobby, while Brad went to Schoder's office, two blocks away in the county health department. As a veteran of the Pontiac police force, he would have known the drill.

Brad went over his story again in the taped interview. Diane left Thursday morning for Detroit and he went to work at Western Michigan University. On Friday, he worked in the barn, puttered around with a bird feeder and went rabbit hunting with his .16 gauge shotgun. On Saturday, Diane was visiting with her cousin, Elaine, and hoped to see her sister, Denise. "Just let me know when you leave so I know when to expect you. Have a good time. Love you. Hug the kids for me," Brad said in their last conversation. It lasted only two or three minutes, because he doesn't waste much time on the phone.

"I know this is a difficult time for us to be talking, and I appreciate it. But you went into Marshall, made a drive through McDonald's and came directly back, is that accurate?" Schoder asked him, trying to nail down specific times for Saturday.

"I stopped and got a movie at the video store."

"Oh, did you?"

"Yeah. I was gonna watch a movie."

"That evening?"

"No, while I ate lunch. I was bored."

"What movie did you get?"

"*Next of Kin.* With Patrick Swayze. It's a nice violent cop movie."

"Nice violent cop movie, huh?"

"So I ate lunch and watched it."

"Oh, you watched some of that."

"Yeah, I watched it. You know, I think I watched it all, now that I remember."

"You still got the movie?"

"No, I took it back. I dropped it off Sunday."

"Did ya? You think you watched that, 'cause I just want to get clear on this."

"I know I had it, but I did watch it. Maybe I didn't even watch it."

"Maybe you didn't?"

"It was in the case."

"The other day you didn't mention that."

"I didn't even remember. I bet I didn't watch it. I didn't watch it."

"You didn't?"

"Bought the movie and set it down, was gonna wait 'til later. Come to think of it, I'm sure I didn't."

"We'll move on."

"That bothers me though, Jack. I don't remember stuff. I had the damn movie."

"You had the damn movie. Now you go back out, do some more outdoor work?"

"Yup, I went back out and worked on the porch."

"Then if I remember right, you went back in."

"Yeah, I got cold. I was also getting tired of doing it by myself. Lonely. I'm not away from my family much."

Brad told the detective he was napping when Freida called him at four-thirty. He lay down again and thought about fixing dinner, but decided on a pizza instead. He went back outside to work on the porch, then changed his mind and picked up wood scraps. After a trip to the bathroom, he went for a walk about six o'clock, heading south to the hay bales to look for deer. During his ten-minute stay, he thought he heard a gunshot. On the fifteen-minute walk back to the house, he didn't hear anything except for the steady drum of traffic on Interstate 69 just to the west. He didn't hear a car door slam, didn't hear or see anybody running through the swamp, and didn't hear a second shot.

"I know there were two bullets in her body, you know. I read all the stuff, and you told me that. And that is what perplexes me. Why didn't I hear the other shot?" Brad said.

"You heard that gunshot in the area of six-fifteen, six-twenty, by our calculations here. Diane couldn't have been home yet," Schoder told him.

"That's right."

"And now we bring it up forward, and you're walking up here, and you don't hear any gunshots?"

"I just don't."

"See that's where I'm getting messed up. I tell you Brad, I'm getting messed up. And I've analyzed this shit, man. I've looked at this up one side and down the other."

"I can tell you're frustrated."

"I'm frustrated as hell."

"I know I'm in the area and I can't help you."

"Brad, I'm gonna be real truthful with you. I've been in this business twenty-one years. You were in it twelve. I gotta get through this with you, man."

"I know."

"I can't conceive, nor can I rationalize in my mind, with the information that we have there, I can't eliminate you as being a suspect."

"I understand."

"And I'm going to tell you another thing, Brad, and it's man to man here, and I'm not going to pull any punches with you."

"I don't expect you to. I just want the truth."

"Based on the information I've got here, I believe you're involved. I believe, Brad, that you're responsible for this. I cannot for the life of me, Brad, and I've worked on this for two days. I can't explain away a number of things. Your explanation of things does not follow logic. And I'm having a big problem, Brad, 'cause I like you as a guy. But objectively, man, listen to me. I can't explain away, most important, that anyone other than you and the family in Detroit knew when she was coming home."

"I know."

"You and you alone knew she was coming home. Second of all, you're out there all day, Brad. A person who is going to sneak or stalk is scared of being detected. Similar to a burglary, lights and sound scare them. Man, you were there all day, Brad."

"I know."

"No one else was there. Cars aren't running by your house all day, and it's a lonely road. There is no one in the area that we can see. There is no place somebody could have a vehicle, and there are no neighbors around there. I can't for the life of me figure how somebody could get into that barn and go in there with the dog being there. Now you say your dog is a friendly dog, and I observed that. But a person is not going to confine themselves to a building where they can only get out via the front door, with you being there all day, Brad. Diane's car is gone the entire goddamned day. If somebody is stalking Diane, Brad, they know you're there and she ain't. And they're not going to sneak in your barn while you're there and when she's not there if she's the object of some unknown stalker."

"That's what I would say."

"I cannot for the life of me explain away how you did not hear gunshots. I been out there. You would have heard the gunshots. There were two distinct gunshots. Let me tell you a couple of things, Brad. I been married for a few years and everything has not always been perfect."

"True. Ours has not been perfect either."

"And you guys have been receiving counseling? For your marriage?"

"Yeah. We thought we needed some help. To get back on track."

"And I tell you, Brad. We're both adult men here. You know as well as I do that there is a very fine line between love and . . . and sometimes you cross over that line. You add up the pressures of life. You've got your part-time job. You've recently lost your job with the probation department, some other things that aren't going quite well for you, Brad. I understand why things can fall apart and your wheels can come tumbling off and I think that you probably need some counseling yourself. 'Cause I think what has happened in your life, as a person, Brad, is the fact that wheels have come off and you're kinda skidding along. And you reach a point of total frustration. And you couldn't handle it. And I think you went for a long walk to kinda sort things out for yourself, and I think that you had enough psychological and mental pressure that for just a minute, just a couple minutes, you snapped. You broke. And you lost your head, Brad, and I'm really sorry about that."

"No."

"Brad, that's what I think happened."

"I understand that."

"Brad, listen to me, man. You cannot go on with what happened there in your life without getting some help."

"Well, I know I have to see somebody."

"I'm talking about your involvement with this. I am convinced that you're responsible for this. I am convinced to the point of proving that in court. There comes a time when the pressures add up and the wheels fucking fall off, that you gotta reach out and you gotta grab someone, man, and you gotta hang on."

"I was trying to grab my wife and hang on with her."

"I'm not talking about that. I'm talking about you. I'm talking about since this incident. You're gonna have to hang on to something. We were out there this afternoon, Brad. We found the murder weapon. And we have other evidence of your involvement in this."

"I didn't do anything to my wife."

"All I'm saying is that good people in today's society sometime face stresses that they can't handle."

"I know that."

"And they break . . ."

"That's why we were seeing a counselor."

"Just a minute. I'm talking about you. And you broke down for a few minutes, and I know that you did something that you would never again even consider, but you broke down and lost control for a few minutes. I don't know whether they call it insanity. You just broke down and you lost control. And I feel bad for you. But what we have to do is come to grips with it. Because you know as well as I know, that for you to go from this point forward with that on your head, without getting some kind of help, is going to break you down and it's gonna shatter your total insides."

"You don't know."

"Just a minute, Brad. You understand what I'm saying? We found the murder weapon in the creek. And we have more evidence, Brad. Everything doesn't happen in a vacuum. We have evidence that convinces me, and it's gonna convince other people, you're responsible for this. The gun is at the crime lab right now."

"I didn't do it."

"Brad, I think it's important for you to come to grips with this. And deal with this issue. And I appreciate the fact that things could be going bad. And you just get broken down. And I understand that. I been through those kinda points myself where I want to throw up my hands and say screw it, man, I've had it with the world."

"Don't we all."

"But that doesn't make you a totally bad person."

"Well, of course it doesn't."

"There is nothing that you have told me that does anything but implicate you. There is no other explanation. And when I add the other evidence that I have, and I'm not gonna tell you all the evidence that I have, and all the witnesses that I have—you'll see it in court, Brad. 'Cause we're gonna be going to court. We do have the murder weapon. Okay?"

"I hear that."

"And we're gonna tie that weapon directly into you. And you've been in this business, Brad. It's over, okay? I want you to begin to accept that it's over. Brad, I'm not asking you about it. I'm telling you. I'm convinced to the point that we've got the evidence. And what I'm talking to you about is, how are you gonna handle it? How are you gonna deal with it?"

"I didn't kill my wife. Why would I kill the woman I love?"

"Not everything runs smooth as it seems."

"I know that, but that doesn't make somebody kill their wife. Come on, Jack."

"Brad."

"I can't believe this."

"Based on what you've told me . . . I don't at this time purport to know everything that was going on in your life, in your relationship with your family, and with you. We've been at this a day and a half now. But I do know enough to be able to re-create what happened out there. What I want to do is sit down with you, and I just want to understand how this happened and what other things are going on in your life that causes you all this stress. There are a number of things, I'm sure. What else is causing you problems, Brad? Not working?"

"Of course it is."

"Financial?"

"Not dire financial problems."

"Okay."

"But it doesn't have you kill somebody."

"What happened here?"

"I didn't kill my wife."

"Explain to me any other scenario that might fit. You please explain it to me, Brad."

"I'd like to know."

"We've got a gun."

"Understand."

"You have any idea where we found that gun?"

"No."

"We have it. Remington, bolt-action .22. Scope, what is it, Scopemaster?"

"I don't know what you're talking about."

"Scoremaster, Model 511. Bolt action. The clip is missing. Brad, please, help me out. I live with these cases."

"I know. I've lived with them, too."

"And I take this stuff real serious. Help me out, Brad."

"That's part of the job."

"Give me something to hang my hat on. Give me someplace else to go look, Brad."

"I wish I could. I mean, I've been trying to explain it to myself how this all happened. Why, why would somebody do all this is what I'm trying to figure out. And I don't know. Jack, I know we had our problems—everybody has in life—and we were doing what we thought we could do to try and straighten them out. 'Cause we cared very much for each other. And it wasn't worth giving up."

"Okay."

"You know, so is that . . . I mean . . . I know, Jack, there is so much stuff that is unanswerable about this. I know that. I mean why? But that . . . Oh, God. That is what's bugging me. I just can't even believe . . . And I know, there is a lot of stuff that is not answerable. A lot of stuff. Does that mean since it's unanswerable that I personally did it?"

"You're asking me a question, and I . . ."

"I'm asking myself the question."

"I say the reason, Brad, that I'm bringing this up to you, man—and we're gonna have this out—because I gotta get . . . Based on the evidence of this case right here, based on the witnesses we've talked to, based on the physical evidence we've found, basing on finding the Remington Model 511 gun where we found it, I'm convinced you're responsible for this, Brad. I'm convinced of that. I am totally convinced that what happened is not that someone else came up and got into a loft that they couldn't get into . . . What I'm saying Brad is that you broke down, and this incident happened as a result of your having too much pressure on you, to the point where you cracked. You absolutely cracked. You made a bad decision. That's where I'm coming from."

"I know that's where you're coming from."

"I have come to that conclusion in my mind. You're responsible."

"I did not kill my wife. It is the last thing in the world I would want to do."

"Listen, Brad. How old a guy are you?"

"I'm forty-four."

"I'm forty-three. You been through the military?"

"Uh huh."

"Been through twelve years of the police department, and from there held a bunch of other jobs."

"Uh huh."

"Here, there, everywhere. Met Diane. Got a couple kids. Got the problems everybody else has."

"That's right. Not insurmountable if we stick together and work them out."

"I understand you're having some financial problems. That those problems just got to you, and they just became a little bit more than you can handle. Well, let's go through this again, okay? There was nobody else down the track. You go over to where we found the gun. No one else has been over there. There is one person that went from that barn to where we found the gun. There are no other people that did that."

"Hmm."

"There is no one else been around there. No one else is in the area, except you. You're the person that's there."

"Yes, I was there."

"Let me ask you a question. Is there any reason we should find a fingerprint on that gun that belongs to you?"

"No."

"So we just absolutely won't? We went up to the lab today. I'm sure you understand that water, you know, muck, doesn't remove fingerprints."

"Of course not."

"Nobody knew when she was getting home. Brad, you weren't there when she got home."

"I know I wasn't. If I were home when she got home, maybe it wouldn't have happened."

"You really think that we're gonna believe, Brad, that somebody else got in there within a short period of time when her car is not even home, and got themselves trapped in a barn situation where they gotta come out the front door, know that you're in the area? Absolutely not."

"It's not highly logical, no."

"No, not at all. And the problem is, I don't think anyone is going to believe that."

"I know, I understand that."

"And then we take other evidence into account. I think we can convince some people that you're responsible for this. I'm sure. I want to get down inside of you and find out what's been going on with you."

"Not killing my wife, that's for sure."

"Okay, let me ask you this. Would you agree to a polygraph test? I gotta have some answers. I gotta have some logic in this thing. Something has got to make sense to me. This doesn't."

"Doesn't make sense to me either, Jack, and it's coming out of my mouth. I only can say what I know."

"Okay."

"If I were just some Joe Blow off the street that had never had to sit in your chair, you know. Here I am talking to you, knowing the process, knowing about investigation."

"Sure."

"And knowing that what I'm saying doesn't make a shittin' bit of sense. At all."

"It don't."

"I mean there's a lack of logic."

"By your own admission?"

"Of course. But that's what transpired for me, and I know, I mean, Randy and I sat and talked and talked and talked, you know. Why would a guy just sit and wait? And you know, I don't have an answer to that. I don't."

"Let's get back, 'cause I don't have answers to this. And we've talked to the point where you're not helping me find the answers."

"I can only tell you what I know, Jack. Do we have someone that saw it happen?"

"Pardon?"

"I mean if we had somebody that saw it happen. You know."

"Well, we'll see."

"I wasn't there to see."

"We'll see. I think we'll wrap this up for now, okay?"

CHAPTER 12

The mood at the Calhoun County Sheriff's Department suggested that an arrest was imminent. Bradford King failed to crack under questioning from Detective Jack Schoder, and no lie detector test was given. But his story remained shaky. Schoder was convinced he had his man. And the public pronouncements from Sheriff Jon Olson made the stalker scenario seem less and less likely.

At a news conference, Olson said the murder weapon had been found—a Remington Scoremaster Model 511. Seven shell casings were also uncovered. Preliminary indications from the Michigan State Police crime lab were that Diane King had been shot from a distance rather than at point-blank range. And the investigation was zeroing in on one person.

"At this time the investigation is beginning to focus on an individual suspect. But we have not eliminated anyone," Olson said. "This person is presently free to roam around in the community. We have not issued any warrants at this time and don't expect to make an arrest tonight, but we feel that we do have a solid case."

Olson said that Diane King "had a personal relationship" with the suspect. And if you could read between the lines, he started deflecting inquiries about an obsessed fan.

"I can only say that the person who wrote the letter has not been identified. We are still looking at all the angles."

Olson wouldn't specify where the gun was found, but he hinted Brad would have known where it was. "The weapon was in an area of plain view. The site was accessible to both family members as well as non-family members."

Calhoun County prosecutor Jon Sahli was aware of the zeal the sheriff's men had for arresting Brad. But arresting someone and convicting him are two entirely different things. Sahli, a conservative man, liked to have an airtight case. This one had some major gaps.

For one thing, the rifle came back clean from the fingerprint lab. If the police were to link the gun to Brad, they'd need another way.

The ballistics tests were a mixed bag. Detective Sergeant Robert Cilwa of the Michigan State Police crime lab had to clean the muck, mud, debris, and light coating of rust from the barrel before he could fire it. A barrel is rifled, meaning it is bored with a series of special grooves. The idea is to impart a spin on a bullet to make it fly more accurately to its target. The grooves can twist either to the right or left. The rifling of a gun makes imprints in each slug that is fired. Imperfections in the metal and other factors ensure that no two rifled bores are alike, which makes them like fingerprints. Under a special microscope, Cilwa found that a slug fired from the rifle was imprinted with six lands and grooves with a right-hand twist. The slugs removed from Diane King also had markings consistent with having been fired from that rifle. But they were so deformed after hitting her that Cilwa couldn't say with absolute certainty they came from that gun.

Another telltale mark is left by the firing pin that strikes a cartridge and causes the internal explosion that propels the slug out of the barrel. And the apparatus that ejects the spent shell to allow another round to be chambered also makes a unique imprint. Cilwa could say with certainty that the shell casing found in the bar loft was fired from the rifle jammed barrel-first into the mud. The seven casings found on the creek bottom also were fired from thc buried firearm. But the casings were a different make than the boxes of ammunition found in Brad King's attic. They had to come from a different source. The Remington Scoremaster Model 511 is one of the most popular .22 rifles ever made. Hundreds of thousands of them have been sold, and this had no serial number on it. That meant it was manufactured prior to 1968, when Congress passed the Federal Gun Control Act following the assassinations of Robert Kennedy and Dr. Martin Luther King, Jr. It was impossible to trace. What all this meant was the police had some promising information to work with, but they lacked a direct tie between Brad and the gun.

No casts of footprints had been made, and the ones spotted the night of the murder had vanished. And the work of Travis the tracking dog was fruitful, but police couldn't say for sure what person he was following that night. Travis is trained to identify a track; if he comes across the person he is following, he sits and wags his tail because he expects a reward. But Brad King had been taken downtown for questioning Saturday night when Travis wrapped up his work at 11:47 P.M. He never encountered Brad after running his track. So any talk of a pending arrest was premature. Besides, if Brad were arrested, the investigators would likely relax in their labors. Having him at-large would prod them to keep digging. Sahli also knew what the perception would be if he arrested Brad and then tried to fit the case around him. He knew he had to make the case first.

While the police wrestled with their problems, an anguished scene was playing itself out at the Craig Kempf Funeral Home. Brad had decided that there would be a viewing of Diane's body that Tuesday before he had her cremated and buried at the Fort Custer National Cemetery. But he failed to consult the family on their wishes, and his decisions touched off a firestorm of protest. Nothing in Mohawk custom allows for burning of a body. And the family wanted to bury her next to her father in Sterling Heights.

"He never consulted the family at all. He was going to have her cremated, to get it over with as soon as possible. That's not normal behavior," said Diane's sister, Denise Verrier.

She was the first person at the funeral home on Tuesday. And she noticed what a remarkable number of others saw, too. Something about Brad's behavior was noteworthy in a man whose wife had just been murdered.

"He was very phony. Very rigid. He seemed to be putting on an act. There were no real tears ever. He tried to act solemn, but it was so fake. He hugged me. It was like ice. I couldn't hug him back," Denise said. "He could be talking normal and then he'd bawl and then he'd take a breath and talk normal again. We asked him what happened, and he kept saying, 'I don't know.' He never mentioned Diane. He never, ever, ever, ever said he didn't do it, even when we knew he was a suspect."

Freida Newton arrived to discover to her horror that Brad planned a cremation later that afternoon. Within a short time, a group of Native Americans encircled Brad and implored him to change his mind.

"Cremation is not the Indian way. That's not what Diane would have wanted," a whole circle of friends and family was telling him.

Brad didn't stay long at the viewing. He elected to return home. Later, when a TV news report focused on the discovery of the .22 caliber rifle, Denise heard him say to no one in particular, "I sold my gun in Colorado." She wondered what prompted that remark until she learned that the police suspected him.

Death poses such awkward moments because people are uncomfortable dealing with it. The scene at the farmhouse was especially clumsy because not only was Diane dead—she had been murdered. Diane's family suspected Brad and they knew the police did, too, but they tried to be civil out of respect for Diane, who wasn't even in the grave yet. Brad had already been grilled by Jack Schoder and was still on the hot seat. His mother was overheard telling her husband, Cliff Lundeen, "We've got to do something. These people suspect my son."

Freida Newton and much of the family stayed at the farmhouse. And Allen was still tending Diane's ceremonial fire in the front yard. But Denise bolted and spent the night thirty miles away in a motel near Jackson. "The more it went on, the more and more spooked I got. I called the farmhouse and told them, 'You guys got to get out of there.' The police had found the gun and said the person was known to Diane. I was so spooked I couldn't get closer. They kept telling me not to worry," Denise said.

She wasn't the only one who was nervous. Joanne Karaba had gone to the hardware store to buy a security light and other things because she assumed Diane's killer was a stalker. Then she did the neighborly thing and took food over to the farmhouse for the mourners. Nothing specific triggered her reaction, but she began to wonder about Brad, too. "It was the whole picture. He didn't grieve. He wasn't crying. It was like, 'Well, she's gone.' He was bubbly. He had his hands in his pockets, just standing there," Joanne said.

A weird feeling overcame Regina Zapinski on the morning of the funeral, a Wednesday. Calling out to her, Brad walked toward Regina like a zombie with his arms outstretched. When he greeted her, Brad always kissed her on the lips and gave hard, tight hugs. Something was amiss this time. "I know everybody grieves in their own way. But he never acted like a man who just lost his wife. His face was just blank. I kept telling myself, 'I shouldn't be thinking these things. I'm looking for signs.' And it wasn't just me, it was everybody," Regina said.

Two years ago to the day, Diane King started working at WUHQ-TV, on February 13. Now everybody at the station was attending her funeral in Marshall. About 350 people jammed St. Mary's Roman Catholic Church, a gray stone cathedral with sharply angled roof and stained glass windows. Outside, a Native-American group called the White Thunder Singers sang traditional songs of grief to the pulsating beat of a washtub-size drum. To the Indians, a drumbeat symbolizes the heartbeat of Mother Earth. The rhythmic vibrations would carry their prayers to Diane in the spirit world. Men in braided black hair howled with sorrow. "The Iroquois believe, and so did

Diane believe, that the truly giving person is the person who did something for her people," said Julie D'Artagnon, one of the singers and a personal friend of Diane and Brad.

Bradford King wore a tan trench coat, stylishly belted, over his suit and tie. He carried an eagle feather in his right hand, a gift of the symbol of vision that Andre D'Artagnon presented to Marler. Several times, Brad wiped his cheeks with the same hand that carried the feather. He had Freida Newton at his left side. But an astute observer would have noticed they never made eye contact and spoke very little.

Inside the church, the scent of Catholic incense and candles mixed with the aroma of Indian herbs—sweet grass, cedar, sage, and tobacco. The herbs are burned to cleanse the air, much like holy water is sprinkled from church fonts. And the smoke lifts prayers and well-wishes to the spirit world.

Camera crews and photographers were barred from the church, but a gauntlet of crews waited outside to capture the funeral procession of family, friends, and mourners. The news value was readily apparent. Diane was a TV person hounded by a stalker, the crime of the nineties. She and Brad seemed to be the ideal couple in an ideal location, the heartland of America. And there's always a fascination with murder, the oldest human crime, part of the alpha and omega of human existence, especially when it occurs in a place where it's not expected to intrude. So the three networks and CNN were represented. So was *A Current Affair, Hard Copy,* and *Inside Edition.* Print reporters ranged from *People* magazine to the *London Daily Mail.* The story was even carried by radio columnist Paul Harvey, himself a staple of Middle America.

To this diverse group, Rev. Jim Barrett spoke from his pulpit. "Diane was a vibrant person, excited, I might say. She was excited about her new baby girl, Kateri, her son, and her husband. She was an exciting person on television. She loved her work. She loved the service she provided through that medium, and she was excited about the traditions of her Native-American background. Maybe the memory of Diane Newton King can cause us to become excited."

Among those at the funeral were Julie Cook and Ann Hill, the two Western Michigan University students who did not know they had shared Brad's attention outside of class. Ann had tried to call Brad after the killing, and had talked to Diane's brother, Allen. She spoke to Brad for a few seconds after mass.

"Glad you came. I have got to talk to you," Brad told her. She noticed his demeanor changed with every person he talked to.

Julie Cook left through a back door. "I gave him an A-plus for acting. He would cry, but he also looked up to see who was watching him," she said.

There was a meal for the mourners after the service. Emotions were raw. Things weren't getting any better between Brad and Diane's family, especially when Denise heard that Brad was talking about leaving Michigan.

"He better not try to leave the state with the kids," Denise Verrier told someone.

The comment got back to Brad, and he tried to reassure his sister-in-law.

"Denise, I'm not going to be leaving with the kids. I'm going to stay right here and get my doctorate—just like Diane wanted me to," Brad said.

Denise's impression: He's a fake and phony.

Sister Ann Jeffrey Selesky, the director of Native-

American ministries for the Catholic Diocese of Kalamazoo, noticed something, too. She had counseled Diane as to which Mohawk music and prayers would be acceptable at Kateri's Catholic christening. And she was present on Monday when Brad told Marler his mother was dead. As a social worker, she saw plenty of people in times of stress. In regard to Brad at the funeral, she said, "I thought it was unusual to turn on and turn off the grief as easily as he did."

Stella Pamp, the Chippewa woman who had comforted Diane after she received the threatening letter, had a difficult time dealing with all of this. It took some inner prompting to view Diane's body in the casket at the funeral home.

"Brad grabbed my hand and said, 'Now I can say good-bye to her.' We went to the casket. And I told him, 'She shouldn't be here. She was too alive, too fully loving to be here.' He didn't respond. He let go of my hand and walked away," Stella said.

Then, the day of the funeral, Pamp went to the farmhouse to pay her respects. She went to the spot in the driveway where Diane was shot, the spot where Diane had voiced fears for her own safety just a few months ago. And some dark but unmistakable notion swept over her. "This feeling came over me. I knew it was Brad instantly. I knew he did it," she said.

Back at the police station, the out-of-town reporters were hounding Sheriff Jon Olson for information. As many as thirty-five showed up at his news conference. It was the biggest crush anyone could remember for any criminal case in Calhoun County. Within five days of the crime, the sheriff's office had logged more than seven hundred calls on the King case, mostly from the media.

"We believe the suspect and the deceased were personally known to each other. He knew her and she knew him. I think we have the individual. It now becomes a question of being able to convince the prosecutor and develop a case that won't blow up in his face. I can only say that the person who wrote the letters has not been identified. We are still looking at all the angles," Olson said. He couldn't say for sure if the letter Diane received was from an admiring fan or if it was a diversion to draw attention away from the killer.

But the prosecutor's office was still moving methodically. Although some family members were told an arrest could happen right after the funeral, Sahli insisted he wanted to see the results of lab tests and other evidence before making a final decision.

"We're not going to use an arrest warrant at this point in time. Further investigation needs to be done. I want to be sure and have everything answered. I don't want to get into trial and have something come up. It's not back to square one, but I do have some questions that I have to have answered."

At WUHQ, the phone rang off the hook from people who wanted to express their sympathy and to find out more about the murder. The station set up a trust fund for Diane's children. And a security guard was hired to control the nonstop crush of media.

On Thursday Diane King was buried in Mount Olivet Cemetery next to her father, George Herbert Marler. Brad still carried his eagle feather and wore a fur hat as protection against the February snow shower. Diane's mother had purchased a granite headstone engraved, "In loving memory of a daughter, sister, and mother." The word wife was omitted. Brad didn't offer to pay anything for the stone.

After a brief service at the cemetery, everyone was

invited to a lunch at the Lakeside Bible Chapel, the church of Donald and Denise Verrier. Once again, Brad's behavior stood out.

"He was controlled, almost theatrical. It wasn't genuine. It was like somebody acting," Don said. "He said something like, 'It took something like this for me and Freida to get along.' I just thought, 'Yeah, right.' "

The war between Freida and Brad heated up in the next few days. The big issue was the kids. To give Brad a chance to get on his feet and look for a full-time job, Freida volunteered to take Marler and Kateri with her for a week. Then it was two weeks. Finally, she obtained a court order granting her temporary custody of the kids. Brad was a prime suspect, and an arrest could come any day. But Brad counterattacked in the courts. A judge awarded him custody of the children.

There was one final ritual associated with Diane's death. It was an Indian custom called a Ten Day Feast. Ten days marked the minimum period of mourning in Native-American thinking. The feast is like a passage; at the end of it, those who had loved Diane were expected to collect themselves and get on with their lives. Food was served and a special place set for the deceased. Favorite dishes were prepared and arranged, then buried. And items that belonged to the deceased were passed out to the guests, so the spirit would live on.

Julie and Andre D'Artagnon, two traditional Native Americans, had the feast at their home in Kalamazoo. Indians believe it is disrespectful to say the name of the dead for a year, so Diane's name was mentioned very little. Whenever someone said "she," though, everyone knew they meant Diane.

There were standard Indian dishes—venison, sweet meats, corn soup, Indian bread, wild rice, and the three sisters of the Mohawk culture: corn, beans, and squash. After the meal, Diane's valuables were given away. Julie got a gold bracelet. Regina Zapinski was given earrings. Sister Ann Jeffrey took a leather headband. Nancy Rapo received a pin.

Brad didn't object to any of this; he attended the Ten Day Feast and thought it was a good idea.

There was no legal will.

During this time, Freida was caring for Marler and Kateri with Brad's grudging consent. He agreed to let them stay in Sterling Heights for two weeks while he looked for a full-time job so he could support them. He had given power-of-attorney to Diane's sister Denise so that she could administer health care to the kids if something came up. The custody fight for the kids began to brew after Brad moved out of the farmhouse and the family found out through the police that Brad was a suspect.

Brad had strong feelings about going back to the farmhouse the night of the Ten Day Feast. He didn't want to be by himself, especially back there. So Andre and Julie invited him to stay over and sleep on the couch. Then they talked it over and asked Brad to stay with them for a while. Their home was converted into three apartment units, and Brad could stay in the basement, which had a kitchen and a bath.

"We offered him that. He wasn't having any luck finding work. He wasn't sure where he wanted to go, or where he wanted to stay," Julie said. A short time later, she went back to Division Drive with Brad to get the remainder of his belongings and clean the place up. "It was pretty much all empty. We hardly talked at all. I didn't want to be there. It had to be done. We got it done as quickly as possible and came back. It was very difficult."

The police had been back again as well. Actually, it was February 19—the day of Diane's feast—when they entered the house armed with a search warrant. They were looking for guns, ammunition, a clip for the Remington Scoremaster rifle, film, cameras, videotapes, footwear, insurance policies, financial records, telephone records, personal papers, newspapers, and magazines. They seized twenty-eight items in all, including unpaid bills, collection letters from the IRS, a bill from the Marshall ambulance service for the night Diane was killed, and a book that hinted at marital trouble—*The Kids' Book of Divorce.*

They conducted a test with a laser beam, fixing the distance from the barn loft to the Jeep at ninety-one feet. Also, Deputy Guy Picketts was sent back to the spot where Brad said he went for a walk while the gun retrieved from the creek was fired from the barn. Picketts heard it clearly.

On the way to Kalamazoo, Nancy Rapo and Allen Marler stopped at the farmhouse. Jack Schoder and some deputies were there with their search warrant. "Look to see what kind of shoes Brad has on," Schoder told them.

Returning to Detroit, Nancy and Allen stopped at the police station. "We know he did it. We're going to nail that bastard for what he did," Schoder told them. For the first time, Allen realized what so many others already had—that Brad might be the murderer. On the drive back home, Nancy noticed he was so angry his knuckles were white with gripping the steering wheel.

CHAPTER 13

It was a time of shifting destinies. For murder suspect Bradford King, every passing day without an arrest meant the case against him was too weak to prosecute. For the investigators, some regrouping was necessary.

Friends were puzzled that Brad showed little interest in the probe. He had been a policeman for fourteen years, and he taught criminology at Western Michigan University. Since the investigation was stalled, why wasn't he helping to catch the killer? And some of his comments sounded like not a grieving and frustrated husband but a sanguine survivor.

For the first two weeks after the murder, the children stayed with Freida in Sterling Heights. After they went back to their father when he got the apartment with the D'Artagnans, there were visitations arranged with the family. It was a bit of shuttling; he would drive them to a spot halfway to Sterling Heights where the family would meet him. Then they would be returned at a prearranged time and spot. Sometimes either Marler or Kateri would stay an extra week with Diane's family.

Within two weeks of the crime, Debbie Rich called from Grand Junction, Colorado, to find out what progress had been made. Her call found Brad at home watching videos and not trying to find the creep who did this.

"Why aren't you out there?" Debbie asked him.

"That wouldn't be appropriate," Brad said.

"Who cares what's appropriate? This is your wife that was murdered. What are you doing about it?"

"I wrote to the president on how this nation has a serious drug problem and we have to do something about it. I'm also writing a book on how our colleges are producing criminals."

Debbie wanted to ask if he was one of the criminals produced in college, but she remained silent. The conversation was really weird.

"They'll never catch the guy. They destroyed every piece of evidence that was on the property. They fucked it all up. The footprints were run over with a car. These guys are really stupid. They're idiots," Brad said. Instead of being upset, he sounded cocky. Footprints had been erased and no fingerprints had been found.

Now how would Brad know what evidence there was, Debbie wondered. She got the distinct impression she was talking to the smug perpetrator of a perfect crime. Finally, she asked him directly.

"Did you kill her?" She expected him to say, How can you ask me a question like that. That's ridiculous. How can you even suggest that?

His answer was, "Well, no."

The denial was so soft that it didn't convince Debbie Rich.

Theresa Nisley, Marler's godmother, had a similar

conversation with Brad. She was upset because Brad had quit calling, and she phoned him to find out what was happening in the investigation. His tone was cocksure.

"Do they know anything?" she asked.

"No, and they'll never know. They fucked it up so bad, they'll never catch him."

The day Theresa found out about Diane, she figured it had to be the stalker. But now she and her husband suspected Brad.

"He was real distant. He had hit her when she was pregnant. The marriage was falling apart. She was going to quit her job. He was going to lose his income. I'm sure he didn't like that. And he bounced back real quick. He didn't seem too upset about it. He was the only one who knew when Diane would be home. He left those kids in the car all that time after she was shot. They worked out this elaborate security plan, and he messed it up to go for a stupid walk. He's full of it," Theresa said.

People also noticed some peculiar behavior on the Western Michigan campus. The place was rife with rumors. The police had come to Brad's office in Sangren Hall. From his desk they confiscated scissors, razor blades, and magazines—ordinary stuff, but what you'd need to send someone an anonymous note.

About three weeks after Diane's murder, Brad ran into a former student. They talked for a while about Brad being in grief counseling and how the case was going. "It doesn't matter, because they can't prove a fucking thing," Brad told her.

On February 21, Brad called Ann Hill, although he hadn't been sexually involved with her since last December. Her answering machine was broken, so she had missed some of his earlier calls. They met at the student center on campus.

Ann offered her sympathies, and he said he was in grief counseling. He also asked if she had been contacted by the police. "I'd rather they not get in touch with you," Brad told her.

According to Brad, Calhoun County had an axe to grind against him because he had been fired as a probation officer. He also claimed that the sheriff was prejudiced because he had married an American Indian and because he was half-Indian himself (a lie, of course).

Brad also bumped into Julie Cook one day. They exchanged pleasantries at a vending machine, and Brad gave her his new phone number and address in Kalamazoo. Brad had a new look. He was wearing the wedding ring he had removed last semester. "He said it had been in the shop to get repaired," Julie said. He was also driving the Jeep instead of the Reliant station wagon. In the new year, Julie Cook had a conversation with Ann Hill. Each of them learned about the other, so there were no secrets about Brad's bedroom patterns. Julie had already been questioned by Detective James Statfeld, and she gave his number to Ann.

Brad had called Frank Zinn, the property owner, to tell him he had moved out. "He left because he said he couldn't live with the memories. Rubberneckers were driving out by the house. It was awful. People would just slow down and stare at the place, like it was a real tourist attraction."

A month after the killing, Brad visited Nancy Rapo and Allen Marler at Nancy's house. The talk centered on the skills of the Calhoun County detectives, which Brad hinted didn't compare to his own, having worked on seven homicide cases in Pontiac.

"He called them small-town cops. Assholes. He didn't think these guys had the knowledge and skill to solve a murder. They don't know what they're doing. It had been four weeks, and he said they'll never catch the guy. He said the only way they'd catch him was if he killed again or got drunk and shot his mouth off in a bar. He was proud, like he beat them. He felt and believed he was such a smart cookie. He was one up on them. No grieving husband is going to say something like that. It was like he was saying, 'I got away with it,' " Nancy said.

The Salvation Army had decided not to name a new Christmas chairperson to replace Diane King. The post would stay vacant in her honor. And Robert Randels of the Food Bank of Southwest Michigan wrote a tribute to Diane in his newsletter.

> I last saw Diane at our January Food Procurement Task Force meeting. As always, with grace and beauty, she was with us . . . friendly, cheerful, unpretentious, full of life. It seems she was always ready to do her share. Indeed, always ready to do more than her share.
>
> Last year, she co-chaired our April food-raising activities. Always with exuberance, always professionally, always with love. Our theme of this year is the same as last year—You Can Be There When A Child Is Hungry.
>
> Diane understood this theme. She wrote, "If we don't take care of our children, we're not taking care of our future." She helped us to make sense of these things. Helped us to find the practical ways one can be there when a child is hungry. She offered us directions to arrive there where children hunger. There where life is not as good for others as it could and should be. There where life must be made better.

Dear friends, let us mourn the life of this good woman. Let us, here and now, resolve that the needless suffering of a child in hunger [will] end.

Here and now, let us go there. There where she, with all her charm and clarity, had already arrived.

Brad stayed busy on the Native-American circuit. Before the murder, Diane and Brad had made plans with the D'Artagnans to attend an Indian powwow in Lansing, and Brad kept the date. All of them also attended a University of Michigan powwow in March, and the following month they went to the Central Michigan University powwow in Mount Pleasant. There a man named Joseph Bravehcart gave Brad a Sioux headdress made from a wolf's head. The fur trailed all the way down his back as Brad danced to the beat of the drums. It didn't go unnoticed among Diane's friends that Brad was dancing in Indian garb when he still should have been mourning. And Native Americans took a dim view of anyone who tried to pass himself off as one of them. It was like blasphemy.

Thanks to a round-trip ticket provided by John and Susan Van Vleet, Brad attended the March powwow in Denver. He brought his new wolf's head regalia with him.

"He was about as clinically depressed as you can get. Just barely moving," John Van Vleet said.

Apparently Brad showed different faces to different people, and his friends in Colorado were convinced that he was a typical grieving husband. They encouraged him to go to the Indian festival because it would take his mind off things.

His funds were limited. He was still drawing a small paycheck from his part-time job at Western Michigan

University, and day-to-day living expenses came from Diane's final pay at the station. He was literally living off the final money earned by his wife.

Brad was frustrated in his attempts to collect Diane's life insurance at WUHQ. It was worth $54,000 and had a double-indemnity clause, but the Union Mutual Insurance Company refused to pay because of the open police investigation. He stopped by the station periodically to keep up payments on the kids' health insurance.

Nancy Gwynne said Marler, shaken by his mother's murder, kept saying, "My mommy fell down. My mommy fell down. I want my mommy." The child became withdrawn and developed a stutter.

Brad wasn't the only one in grief counseling. Freida had joined a support group called Parents of Murdered Children, which was established in 1978 by a couple whose daughter was murdered. Parents naturally expect their children to outlive them, so the death of a child is especially traumatic. When murder is involved, it is even more traumatic. The grief can last twenty years. Freida's mourning was compounded by a self-imposed guilt. "I was the one who told him when to get up in that loft. I called to say Diane was on the way home." Bumper stickers appeared on family vehicles that said, "Someone I Love Was Murdered."

The rift between Freida and Brad had widened because of the custody fight over Marler and Kateri. At first, he had given the family the kids' health insurance card and power of attorney so the kids could get medical care. But things were souring. Brad voiced some of his sentiments in a March 12 letter sent to Keith and Nita Clark, a ranching couple the Kings had known when they lived in Grand Junction. In it he told the Clarks how Diane's mother was trying to take the children from him, and the legal battle he foresaw fighting. In addition, he felt the police had no real leads, thus leaving him as the lone suspect to concentrate on—making it increasingly difficult to go on with his life.

The custody battle was also on Brad's mind in a letter he wrote to Regina Zapinski, in which he included his new address and phone number in Kalamazoo. In this letter he explained how Freida attempted to take the children away from him through court order, but Brad had the court date moved up without informing Freida—leaving him with the children. He was struggling with the fact that the children should see their relatives because that was how Diane would have wanted it.

Regina wrote back that she was agonizing over the loss, typical of the grief process of shock, denial, anger, and depression. She had given up trying to numb her pain with alcohol, but she was disturbed by so many unanswered questions. She was also haunted that she hadn't spent more time with her long-time friend.

Kristina Mony had noticed a profound change in Brad's personality. This was a man who always greeted her with a hug, who had called to wish her good luck on prom night, and who had come over to her house to share strawberries for dessert. But Brad failed to say one word to her at Diane's funeral. He hadn't stayed in touch at all. And Kristina, who once was treated as part of the family, now felt like she no longer existed in his life. On April 12, she and her mom had gone to Brad's new residence in Kalamazoo to retrieve a book she loaned to Diane. It was Barbara De'Angelis's *Secrets About Men Every Woman Should Know.* Brad was infuriated when Diane got the book; he called it a bunch of garbage. Now his anger was directed at Freida for trying to get custody of his kids.

"She might think she can walk all over me. But nobody crosses me," Brad said.

There was an icy stare in his eyes when it said it. Kristina said looking into his eyes was like looking into a black hole from which no feeling could escape.

"My mom and I took it as a threat. It sent chills down my spine," Kristina said. "He never once mentioned Diane. It was like she never existed. There was a strong feeling that this man was not the husband and father we once knew, but a man who was capable of committing a serious crime."

In a letter to Detective Jack Schoder about the incident, Kristina wrote:

> More than one life has been destroyed. The little boy that used to have charisma and a smile that would warm your heart has become insecure and scared of the world around him. It breaks my heart that her beautiful baby girl will never know what a wonderful woman her mother was. She will never have her wonderful mother to confide in, to attend her school play, to help her get ready for her first prom, or to watch her receive her diploma. I hope and pray every day that you will find the monster that murdered my best friend. Diane King was a woman that touched many lives and had so much to share with her precious children.

The raw anguish in her words contrasted with the concern for his own feelings that Brad expressed in his letters.

Brad had lost his job at Western Michigan. He failed

to show up for the last two weeks of classes in April, and a substitute finished up the term and gave the final exam. University officials said his grief caused his absences.

But he was still involved with campus life. Julie Cook hadn't been with Brad since two days before the murder. At the end of the spring semester in late April, she and a friend, Michelle Miller, saw Brad one night at Waldo's bar.

"I bought him a beer. He was with a bunch of guys. Then I was sitting at a different table. I sent him over another beer, and he came over to talk to me right before he left. He put his arm around me and said he'd call," Julie said.

She left the bar, too, and went home to bed. It was about two in the morning when one of Julie's roommates came upstairs and said, "Brad is at the front door."

"Let him in, and tell him to come upstairs," Julie said.

Once in Julie's room, Brad sat at the end of her bed and started to unbutton his shirt and peel his clothes off.

"Take off your clothes and stay awhile," Julie said with a trace of sarcasm.

"Do you want me to leave?" Brad asked.

"No. What makes you think I'm going to sleep with you."

"Because if you weren't, you'd kick me out."

So he climbed into bed and they had sex. Brad stayed for a couple of hours, leaving about four in the morning. One of Julie's roommates was extremely agitated that a suspected murderer had been in the house. She ranted so much that Brad wasn't allowed in the house again.

But Julie didn't stop seeing Brad. On Wednesday, May 30, Julie and Michelle Miller were at Waldo's again when they encountered Brad. He saw her as he was leaving, and he approached for some small talk.

About two o'clock that morning, the phone rang at Julie's house. It was Brad.

"Can I come over? Please, please, please," he said, sounding half-drunk.

"No, I'm sleeping," Julie told him.

"Do you have plans for Thursday night yet?"

"We're going to Waldo's again."

"Maybe I'll see you there."

Brad failed to show at the bar. But he was on the phone again at three in the morning, pleading to come over. Julie again said no. "Did you ever hear of calling someone in the daytime? Do you have a problem with that?" she asked. He phoned her again at a more reasonable hour and said he'd see her on Saturday, June 1, because they were both taking a graduate entrance exam from eight A.M. to noon.

After the test, Brad and Julie met for lunch at Wendy's, about two minutes from campus. They were soon holding hands and exchanging kisses in the parking lot. Julie's place was off-limits. Julie grabbed a blanket, and Brad drove to a park in Kalamazoo. He held her hand as they walked in the woods, making small talk about wildlife, such as the different berries deer eat. She saw some strange-looking character in the woods and said, without thinking, "Oh great. You brought me to a place where there are psycho killers in the woods." Brad never reacted.

He unfolded the blanket, and they were locked in an embrace. But in the middle of the afternoon, there were people walking nearby and Julie was skittish.

"You're not very comfortable, are you?" Brad said. He didn't seem to care about the other walkers.

They stayed for about ten minutes before going to a motel for some privacy. Brad drove to the Holiday Motel just off Interstate 94, where he paid $26 plus $1.82 for a room for two. He registered his address as 1270 Gratiot, Port Huron, Michigan, which was where he grew up. After sex and a stay of several hours, Brad dropped Julie off at her house. She kept a matchbook from the motel.

"Well, goodbye. Have a nice life," she told him.

"What's that supposed to mean?" Brad said.

"I'm not going to see you again." Julie knew she was leaving at the end of June to go back to the Detroit area, where she planned to enroll in Wayne State University. And she got the impression Brad wasn't going to stick around much longer either. He had hinted at going back to Texas or Colorado.

"Maybe you will," Brad said.

"Whatever. Good-bye."

And that was the last contact Julie Cook had with Brad. He had never mentioned Diane's murder. He never showed any remorse or asked for any sympathy. She suspected him from the start but she never once confronted him. He never said he didn't do it. "Looking back, I guess I should have been afraid. But he had no reason to harm me. He was always a perfect gentleman. He never made me feel uncomfortable. It was an unusual relationship. I don't even know how to describe it. I must have been crazy," she said.

But she had noticed a change in Brad's behavior.

"He was very, very carefree. As if he had no cares in the world. Very, very upbeat. He appeared to be just more relaxed. He was just real nonchalant about everything," Julie said.

Brad had been thinking for some time about going back to Colorado. He had friends there. And he was tired of the police being on his back. At this point, there was not enough to charge him with a crime, and his lawyer, James Brady, advised him to take off. He wrote to Keith and Nita Clark on May 21, telling them of his intention to move to Colorado, and how much he missed Diane. He told them how much he looked forward to seeing them upon his arrival in Colorado.

But the Clarks were in no mood to greet him. They had been friends of Diane's. They met her through a story she was doing on radioactive mill tailings from a uranium mine. And the Clarks knew Brad was the prime suspect in her death. Keith wrote back to him on June 1, and there was no welcome mat.

When he left Michigan, Brad left behind his second car for the D'Artagnans as compensation. He had paid some money for rent and contributed for food occasionally. But Julie and Andre never did get the Reliant running. Brad loaded up the Jeep Wagoneer and headed west with Marler. He left Kateri behind with the D'Artagnans until he was settled. He left without saying good-bye to Diane's family, and he failed to leave a forwarding address or telephone number. He mailed a letter on his way through Indiana on personal stationery adorned with images of an Indian peace pipe and a band of beads, telling Freida that he and the children were in the Denver area. He told her that he did not feel he could trust her because she had tried to take his children, and that he had a job offer in Denver.

Freida knew that Kateri was still at the D'Artagnans. She had her connections in the Native-American network with the moccasin telegraph. She attempted to keep tabs on her granddaughter by tailing Julie, which further distressed Brad. He wrote her again soon after he got to Denver, and he again lied about having Kateri with him.

* * *

The timing of the Colorado move couldn't have been worse. Brad's friend, Susan Van Vleet, had her own personal tragedy to deal with. Her mother died on June 10, the day Brad and Marler arrived. They stayed with other friends instead. To help Brad get on his feet, Susan advanced Brad three months' rent on a new place at the Tamarac Apartments in Denver, plus rented some furniture for him.

"He had a support system here. This was the place he and Diane were the happiest," Susan said.

But he didn't have a job offer as he had told Freida. While he was hunting for work, he painted houses. He had a lot to learn about the business, though. He painted one woman's house without first securing a deposit, and after he was finished, she refused to pay him.

Brad considered enrolling at Colorado University to complete his doctorate. He had a letter of recommendation from Lewis Walker, his department head at Western Michigan University. "I encouraged him to do so. He felt he was being harassed. He wanted to get on with his life," Walker said. But it just wasn't practical trying to raise two kids and study for his doctorate. Brad finally took a job with an insurance company.

"It was back to ground zero," John Van Vleet said. "Selling insurance wasn't his big passion or anything. It was a job to make some money. He was tired of being broke, tired of scraping by. He had no job, but he wasn't in any shape to work. He had no energy left. Marler was having nightmares every night. Every time he closed his eyes he saw his mother being murdered. Brad was trying to get it together for the kids. The most common thing he said was, 'I hurt so bad. I wish she was back. I miss her so much.' "

The Van Vleets also paid for Julie D'Artagnan to fly out with Kateri, so he had his hands full with the kids. He enrolled Marler in the Native-American school, and he attended powwows whenever he could. When he was settled, he wrote Freida with his phone number but didn't furnish an address: In the letter he stated that he had heard through some people in Michigan that she was concerned about the children's safety. It was written in the cold tone of someone who felt he was being accused. Brad questioned her concerns about the kids' safety, and he felt he was owed an explanation of why she tried to get custody of the kids. Finally, he stated that Freida cost him $1,700 in trying to take the children, and he would like to be paid back.

The cloud of suspicion still hung over Brad, and many friends in Grand Junction avoided him. "He was running. A lot of people turned their backs on Brad. They had heard some bad things," said Theresa Nisley.

But the Van Vleets stood by him. They were aware that Brad was suspected of murdering their friend Diane. They wondered about the possibilities, but they accepted his story. "You gotta ask yourself the question: Is this possible. The answer always came back no," John said.

Part of their reason was what Marler, who had turned three in March, had told some of his playmates. He told a ten-year-old friend that it was two men wearing cowboy hats who killed his mother. To a five-year-old chum, he said it was two guys wearing black hats and black boots and who drove a black car. And to a baby-sitter who saw Marler two to four times a week while Brad was out looking for work Marler said that it was two guys in cowboy hats and cowboy boots. Both of them had long guns, but only one of them shot her. They ran off in two directions. Marler stopped talking after he'd tell this story and just shut down completely for a while. The sitter said Marler wondered why his dad didn't take him out of the car. He and Kateri were crying a lot while he was yelling for his dad.

A mutual friend, Cindy Zebelman, overheard Marler tell the same story about two guys in cowboy hats and boots.

The investigation into Diane King's murder sputtered and stalled. Brad King was still the prime suspect in the minds of the Calhoun County Sheriff's Department, but no progress had been made in the case.

At a March 8 news conference, Sheriff Jon Olson said the killing was premeditated.

"There is nothing to diminish our focus on the primary suspect," said Olson, who was still being pressed on the stalker. "We have the motive and we have the opportunity and we are developing those issues further."

The murder weapon was a sticking point. The Remington rifle found in the creek was their strongest piece of evidence, but the link to Brad had yet to be confirmed.

"We can put the weapon in his hands at the time of the crime," said Olson, who was holding the gun for emphasis in front of the cameras. "We are trying to identify the history of this weapon. We want to find out how and when it was acquired. It is a critical link, but not the last link."

In the month since the murder, rumors abounded in the community. Police had been downplaying the "fatal attraction" angle, but public pronouncements that the killer knew Diane were worrisome. Residents were afraid that a killer was in their midst.

"I don't think there's reasonable cause for alarm to the general public," said Olson. The police believed the motive involved domestic pressures, which meant the killer wasn't likely to harm anyone else. But few in Marshall felt reassured.

Olson also made a cryptic comment about the suspect's identity concerning fingerprints. "I have good reason to believe there will be prints on file," Olson said. Because Brad King once worked as a probation officer for the county, his fingerprint samples would be available.

But Olson clammed up about the suspect's identity. Even two months later, in an interview with the *Battle Creek Enquirer,* Olson said, "My heart is screaming to tell who it is, but my professional ethics will not allow me to do it. I don't want to see the prosecution's case undermined."

The strain was building in the sheriff's department. From the start, Olson's public pronouncements raised expectations that an arrest was forthcoming. If it was a single male suspect who knew Diane, and the murder weapon had been found, why wasn't there any action? The only conclusion in the rumor mill was that something must be wrong with the investigation. Detective Jack Schoder shouldered a significant amount of the pressure. Privately, he too was frustrated and anxious to proceed. It was a bit like gripping a fistful of sand; the harder he squeezed, the more sand seemed to slip out. Schoder was convinced he had his man; and if there's a bad guy out there, Schoder felt, he needs to be locked up. What's worse, Brad was running around calling the investigators assholes and small-time gumshoes who screwed up the scene and would never catch the guy. "Just keep talking, Brad. Your days are numbered," Schoder thought to himself. The criticism stung. But personal frustrations had to be put aside. The only way to build the case was to get results.

There was some friction between the investigators and the prosecutor's office. The sheriff's department was pushing for an arrest, but cooler heads prevailed among those who had to bring this case to trial. They were issuing terse "no comments" to the media while their work was being done. Public pronouncements could only hinder their case, and there were private feelings that the sheriff's department should do less talking and more producing.

In Michigan, prosecutors labor under the 180 Day Rule. Someone who is charged with a crime must be brought to trial within 180 days or the case is dismissed. Consequently, it is better to build a case first and then make an arrest, not the other way around.

Brad King's arrest was a long way off. First off, it had to be determined that Brad was the killer. That meant eliminating any other possibilities. In a way, that meant proving a negative—if no one else could have done it, Brad must have done it. The work wasn't going to be done overnight. Given the complexities of a circumstantial case, it might take years to pull together, despite what the sheriff was saying. The prosecutor's office faced the daunting task of methodically, systematically pulling all the bits and pieces together. There were so many pieces of the puzzle, and there would be plenty of dead ends. A case like this is built from the outside inward. And the prosecution also had to play devil's advocate to counter any argument that a defense attorney might use. In the end, though, this was the strategy that would pay off. A quick arrest to appease public sentiment would not.

Things hit their low point in June when Brad moved to Colorado. Some worried that he might be slipping through their fingers, but there was little they could do. They didn't have enough to charge him yet. The investigators wanted him around, both to keep an eye on him and hope that maybe he would slip up and incriminate himself. Even though they knew where he was going, the prospect of an out-of-state move was disheartening.

It was time to step back and regroup. Authorities had acquired the Kings' phone records, which included something like 190 calls in the months preceding the murder. Analyzing those calls could show the difference between what Brad said he was doing and what he was really doing. But it was impossible to do all this with just two county detectives and one investigator in the prosecutor's office. To keep the case from stalling, Calhoun County had to acknowledge its case was nowhere near ready for trial and it needed outside help from the Michigan State Police. The point man would be Detective Sergeant Gary Hough of the Battle Creek office.

Hough's strength was organization and coordination. When Sheriff Olson approached him about setting up a task force to direct the King probe, Olson set some ground rules right away. No politics would be tolerated. It would be a straightforward investigation. And troopers would have the cooperation of the county detectives and deputies. Several state police units had been at the scene the night Diane was murdered. When they saw what was happening, they let the county people do their own thing.

Although the deputies had done some good police work, they had also made some serious mistakes. It would have been ideal to have plaster casts or at least pictures of Brad's footprints so they could match them with those that had been observed on the grounds after the murder. And sealing off the area would have prevented crime-scene contamination. In hindsight, the detectives should have set Brad aside in a corner until they could check out his story about being at the hay piles, considering there were no footprints back there. And Jack Schoder played his cards too early to trap Brad into making a confession. He should have waited for the crime lab reports, and he never should have conducted the second interview alone with Brad. He was dealing with a cagey police veteran; investigators got the impression later that Brad may have made that tape for himself. Brad was correct when he crowed to his friends that the police "fucked it up so bad." But those weren't the only critical factors to solving the crime. If you could eliminate everything else, it still left only one conclusion. The investigators still had deductive reasoning going for them.

Hough inherited a stack of paperwork—from interviews to reports to maps. Most of the interviews were of little use, so people who had talked to the police two, three, or four times were visited again. The investigation needed a focus. There were three priorities.

First, the police needed anything and everything that could link Brad to the gun. Second, they worked on salvaging everything they could from the crime scene. And third, they tried to establish motive, which was the weakest part of the whole case.

Diane's family had been on an emotional roller coaster, thinking that Brad's arrest was coming any day and having their hopes dashed when it didn't. Freida Newton was heartened when the task force was created, but she was more concerned with getting custody of her daughter's children.

"I want those children. I don't care if he walks away. It won't bring Diane back," Freida told Hough.

"I want him," the detective told her.

Having grown up on a Michigan farm, Hough had been with the state police for seventeen years and had been a detective for the past seven years. He was a dedicated cop, perhaps too dedicated; he was getting a divorce after seventeen years of marriage. He was driven by the ideals that motivate all cops who take their badges seriously. "Nobody deserved to die like that. We owe it to the person in the ground to try to resolve this," Hough said. "I'm just doing my job. That's what I do."

Among the other members of the task force were Michigan State Police Detective Phil Mainstone, investigator Jerry Woods of the Calhoun County prosecutor's office and the two Calhoun County detectives, Jack Schoder and Jim Statfeld.

Woods, a former detective in Eaton County, had been reading the files on the King case since the day after the shooting. He had volunteered his services from the start, and on March 9, he began looking through the Kings' phone bills. His arduous task was to find links between calls Brad was making to his campus girlfriends and dates when Diane was away. The information was necessary to form a time line.

The task force set up a "King room." In space donated by Calhoun County, the King room was a large area near the prosecutor's office where the volume of evidence was accumulated and sorted. A time line was started of dates and activities. At first, it was written in investigator Jerry Woods's illegible scrawl, then transferred onto charts and graphs as a clearer picture began to emerge.

A breakthrough came just after the task force was formed. One of the investigators interviewed Barbara Elgutaa, Diane's Native-American friend, and showed her a picture of the Scoremaster rifle retrieved from Talmadge Creek. Barb said it looked like a gun Brad was carrying when she visited the farmhouse in November, just months before the killing. Now the police searched with added vigor for more people who had seen Brad with a gun that he swore he had sold years ago. Eventually, they went to Texas to question Brad's mother, Marjorie, and his brother, Scott. Both of them said Brad's father purchased a bolt-action .22 caliber rifle when the boys were young. Brad had kept it after he graduated from college.

But the critical work was done at the crime scene. The task force called on Detective Sergeant David Minzey, who is with the investigative resources section of the violent crimes unit of the Michigan State Police. A fourteen-year cop and a member of the International Association of Homicide Investigators, Minzey had authored the handbook for Michigan State Police use in crime-scene analysis. A thinking man's investigator, he was studying for his doctorate at Western Michigan University. His expertise is reviewing a scene, comparing the known and unknown, and developing probabilities about what happened. In a case where the evidence is mostly circumstantial, his insight can be invaluable. Minzey first visited the King farmhouse in June of 1991, and assisted investigators through the arrest and beyond.

Finding out what happened sometimes meant eliminating what didn't. The shooting of Diane King was neither self-inflicted nor accidental. She wasn't killed in self-defense because she hadn't threatened anyone. There was no robbery or sexual assault. Consideration was given to a sniper, because Diane was killed sniper fashion from the barn. In these shootings, commonly called "thrill kills," the targets tend to be picked at random. The victim is just in the wrong place at the wrong time. The sniper usually sets up his quarry so he will have an avenue of escape. In this case, a sniper would have had to carry the gun to the scene, at the risk of being observed, and after he shot Diane, he would have come out of the barn in her direction and then head south, where Brad King had gone for a walk. That's just too risky. And to abandon a gun would be extremely rare for a sniper.

An obsessed fan or some deranged soul having a one-way love affair was obviously considered because of the calls and letter to Diane. The cut-out letter—"You should have gone to lunch with me"—was especially significant.

"Notes with letters cut out of magazines from strangers are extremely rare. In my experience I have never found one that wasn't from the person themselves or a close acquaintance. I have never found one to be from a stranger. They tend to come from an individual or someone close to her who is concerned about having his identity revealed. It's likely that the person who was making the phone calls was not the person who made the letter, but the person who sent the letter knew about the phone calls. That note is so sophomoric. I've never seen one like that," Minzey said.

So Minzey considered why someone who knew Diane would want to kill her. Could it be for financial gain, such as an insurance policy? Would the killer gain his freedom to pursue a love affair? Or were there psychological workings—anger, rage, ego? Was the killer enraged because she had hurt him or was planning to leave?

The general category is called self-esteem, because the victim is seen as a threat to the offender's ego. Minzey's report explained it this way:

> The offender feels that the victim is "winning." In fact, the purpose of this type of scenario is to "win." These homicides are generally well planned and organized. The weapon used is one that the offender is comfortable with and is specifically chosen by the offender.
>
> In assessing the Diane King homicide, the self-esteem scenario would appear most applicable. Diane King was executed. The weapon used was not one that just happened to be lying on the ground or the property, the offender brought the weapon to the barn for that specific purpose. The offender attempted to hide the weapon. The likely reason for this was the offender felt that the weapon could be linked to the murder.
>
> Due to the risk factor involved, it would appear that the offender was familiar with the barn and property where Diane King lived. The shot to the abdomen may be significant. It could merely be an "insurance" shot, to make sure the victim was dead. If the shot were fired specifically at the lower abdomen area, this may be an emotional action on the part of the offender. It is the one and only emotional aspect of this case.
>
> Based on the information provided, the offender in this case will be a Caucasian male. Although the victim was a Native American, her primary social

associates were Caucasian, as was the area that she lived in.

It has been my experience that offenders who kill in such a fashion do not have the ability to confront face to face. Because of this, they are dependent upon others. The use of a firearm is the most common means of inflicted death in this country. The use of a firearm also prevents the victim from retaliating either physically or verbally. It is likely the victim was the specific stimulus to this aggression that ended her life (i.e., something she did or said).

The offender will likely have post-high school education. The homicide was planned and carried out in an organized, methodical manner. The primary error made involved the weapon's discovery. This disciplined thinking may be associated with someone who has attended college classes, where it is up to the student to organize and budget their time. This would also be consistent of those individuals that the victim would associate with.

In terms of social class, the offender will likely consider himself middle class. Definitionally, this will probably not be true. The frustration-aggression hypothesis holds that individuals become highly frustrated and are characterized by higher levels of unreciprocity in their formal role relationships. While they feel they deserve better, their income, status, education, etc., are not what they should be, so the frustration is blamed on someone else. Homicide offenders tend to be characterized by these higher levels of unreciprocity.

Because the offender could not face the victim, it is likely that he will have low self-esteem. To compensate for this, he may choose an occupation which is considered "macho" (i.e., construction, truck driver, security guard, law enforcement, etc.). He may also drive a sports car or four-wheel-drive truck, if possible. The type of automobile may be dependent on his financial situation. The offender likely will be well groomed, dress to the occasion, and be in good physical shape. He attempts to dress to the class he feels he belongs.

If the offender was in the military, he would have volunteered. This would be merely another facet of trying to compensate for his low self-esteem.

The organized yet simple plan involved in this homicide may indicate an intelligent individual who has not been arrested. Individuals with criminal histories tend to learn from their experience and in fact become better criminals. The inexperience exhibited in this case points to this being the offender's first homicide.

Individuals who commit these types of homicides, where the victim is viewed as threatening to their ego, tend to be hedonistic. Everything revolves around him. This type of homicide reflects very little emotion. The offender will likely be described as having an antisocial personality. These individuals do not feel remorseful for what they have done, however [they] are quite manipulative. Those who know this offender will describe him as being a notorious liar, manipulator and backstabber. While he cannot confront someone face to face, he will sneak around behind their back and retaliate in more devious ways.

Being manipulative, this offender will attempt to display the "appropriate" emotional response, however those around him will find that it does not

> seem natural. It is possible that the offender may date frequently. This is merely to satisfy his ego and these relationships are superficial and usually sexually oriented.
>
> In examining this homicide, I feel that there are some significant investigative questions. These would include: Who knew where the victim lived? Who knew she was coming home? Who could have felt threatened enough to want to kill her? Who would benefit from her death? Who would have access to a rifle and know how to use it? Who has significant post-offense changes in behavior?

Minzey gave the task force additional fodder on probability. In killings done with a gun, more than seventy percent of the assailants and their victims lived within two miles of each other. Homicide in general takes place among primary social relationships, which are a definite source of friction and potential for violence. Only twelve percent of homicides are committed by strangers. And FBI statistics show that thirty percent of all women murdered in this country are killed by their husbands or boyfriends—which means the bedroom is one of the more dangerous lairs around.

Meanwhile, the Calhoun County rumor mill was working at peak production. Statements by the police had provided the fuel, and gossip was like oxygen that fed the flames. The innocent person being scorched was Tom Darling, the Marshall hardware-store owner who lived just down the road from Diane and Brad King. Every rumor was without merit and not worthy of mention, but the weight of gossip, unfounded though it was, forced its way untidily into the public domain. The story was that Diane was having an affair and that her spurned lover was responsible for her shooting. Tom Darling had an airtight alibi for the night Diane was murdered; he was away for the weekend with his wife and stepson as church chaperons on a ski trip. The idea that he was having an affair was ludicrous. Yet rumors persisted to a degree that neighbor kids heard them all day at school and Tom considered selling the hardware store and leaving town. "It's laughable if it wasn't so tragic. There isn't anybody truer than Tom. It's just preposterous," said Lisa Knowlton, a neighbor. It got so bad that residents were calling the *Battle Creek Enquirer* with nonsensical stories of Tom being arrested and led from his home in handcuffs. The sheriff's office got forty-five media calls in a single day about the arrest.

Sheriff Olson and prosecutor Jon Sahli took the highly unusual step of releasing a joint statement on January 23, 1992, that no arrests had been made. The statement did not identify Darling by name but said, in part, that he was "not a suspect and rumors are without merit."

The *Enquirer* ran an editorial about the gossip and the public frustration that no arrests had been made.

The case had reached critical mass. The task force had gone as far as it could. The criteria for arresting Brad were on the table. It was decision time. "First, you have to believe he did it. You have to be absolutely convinced, which we were. Then you have to think you have a better than fifty-fifty chance of getting a conviction. The prosecutor's putting his career, reputation, and neck on the line. And finally, the case just wasn't going to get any stronger. Once you get to that point, you have to go forward. It's your job," Gary Hough said.

Jerry Woods, the investigator in the prosecutor's office, had done scores of interviews, read over seven hundred pages of documents, muddled through reams of phone records, and sat in on meeting after meeting. And at the end of January, while he was driving to a country-and-western bar called the Robin Hood Inn in Sherwood, Michigan, Woods and prosecutor Jon Sahli went over the entire case. They discussed the obvious weak points and strengths.

"That's all we got. It ain't going to get any better. This is it," Woods said.

"Are you sure?" Sahli asked.

"I am. But you're the one who has to prosecute it."

After a thoughtful pause, Sahli gave marching orders. "Have Statfeld in my office in the morning. I'll issue the warrant."

And on January 30, the Calhoun County Sheriff's Department contacted detectives in Denver and directed them to arrest Brad King for the murder of his wife, nearly a year after she was shot to death in front of her children in her driveway.

CHAPTER 14

The end of January was the end of the line for Bradford J. King. He was months behind in his rent and was being evicted from his residence at the Tamarac Apartments, where Susan Van Vleet had paid for three months' rent starting in July. The landlord seized some of his belongings to pay the back rent. And at 7:25 A.M. on Friday, January 31, five Denver police officers came to arrest him for the murder of his wife. Brad was in the driveway, loading Marler and Kateri into the same Jeep Wagoneer they were sitting in when Diane dropped in her driveway. Now the police, with guns drawn, made Brad lie facedown on the ground while they frisked him and read him his rights. He was taken to jail; the kids, crying hysterically, were headed to the Family Crisis Center of the Denver Department of Social Services until custody could be determined.

"When he was arrested, it was another stage of 'how can this be happening to me,' " said John Van Vleet, who visited him in jail. "He was in stages of disbelief. Incredulity. Our assumption was that it would never make it to trial. He knew he was innocent, that he had done what he needed to do to clear himself. He was also angry his wife's murderer was still out there. He was angry they were focusing on him and not finding the true murderer. The murderers would not be found if they focused on him."

Back in Michigan, Sheriff Jon Olson and Prosecutor Jon Sahli issued a one-paragraph statement saying there had been an arrest in Colorado. The man arrested wasn't even identified. It was a remarkable understatement to perhaps the most celebrated murder case in Calhoun County history.

"I was ready. I have been spending the last couple of weeks reviewing it and decided to authorize the warrant," was all Sahli told reporters.

The charge against Brad was open murder and use of a firearm in the commission of a felony. In the arresting affidavit, police said they had evidence implicating him within two days of the shooting. A .22 caliber Remington Model 511 Scoremaster rifle was found in a stream near the home, and lab tests matched it with the slugs that killed Diane. Brad's mother, Marjorie, and his brother, Scott, had told police Brad's father had given him a similar rifle years before. Brad said he had sold his .22 rifle, but police found boxes of ammunition and a cleaning kit in his home the night of the murder. And footprints near the stream matched the boots Brad was wearing.

Bernie Messer, an attorney retained by Brad in Denver, was livid about how the arrest was made. He said Brad had told police he would come in any time they needed to see him.

"Why was that ignored? Why suddenly race in and arrest him with guns drawn when his kids are with him?

There was no reason to do that. This seems like intimidation," Messer said.

Attorney James Brady said from Michigan that Brad was being persecuted. "He is absolutely innocent. There is no evidence against him. He's just a scapegoat. They made the arrest because of all the pressure from the tabloid media. What more evidence do they have now than they did two days after? It's not his gun. All they're doing is guessing, trying the case in the media. He doesn't know what happened other than that someone tragically took the life of his wife, who he loved very much. They have keyed in on him apparently because they failed in other aspects of the investigation. Whoever did this is either still in the community or long gone. It has been a tremendous burden on him and his family and his kids," Brady said.

If Brad fought extradition, the legal process could take ninety days. A governor's warrant would have to be signed by Michigan Governor John Engler and sent to Colorado. Then a hearing was required to determine if he should go back. But Brad agreed to return to Michigan to face the charges against him if he could attend the custody proceedings involving his children.

Freida and Royal Newton grabbed a plane the morning Brad was arrested to try to reach the kids. For Diane's family, the arrest alleviated frustration that had been pent up for twelve months. She had even taken scissors and razor blades to cut Brad out of Diane's family pictures.

"Have you ever heard the expression happy as a pig in shit? We suspected it all along. The detectives and the prosecuting attorney never investigated anyone else," Royal said.

Darlene, Diane's older sister, said Brad's moving back

to Colorado with the kids didn't ease any of the suspicions the family felt. Her anger hadn't subsided either.

"I have always believed he murdered my sister. I just don't have anything good to say about that man. We just don't know why he did it. I just wish he would admit why. This has been a long year. I never believed he would get away with this, and now that he is arrested I am hoping he thought he was going to get away with it, and being arrested was a nice shock for him. I hope he gets what he deserves. I hope he suffers really bad," Darlene said.

She also voiced concern for Marler and Kateri.

"We might not like him, but we love the kids. I'm very much worried about the boy. He's the one who has gone through hell," Darlene said.

If the custody dispute in March was a squabble, the one in Denver was a war. Freida and Royal Newton had petitioned Denver District Court to seek custody of the children. Native-American law requires that they be placed with Native-American relatives or other tribe members, they argued. But Brad was dead set against that. After waiving extradition on the morning of February 4, he appeared in juvenile court to argue that the kids be placed with his friends, John and Susan Van Vleet, instead of the Newtons. Brad's attorneys argued, "[The Newtons] believe he's responsible for the death of their daughter and will poison any relationship the child could have with their father. His children have been through enough. He wants them to remain in Colorado rather than being subjected to the trauma of a new home." Brad's mother and stepfather, Marjorie and Cliff Lundeen, flew up from Texas. They were unable to take custody, but they supported Brad's wish of having the kids stay with the Van Vleets.

"The Department of Social Services came to check

out our home. I would have bet money we were going to get the kids. We were scrambling to prepare the house for the kids," John Van Vleet said.

But at a hearing on February 7, the juvenile court judge, Melvin Okamoto, split custody of the children between the Newtons and the Lundeens. He disregarded allegations raised by Brad's lawyers that Diane's family was tainted by alcoholism, run-ins with the law, and abuse. The Newtons' attorney, Frank Moya, said the charges were scurrilous and challenged Messer to support them. Okamoto ruled that he thought the grandparents were fine people who had the purest of motives and strongest of love and commitment for the children. And to everyone involved, Okamoto said, "I give you one final order. That is to give these children plenty of hugs and kisses and let them know they are loved by both sides of the family and always will have that." The Lundeens relinquished their right to joint custody, and on February 14, the Newtons got temporary custody. Freida said it was the best Valentine's Day present she ever had.

Meanwhile, Brad was back in Michigan to face his accusers. He had taken United Express Flight 2718 from Denver through Chicago to Kalamazoo–Battle Creek International Airport. Wearing a yellow Western Michigan University sweat shirt and restrained in handcuffs, he was led by detectives James Statfeld and Jack Schoder into an unmarked car on the tarmac. He was arraigned on February 11 before Calhoun County District Court Judge Franklin Line and held without bond. In the brief court appearance, Brad wore a wrinkled orange prison outfit—a "pumpkin suit" in the vernacular of the cops—and was chained. He spoke briefly, giving his address in Denver and answering "yes" when asked if he understood the charges against him. Because of his past service as a policeman, he was placed in protected segregation in the county lockup. Attorney James Brady again proclaimed Brad's innocence: "The investigators let the tracks get cold, letting the real killers get away. They needed a scapegoat and here he is."

By now, a new controversy was percolating in the community. The bullet that destroyed Diane King's heart had now struck a societal nerve. The issue was the dominant wife, who was aggressive and assertive in her career. Some of the comments made after the arrest implied that Brad, if he did do it, was provoked by his bitchy wife. And some of the strongest statements came from Mike Moran, Diane's old boss and the news editor at KJCT-TV in Grand Junction, Colorado.

"He was very dominated by Diane. Diane ran the family. She wore the pants in the family. He did whatever she said. If she wanted to go to a party, they went to a party. If she wanted to move to Michigan, they moved to Michigan. Her career and her life are what mattered. Putting that in the puzzle, with a domineering wife like that—Diane could be very abrasive and pushy—I can see how the guy could snap. Anything you could describe as a domineering person Diane was all the way," Moran told one interviewer.

"Bradford was abnormally in the back seat. Diane would do all the talking. It was almost one of those situations where the husband goes to say something and the wife answers for him," he told another. "Diane was a person who could push you to the edge. She was not afraid to tear into me. She'd do that often. She was not afraid to tell you exactly what she thought. I could see how that could wear on a husband. It looks like the classic case of letting himself blow up in the wrong manner.

That's the scenario I see. If he did do it, he had all this anger he was suppressing and it blew up."

His strongest comments were taped and aired on *A Current Affair.*

"Brad was very dependent on her. She kiddingly said a few times I'm the best thing that ever happened to Brad," Moran said. "It makes sense in a way for something like this to happen to a Diane King because I don't think there was a person she was in contact with that she didn't aggravate. I talked to one of her best friends off and on this week. As she put it frankly, 'Can you imagine living with Diane King knowing what a b-i-t-c-h she can be?' She said, 'I don't know if I as a good friend wouldn't think about shooting her once in a while.' Who knows what goes through your mind when you face a person like this day after day after day? I could see the nicest, sweetest guy in the world just going crazy."

That did it for Jan Hammer, KJCT's general manager. He had established a policy of staff members talking to the media about Diane. When Moran vented his views, Hammer fired him. Hammer dismissed him for "statements previously and currently made toward Diane King and other past statements in violation of company policy." Moran said he wanted, as one reporter to another, to flesh out Diane as a human being. Hammer disagreed strongly with his characterizations, saying, "She was anything but the ultimate bitch."

But Moran was hardly contrite after his dismissal. "I'd say it all again. Someone needed to tell a little bit more of the truth," Moran told reporters. "Nobody else will say this stuff about her."

One other person went public about his view of Diane's personality. That was Jerry Martin, a former cameraman at WUHQ-TV in Battle Creek who worked with

Diane. In an interview with the *Kalamazoo Gazette,* Martin said that in July of 1989, he and his wife lost a son at birth at Bronson Methodist Hospital. Coincidentally, he went with Diane to the same hospital and in the same room that his son died in to do a story on the natural birth of twins.

"I started getting really sick, so I put down the equipment and left the room. She chased me down the hall and said, 'What the hell are you doing? You're going to have to shoot this.' That's the kind of heartless person she was," Martin said. And of Brad, he commented, "I think he had justified motivation. If she treated him in their private life the way she treated everybody in her professional life . . . You can only take that for so long."

Others at WUHQ disputed Martin's story. And there was plenty of reaction to the comments.

Renee Donovan, a reporter for a radio station, had a different view of Diane King. She recalled a time on January 28, 1990, when Governor Jim Blanchard was making a speech at the Woodward Elementary School in Kalamazoo. Reporters gathered around Blanchard for an impromptu news conference, and Donovan, who was pregnant at the time, struggled to get her microphone close to him. She was jostled in the crush of bodies, which reporters learn is part of the competitive job.

"I was struggling to push my way in. You have to fend for yourself. But Diane took my mike and held it for me, even though it had my station's flag on it. Nobody wants anybody else's flag in their camera shot, but she was sensitive to other people's feelings. She wasn't the ultimate bitch. Yes, she was aggressive. When the pressure was on, she would do it. I've heard men debating this behavior. I cannot fathom this way of thinking. I just don't think that's a cause for murder."

Barb Lilly also thought the blame was misplaced. Lilly helped organize a benefit concert on behalf of the Solis-Parmer Chapter of the Vietnam Veterans of America, which wanted to honor Vietnam vets with a memorial. The concert featured Mitch Ryder and the Detroit Wheels at the Kellogg Arena on April 28, 1989, and Diane covered it as a news story for WUHQ. During one part of the show, veterans from all of America's wars and all those who served in the military were asked to come forward. When the women veterans assembled, Diane went with them because she had been an Army lieutenant. A band played a Willie Nelson song, "Angel Flying Too Close to the Ground."

"Diane came on stage and stood proud with us. We had a special bond," said Barb Lilly.

Diane also made a videotape of the event and presented it to the veterans. From time to time, Lilly would see Diane coming through Hudson's department store, where she worked at the Lakeview Square Mall. "She'd always come up to me and give me a big hug. It was not a show hug, it was a warm hug. It wasn't like she felt she was the queen of television in Battle Creek. She was approachable." Lilly was outraged at some of the talk about Diane.

"She was a very strong woman, yet I saw her as having a soft and feminine side. And what if she was the world's biggest bitch. Where I come from that's not an excuse for murder. They have an institution called divorce. This whole thing is bizarre. I know people are presumed innocent, but it's almost like Brad toyed with people, that he was a police officer and a criminology teacher and he can get away with this. If it's true he killed her, it's such a cold, calculating act. How insidious. And the terror of her little son. That's what gives me the shivers."

Women readers also sent letters to the editor of the *Battle Creek Enquirer* about the tone of stories regarding Diane King. Susan Serafin-Jess of Vermontville wrote

> "Pity the poor man whose shrewish wife was more successful than he. Can you blame him for losing it?" is just another variation of the theme "she asked for it" said of so many female crime victims. Tell the whole story, but use balance and objectivity instead of stooping to the simplistic shorthand of stereotypes that take resentment against successful women.

Another letter, signed by Linda M. Keller and Susan D. Barber of Battle Creek read

> If proven guilty, no amount of justice will bring back Bradford King's wife, Diane. If proven innocent there is no amount of compensation for the loss of his wife or the year of anxiety he has been through . . . When people read such statements as Diane was "up front, abrasive and pushy. Anything you could describe a domineering person Diane was all the way," or statements such as Diane "wore the pants in the family," it conjures up views of a woman's tragic death as being deserved and justified. Why is it deemed appropriate for women to uproot their lives to follow their husband's career, yet a man who does the same is somehow viewed "as a man living in the shadow of an ambitious, career-minded wife"? Are we still living in such a male-dominated society that only men are viewed as

legitimate speculators of a woman's life? We are once again being force-fed the old standby of the double standard.

Before there could be a trial, a preliminary hearing was necessary to determine if a crime was committed and if enough evidence existed to put Brad in front of a jury. It was held without a jury in front of a district court judge. Sworn testimony was taken to determine if there was "probable cause," a lower and less difficult standard than "reasonable doubt" applicable in a jury trial. Brad's hearing included four days of testimony stretched over two weeks. He objected to the proceeding being held in the district court from which he was fired as a probation officer, but the hearing went ahead in front of Judge Marvin Ratner in a Marshall courtroom.

Brad entered the courtroom wearing chains on his ankles and handcuffs locked to a chain padlocked around the waist of his wrinkled orange outfit, his pumpkin suit, lettered in black stencil that said Calhoun County Jail. Gone were the est days of high fashion. He shambled into the room in his prison-issue flip-flop shoes over his white socks. The rim of hair had grown back around the sides and the back of his once shaved head. A gaggle of media from three television stations, three newspapers, and several radio stations sat in the jury box as Brad sat down noisily at the defense table, his chains rumbling against the wood. His attorney, James Brady, who had been retained with hefty contributions from Brad's mother and friends such as the Van Vleets, objected to Brad's chains because of the media exposure. If Brad was pictured in manacles, people might conclude he was guilty instead of presuming him innocent. "I'm very concerned how that's going to be perceived by potential jurors," Brady said. He won the point, and the chains came off. An armed deputy sat just behind Brad through the proceeding. Brad lowered his eyes to avoid eye contact with Freida Newton, her husband, and her two sons, Diane's brothers, Gordon and Allen.

Judge Ratner heard twenty-four witnesses talk about everything from the crime scene to the tracking dog, from the ballistics tests to Dr. Stephen Cohle's autopsy report on two gunshots. Brad's demeanor, his marital problems, and his extramarital affair with Ann Hill were discussed, as well as Diane's security routine when she thought she was being stalked. And foundations were laid linking Brad to the Remington rifle he claimed he sold years before in Colorado.

Two critical witnesses were Christopher Sly and his stepfather, Tom Darling, the hardware-store owner and the center of the rumors that swirled since the previous summer. Sly was thirteen years old in the summer of 1990 when he cut the Kings' grass for pocket money. On one of the eight or nine times he did his lawn chores, he was on the back porch waiting for Brad to pay him when he spotted a rifle atop a waist-high freezer. It was a bolt-action gun with a dark wooden stock. Although he never picked up the gun, Sly said he was within five feet of it and got a good look at it. When prosecutor Jon Sahli held up the rifle the deputies had retrieved from Talmadge Creek, Sly said it was the gun. Before the hearing, he had identified it from four pictures of Brad's rifle and shotgun the police showed him. "This is the one that looks like what was on their porch," he told Detective James Statfeld.

But he was more sure having seen the real weapon, and Brady asked him how it he knew it was the gun.

"Because I recognize especially the pull-back chamber and the wood handle. I had seen it," Sly said.

Why did he tell his dad about the gun during the investigation?

"As soon as I had known about the murder, I had to let him know. He was asking me if there was ever any things around their house such as a gun or if I had ever noticed anything strange. And I said, well, that one time there I was mowing their yard and I did see that rifle on the freezer," Sly testified.

Tom Darling knew the Kings from the times they came to his store to purchase rakes, garden tools, shovels, and nuts and bolts. He and Brad once went hunting for rabbits with their shotguns. But Darling also recalled seeing a .22 rifle in the house. When the police found the gun and asked anyone with information about it to come forward, Darling contacted the sheriff's department and told them, "Something tells me I've seen that gun before." Although he couldn't be certain it was the same gun, he said it looked similar.

Darling also recounted a gun story dating to the fall of 1990. Brad and Diane had come to the hardware store looking for advice on how to get rid of a pesky groundhog that was rooting around their garbage. Darling told Brad there were two ways to dispose of the critter: shoot it or trap it. Darling even offered Brad the use of his .22 rifle.

"No, if it comes to that, I will use my own," Brad said.

One more gun connection came from Barbara Elgutaa, the Native-American woman who cared for Marler and Kateri in the hours and days after Diane's murder. While visiting Diane in November of 1990, Elgutaa said Brad came in from hunting carrying a gun with a long barrel. She was it wasn't a shotgun with two barrels, but a rifle. Brad's hand blocked her view of the bolt-action, but Elgutaa said it resembled the rifle police pulled from the creek.

There was also testimony about ammunition. All of the eight casings found in the barn and the creek were CCI brand, but none of them matched the bullets found in the Kings' attic. However, Mark Karaba testified that he noticed some shells were missing from a box of CCI .22 caliber shells he had purchased. Karaba kept the box in a shelf on the back entrance to his home on Division Drive, so it would have been in plain view of someone passing by. Coincidentally, his wife, Joanne Karaba, testified that Brad and Diane had stopped by in January while she was baby-sitting their kids. She said Brad spent some time alone near the cabinet where the bullets were, and the inference was Brad had the opportunity to take some shells that could never be traced to him.

Finally, prosecutor Jon Sahli summarized his case.

"Judge, this is not some unknown person that shot Diane King. There was no one around the house except the defendant. An unknown person would not have known when Diane King was coming home. The defendant was having a sexual relationship with Ann Hill. He was not happy with his wife. He said he was separated, that they were getting a divorce, that he had temporary custody of his son."

He noted that on the day of the murder, February 9, Ann Hill had returned Brad's call from the previous day and was told he was just leaving and wouldn't be back until late that night or early Sunday.

"Judge, I submit to you that is evidence that the defendant did not want Ann Hill to come to his address because he was, in fact, planning on shooting and murdering his wife on that date," Sahli said. "I would also ask you to consider the location and angle of the shot to the lower abdominal area of Mrs. King. I believe the location of that shot is very significant. I believe that goes psychologically at least a long way towards proving that the defendant was the perpetrator of this crime."

Defense attorney James Brady argued the entire case was full of holes.

"After listening for these many days to the prosecutor's case, it is substantially and significantly the same as it was in March of 1991. It didn't hold water then, and it doesn't hold water now. Circumstantial evidence should lead the finder of fact to a point at which he or she can infer a fact, not force the finder to make an inference upon an inference upon an inference. And that's basically what the prosecutor's whole case is here. There simply isn't enough evidence to bind the defendant over. This is the most serious crime we have in this state. Mr. Sahli is requesting this court simply to bind this case over on mere and pure speculation."

Judge Ratner mulled over the testimony and the arguments before making his ruling. Much of what he was looking at was circumstantial. Oliver Wendell Holmes once described circumstantial evidence as being like finding a fish in the milk jar; it doesn't prove anything but it's a sure sign something is amiss.

"It's obvious it's an unusual case," the judge said. "It's clear a murder was committed. The more difficult question confronting the court is who committed the crime or the probability as to who committed this crime of murder. No eyewitnesses testified concerning who fired the fatal bullet. Instead the court has been presented with a series of circumstances. The only person who was certainly present at the time and in the vicinity of the fatal shot was the defendant. Barbara Elgutaa, Christopher

Sly, and Thomas Darling all testified they saw a .22 caliber rifle similar to the apparent murder weapon. Another significant circumstance is Trooper Lisle's testimony that he and his tracking dog followed a human scent from the barn loft, the apparent location of the firing of the weapon, around the King property and back to the driveway. This path coincidentally crossed the point where the apparent murder weapon was found. There is circumstance upon circumstance which go to confirm each other. And since this is a matter of probable cause, the court has to consider the matter of probabilities. And when circumstance upon circumstance confirm each other, then each succeeding circumstance confirming the previous circumstance increases the probability of what the People are alleging.

"Taken all together, these circumstances are compelling and convincing and pass the threshold of probable cause. Additionally, the court notes that the circumstances surrounding the homicide establish premeditation. The evidence clearly indicates that the defendant lay in wait for the victim and fired more than one shot to accomplish his purpose."

Ratner ordered Brad to stand trial in circuit court and put him back in jail without bond.

If convicted of first degree, premeditated murder, Brad was looking at a mandatory life sentence without possibility of parole except at the intervention of the governor. Michigan does not have the death penalty; in fact, it was the first English-speaking jurisdiction in the world to abolish the death penalty. The ban stemmed from a case in which an Irishman named Patrick Fitzpatrick was wrongly accused and hanged for the rape and murder of a young girl. The real killer confessed to the crime on his deathbed a few years later. The state reacted with shock and indignation, and in 1846 voted to abolish hanging and replace it with life imprisonment for all crimes except treason. The law took effect March 1, 1847.

CHAPTER 15

Brad's lawyers battled to move his trial to another location, given that just about everybody in the area had heard about the case. No change was granted, however.

In a survey commissioned by attorney James Brady, Kennedy Research of Grand Rapids conducted a telephone poll of two hundred potential jurors. It concluded that ninety-four percent of the potential jurors had heard about Diane King's murder, thirty-six percent thought Brad was guilty of a crime, and twenty-seven percent felt he was guilty of murder. One comment mentioned in the survey was, "I think he did it. He hated his wife. She wore the pants in the family and he killed her."

Brady's motion to move the trial said "a plethora of prejudicial and inflammatory news reports require a change of venue from Calhoun County. The media barrage surrounding the death of Mrs. King has served to thoroughly saturate the Calhoun County area with information, rumors, and allegations regarding her death." Brady argued that the case had been tainted by testimony in the preliminary hearing and town gossip about Brad's extramarital affairs. He said a change should be granted when "actual prejudice, strong community feeling, or a pattern of deep and bitter prejudice exists. All those exist in Mr. King's case."

But Circuit Court Judge Conrad Sindt ruled that he would at least attempt to seat a jury before he granted any change of venue. It was at a motion hearing on August 11, 1992, that Brad King uttered his first public words about his wife's murder and the charges against him.

"I have spent over six months in jail and I'm an innocent man and I'm very angry over all this. I want this trial to go on so I can tell the county I did not kill my wife. I feel I'm unjustly charged and that it's a political issue. The fact that I've been in jail for six months is ridiculous."

The trial had originally been scheduled for September 1 but was pushed back to November. A factor in the delay was allowing more time for Brad and his family to raise money for his defense, although he was in the process of hiring a new attorney who he felt more comfortable with.

And so it was that the great drama of American justice was to be played out in a courthouse named the Hall of Justice in Battle Creek, an industrious heartland city of 53,578 residents located in a river valley and along the Amtrak railroad line. The city has become a federal center, and people who draw government paychecks from various agencies outnumber any single employer. But it still justifiably carries the title of Cereal Capital of the World. Kellogg Company is the largest private employer, with 3,500 workers. The company's net sales of $5.79

billion ensured its rank as the world's leading maker of ready-to-eat cereal; the company also produces frozen pies, waffles, toaster pastries, cereal bars, and convenience foods. General Foods Corporation has 1,100 workers and the Ralston Purina Company has 420.

In many ways, the story of Battle Creek is a chronicle of America's growth as an independent power. The territory was a combination of hardwood stands, rivers, and fertile flatlands that appealed to pioneers once the Potawatomi Indians were removed. The first settlers to arrive in 1831 came from New York, which was already considered overcrowded. They headed west via the Erie Canal to Buffalo, then across the Great Lakes to Michigan. At a point where the Kalamazoo River meets Battle Creek, a frontier outpost became an agricultural trading center and later an industrial power. It has always welcomed social and religious free-thinkers. One of its early residents was Sojourner Truth, the black slave who was friend to presidents and paupers, achieving national distinction for her fight against slavery and for women's rights and temperance.

A group of Seventh Day Adventists relocated their headquarters from New York to Battle Creek in 1855. Earlier Adventists had believed the world would end in the 1840s. When the prediction failed to come true, they modified their stance to say events leading to the second coming of Christ began in the 1840s and would continue until those worthy of joining in the resurrection were identified (leaving the date open). Adventists are fanatics about diet, shunning red meat and stimulants such as caffeine. They turned Battle Creek into the "Food City" and the "Health City." Ultimately, this smallish city changed the world's breakfast habits, thanks to Adventist John Preston Kellogg, whose sixteen children included

John Harvey and Will Keith Kellogg. John Harvey Kellogg became the leader and promoter of the world-famous Battle Creek Sanitarium, which was founded in 1866 as the Western Health Reform Institute. The "San" offered refreshment for mind, body, and soul. In its kitchens, palatable whole-grain treats were developed to brighten meals. Presidents, kings, and celebrities heard the Adventists preach "You are what you eat." John Harvey invented a substitute for coffee made from roasted grains. He also invented something called Granola, which, in its original form, was twice-baked graham bread crumbs. Then, in 1894, while he was looking for an alternative to hard breads, he learned how to make the world's first baked wheat flakes. He and his brother, Will Keith, had boiled some wheat and rolled it into a thin dough. The men were called away, and the dough was stale when they returned, but they forced it through baking rollers and discovered each wheat berry became a flake. John Harvey called the stuff Granose, and a new industry was born.

The Kellogg brothers began production in a barn behind the sanitarium. Breakfast food was now made in a factory, not in the home, and was served cold, not hot. In time, Battle Creek became known for cereal the way Pittsburgh was known for steel, Milwaukee for beer, and Akron for tires.

One guest who came to the San was Charles William (C.W.) Post, an advertising wizard from Texas who suffered from dyspepsia. Post improved on the Kellogg diet and urged that the products be sold to the general public. When Kellogg demurred and insisted on selling them only via mail orders, Post started mass marketing the products. Post invested $46.85 in some basic items in 1894: a second-hand gasoline stove for roasting bran, a peanut roaster for roasting wheat, and an old-fashioned coffee grinder. With an initial supply of wheat, bran, and molasses, he sold a coffee substitute called Postum. And with the profits made from jars of Postum sold from a pushcart, Post opened the Postum Cereal Company in 1895 inside a tiny white barn. His version of Granola was called Grape-Nuts. He borrowed another idea from the Kelloggs and made cornflakes, which in 1902 he called Elijah's Manna. It later became Post Toasties. Post's only child, Marjorie Merriweather Post, inherited her father's wealth and turned the company into a food empire. With the assistance of the second of her four husbands, E. F. Hutton, she parlayed the Postum Cereal Company into the nation's largest food manufacturer, General Foods.

The Kelloggs, the people responsible for the cereal boom, almost missed out because John Harvey Kellogg wasn't interested in profit. But Will Keith (W. K.) Kellogg, a broom salesman at age fourteen and a bookkeeper under his brother, created an empire. In 1898 W. K. Kellogg made flakes of corn, then refined the product to commercial quality by using grits (the sweet heart of the corn). Originally, he called them Sanitas Toasted Corn Flakes. People wanted them for nutrition, but they kept eating them for flavor, convenience, and value. W. K. started the Battle Creek Toasted Corn Flake Company in 1906, with an initial output of thirty-three cases a day. Three years later, he changed the named to Kellogg's and printed this note on each box: "None genuine without this signature—W. K. Kellogg." It was needed, because there were 108 brands of cornflakes being packed in Battle Creek. Nutritious, tasty breakfast food was a hit with the American public.

The Kellogg Foundation was established in 1930. In addition, Battle Creek boasts such fixtures as the Kellogg

Airport, the Kellogg Arena, Kellogg Community College, and the like.

It was in this setting that the grisly business of a murder trial would be settled in the fall of 1992. Brad had jettisoned his first lawyer, James Brady. Brad's mother and his friends had put up money for his defense, but there were grumblings that Brady's fees were too high. Brady had retained a women co-counsel, Virginia Cairns of Marshall, ostensibly because she knew her way around the Calhoun County court system and it wouldn't hurt Brad's image to have a female lawyer with him while he defended himself against charges he murdered his wife. Virginia developed a bond with Brad, and she was kept on in the legal shuffling. She had recommended other lawyers to Brad, including John Sims of Albion. The major portion of Sims's practice was civil rather than criminal law. With a 1977 law degree from Brad's alma mater, Western Michigan University, Sims had joined the law firm of Wilcox and Robison and became a named partner. His fees were more in line with what Brad's mother could afford. He exuded a cocky confidence. Brad liked him because Sims was convinced he could win an acquittal in a circumstantial case that he believed was full of holes. Sims was a tough legal foe; he attacked weaknesses with a relish and had the manner of a street fighter in the courtroom. Plus he knew the law; he prepared a slew of pretrial motions aimed at keeping damaging evidence and testimony out of the courtroom.

Sims didn't overlook things that he could use to his client's advantage, either. He went to where Brad's three-year-old son, Marler, was living with Freida Newton in Sterling Heights and subpoenaed the boy for an October 16 pretrial hearing. There was speculation that Marler, just two years old when his mother was murdered, might be called to the witness stand in Brad's defense. Sims was aware that Marler had told his playmates in Colorado about two men having killed his mother. The prosecution, meanwhile, was ready for this tactic. Marler had been interviewed by a child psychologist from the University of Michigan, and it was his expert opinion that Marler's story was a fabrication, something that he would have been told by someone else, not something that he would have witnessed and remembered by himself. With the value of his testimony in question, Marler was spared the trauma of being placed on the stand under oath. Sims agreed to drop the subpoena if the prosecution—and Freida—agreed to have Marler meet with Brad; they hadn't seen each other since Brad's arrest in Denver, and Marler and his sister had been living with Freida ever since under a temporary court order.

There were specific ground rules. There could be no physical contact because no social workers were present, and lawyers from the prosecution had to monitor the meeting in the law library of the Hall of Justice. It didn't go smoothly. Brad reached for his son, but the lawyers intervened and the twenty-minute meeting was over. Brad shouted at them: "You fucking assholes."

A couple of things had happened on the family front. Kateri was baptized that summer in St. Francis Xavier Church on the Kahnawake Reserve in Canada. Edith and John Cupples, Diane's aunt and uncle, were godparents. And Diane's sister, Denise, gave birth to her fourth child in October. She was named Diane Marie, after her murdered aunt.

Meanwhile, bail was set at $750,000 under some rigid conditions. Brad's family and friends, including Randy

Wright and John and Susan Van Vleet, were able to come up with the necessary money—but the plan never materialized. Brad was required to stay within two miles of his pastor, Rev. David Robertson of the First Presbyterian Church, and was banned from leaving Calhoun County. Attorneys had found a place for him at the Limewood Apartments in Battle Creek, and two church members had agreed to pay two months' rent for him. But residents who learned of the plan in the newspaper balked at having an accused killer living there. Management circulated a leaflet to all residents saying the story was incorrect and that King was rejected as a tenant because he didn't meet requirements for having a steady income. "The publicity killed his release," Sims said. So Brad was a resident of the county jail when he went on trial.

The judge who would preside over the trial was Conrad Sindt, who had risen through the ranks of law enforcement to sit behind the bench. He was once a beat cop, a corporal, and a detective with the Albion police from 1969 to 1973, when he quit to become a lawyer and work a different beat in the justice system. A graduate of Albion College with a law degree from the Thomas Cooley Law School, Sindt was elected prosecutor for Calhoun County in 1980. He had a windowless office in the basement of a building near the Hall of Justice. He learned firsthand the demanding elements of the job when the first murder case he tried was reversed on appeal; he got a conviction of a lesser charge in the second trial. He was reelected in 1984 and 1988, and his top assistant was a methodical lawyer named Jon Sahli.

In 1990 Sindt was named to the Thirty-seventh Judicial Circuit Court following the death of Judge Paul Nicolish. When he ran for election the following year,

Sindt was endorsed by sheriff's deputies, the Marshall and Albion police, the Michigan State Police, four township police departments, the Calhoun County Assistant Prosecuting Attorneys Association and the *Battle Creek Enquirer.* The newspapers said of Sindt, "We feel that Conrad Sindt has the energy, brains, and temperament to give full attention to all sides of any issue. He has kept the public trust for a decade and deserves to reach this rung on the legal ladder."

Sindt beat Judge Ronald Lebeuf by 934 votes of 27,996 cast, but it was clear he had little appetite for politics. "It's really difficult for me to blow my own horn. I don't talk about myself much. I don't enjoy the tasks that are necessary to run for public office," he told an interviewer. Woodworking is his private passion, so when he is not hammering criminals, he is hammering nails.

Sindt had a working relationship with Jon Sahli, but he bent over backward to be fair and impartial, at times he seemed to go overboard to defuse notions that he favored the prosecution. Sahli was appointed the county prosecutor on January 9, 1991, a month prior to Diane's murder, when Sindt vacated his post to become a judge. A 1978 graduate of the Thomas Cooley Law School in Lansing, Sahli once worked for the Legal Aid Society. He was named an assistant prosecutor for Calhoun County in 1979, and ascended to the chief assistant's job in 1985.

Just before his trial began, Brad granted a telephone interview to reporter Trace Christenson of the *Battle Creek Enquirer* from his jail cell, where he had been penned up with five other inmates.

"I am right, and right always wins. I am not guilty and I am waiting for this to pass. But getting a fair trial, I have my doubts about that because of the publicity that has been given this case for the past year and a half. I have every confidence in my lawyers, but given what has been going on in this county in regards to this trial, that makes me nervous. The judge who is handling this case . . . is very biased toward the prosecution. . . . It's time to get this over with so I can put it behind me and get on with my life, with my family. I am innocent, and I should be treated as though I am innocent until a jury says I am not."

A pool of potential jurors reported to the Hall of Justice at nine A.M. on Tuesday, November 3. It was election day, and Sheriff Jon Olson was voted out of his job. The county sheriff for the past fourteen years, he had been hired as a deputy in 1964 and worked his way up through the ranks. But he lost to James Roberts this time. No one could say for sure, but there was speculation that the sheriff department's handling of the Diane King investigation had contributed to Olson's political defeat.

Among the potential jurors was Marybeth Culverhouse, forty-eight, a wife and mother who held two jobs as a cashier. She received a questionnaire for jury duty way back in the summer. With Christmas coming, November is a busy time for retail so her bosses weren't thrilled about Marybeth performing her social duty. And it would be a financial hardship to miss all that work, but she wanted to do her duty. Because she had only been to the Hall of Justice one time to pay a speeding ticket, she went to check out the place so she'd know where to go. On Election Day, she voted at seven-thirty A.M. and reported promptly at nine.

"So many people today are so wrapped up in their own lives that they don't care about the needs of others. That is what we are here on earth for—to help each other. It's surprising that so many people wanted to get out of it," Marybeth wrote in a personal journal she began to keep when she figured she might get picked for the King case.

There were questions about how long the trial would last and how the jury would be picked. Instructions were given not to discuss the case or read or listen to news accounts, but not much else happened that first day. Marybeth was told to report at one-thirty P.M. Wednesday. Acquaintances volunteered ways on how to get out of the commitment, and she kept asking herself, "Why does everybody want off this case?"

Marybeth had one thing in common with everyone in the jury pool. Each of them had heard about the King case. But the ones picked for the trial, like Marybeth, said they could be impartial because they had an open mind about guilt or innocence.

"I had not made up my mind about this case. I felt I was necessary to Mr. King. That I was an honest person and if I were in his shoes I would want me to be on the jury," she wrote. "It was still amazing to me how many people didn't want to be on this case."

After eighty-one people were rejected by one side or the other over four days, a jury was selected by three-thirty P.M. Friday. The fourteen-member panel of twelve jurors and two alternates included seven men and seven women. Four were black, six were young people with families and eight were older. John Sims had used all twelve of his opportunities to dismiss jurors without cause. "I burned all of them, and if I had more, I would have burned them, too. I would have liked a jury of fourteen people who didn't know about the case." In a sense, the jury had picked itself. Any of them could have been dismissed by just saying they were biased one way or the other, or that it would be a health problem or a work conflict to serve on a trial estimated to last four to six weeks.

"The jury room was now ours. Our home away from home. We could even come and go by a separate door. I surely prayed and talked to God for a while that night. God help me not to get on that stage unless that's where you want me," Marybeth wrote.

The King case was all over the front page. So every time Marybeth rang up the sale of a newspaper at work, she turned it over. To keep from overhearing conversations, she asked for but was denied permission to wear earphones like airline mechanics wear. At home, every time the King trial came on TV she hit the mute button on the remote control.

But before this five-week show could start, there was lots of pretrial maneuvering. A murder trial is not a door that opens to the whole story. Trials are designed to exclude as much as they include, and this one would leave out plenty. Each side gives its own heavily edited version of what it wants the jury to hear, and each tries to poke holes in the other's story. It is a carefully constructed performance for the benefit of a select group of critics—the jury.

Most statements that Diane King made to others about her security routine, the state of her marriage, and her wishes to quit her job would generally not be admitted. Sims argued successfully that introducing those comments would be like allowing Diane to testify from the grave. "The person is unavailable to testify as a witness. I can't cross-examine her," he said.

Also, there could be no direct testimony about Brad's affairs with Ann Hill and Julie Cook. However, comments he made to the women about the state of his marriage could be presented. The basic premise was this:

just because he was a bad character or a philanderer didn't mean he was a murderer.

No testimony would be heard about the financial pressures on the Kings' marriage. The judge ruled that items taken from the house with a February 19, 1991, search warrant were inadmissible because the warrant didn't establish a connection between the murder and the evidence being sought. Much of the Kings' debt records were seized at that time. "The law requires a nexus be established between the crime charged and the evidence to be seized," Sims argued.

Sahli fought on each point, claiming that each would help prove Brad murdered his wife.

"It's all interrelated," Sahli said.

"In a fairy tale," Sims replied.

The tone was set for what was to come.

CHAPTER 16

Spectators who came to hear the opening arguments of Brad King's trial had to endure a dreary, steady Great Lakes downpour to get to the Hall of Justice. Christmas decorations already adorned Battle Creek, and at the courthouse was a man-made hazard of cables, wires, and lights. A sign in the hallway read, "Caution: TV Cables," because *Court TV* was broadcasting the trial nationally. Sports bars in the area that had never shown anything but an athletic event to their patrons tuned in to the courtroom, and the bar crowds sat in rapt attention. A cameraman and his tripod settled into a row of seats, and microphones were spread about the courtroom. Brad was no longer in his pumpkin suit. He wore a navy blue, double-breasted suit over a white shirt and a maroon tie with white diagonal stripe. At 9:03 A.M. on Thursday, November 12, Judge Conrad Sindt told the court bailiff, "All right, let's bring in the jury." Fourteen residents of Calhoun County raised their right hands and solemnly swore to render a true verdict only on the evidence introduced. They were allowed to take notes during the trial, and all but one of them did. Jurors could also submit questions in writing, which the judge and the two attorneys would review before they were asked of witnesses.

Judge Sindt instructed them for twenty minutes, starting with the fact that the opening statements they were about to hear weren't evidence. They were meant to help jurors understand how each side viewed its case. "By law, the defense does not have to prove innocence," the judge said, pointing out that Brad King was presumed innocent as he sat at the defense table. "As jurors, you are the ones who will decide the facts of this case. What you decide is final. You must decide which witnesses you believe, and how much weight to give the evidence. Rely on your own common sense. Don't discuss the case with family or friends or yourselves until deliberations begin. Keep an open mind and do not decide anything until all the testimony has been presented."

Then prosecutor Jon Sahli rose to state the people's case. He set up a series of visual aids to help the jury with this complicated, circumstantial case. There was a slide projector and screen for viewing pictures of the King farm and Diane's body. There were charts of time lines pointing out when Diane received the phone calls and letter, plus the times Brad phoned or visited Ann Hill, Julie Cook, and other students. Sahli was prohibited from talking about sexual affairs, but through the art of lawyering, he was indirectly planting a seed. There was a map drawn by Trooper Gray Lisle of the track his dog Travis followed on the night of the murder, and an aerial photograph of the grounds. Before Sahli even began to speak, defense attorney John Sims objected to the time charts. Although he was overruled, it was a signal that the trial would be a real brawl between two scrappy adversaries.

Sahli's style was methodical and plodding. He told his whole case to the jury, which was a lot to digest because he spoke for two hours and twenty minutes. Sahli began with the phone calls and the letter that Diane received. "You're probably all familiar with these types of notes from watching television programs and movies. In television programs and movies, these crazed killers send these notes to the victim." But, said Sahli, "experts familiar with these types of notes say they come from family members."

Then he detailed how the stalker theory was just a smoke screen. The day Diane got the letter, Brad was with Ann Hill. The day Brad's daughter was born, Brad was with Ann Hill again. The time he reported a breaking and entering while Diane was away, Brad was with Julie Cook. The day Diane left for her final trip to Sterling Heights to visit her mother, Brad was with Julie Cook again.

Sims was on his feet again, asking for a mistrial. "He comes in here with a fairy tale story with psychological mumbo-jumbo. I want a mistrial so I can go home and take a nap and forget this mess," Sims said.

Sahli said he had characterized the women merely as friends of Brad's and had not overstepped the court's ruling on sexual relationships.

"Let's take a poll, your honor. I think everybody in here knows what's going on. And if you think we can't see through that thin veil . . . It is an improper argument and improper information and is circumventing the ruling of this court," Sims said. But it was to no avail.

Judge Sindt had removed the jury from the courtroom during this argument. He studied the motion for a time, then ruled that nothing in the opening statement was grounds for stopping the trial. The jury was called back, and the prosecution's opening statement resumed.

Sahli talked about how Diane had altered her routine so she would never get out of the car until Brad was home, and she got out of the car on February 9, 1991. Brad didn't expect the children to be in the car that night because Diane planned on leaving them overnight at her mother's. Sahli spoke of the casing found in the barn loft, and the angle the bullet followed the ninety-one-foot distance measured by laser beam. He noted the tracking dog and the finding of the gun in an area a stranger would have had trouble getting to. No strangers were seen on the property that day, and no one but Brad knew when Diane was coming home. He pointed out several witnesses would testify they saw a rifle in the home, even though Brad told police he had sold his .22 in Colorado. Other than a few references to marriage problems, Sahli mentioned very little about motive. It is not necessary to prove motive to convict someone, but jurors like to know why someone would do what Brad was accused of doing.

"We're going to spend several weeks talking about the murder of Diane King. Ladies and gentlemen, at the end of this trial, I'm confident the evidence is going to come across at least as strong as I've outlined it to you in my opening statement if not stronger. And if in fact that happens, I will be asking you as members of the jury to return a verdict of guilty of first-degree premeditated murder," Sahli said.

Now John Sims took center stage with an irreverent, sometimes caustic approach that starkly contrasted with Sahli's low-key manner. Wearing a sport coat and quoting Shakespeare, Sims didn't take the prosecution's case apart bit by bit—he dismissed the whole thing as police incompetence and a conspiracy to nail his client. In his twenty minute opening, he challenged the prosecutors to prove their case.

"I sat through this opening statement this morning and thought, 'Golly. We've got everything here, folks.' We've got lasers, we got microwaves, we got videotapes, we got audiotapes, we got film at 11, we've got tracking dogs, we've got experts on personal behavior, we've got ballistics experts, we've got time lines, we've got slides, we got graphs, we got statistics, we got everything. Everything except something to do with why you're all here. There's only one issue in this case, folks. Who did it? I can sit here and tell you my father came here to Michigan in the 1930s from Guy, Arkansas, where he had been born and they had a rough trip coming up and things were rough. But what does that have to do with who killed Diane King. It's got nothing to do with it. And there is no proof you will see of Bradford King's guilt.

"Tragically enough, Diane King was killed. She was found in her driveway dead. I'm not going to insult your intelligence. Mr. King is a widower. He lost his wife. I'm not arguing she's not dead. I'm not arguing she died of some strange disease, or keeled over from some epileptic seizure. Somebody shot her twice. I don't care which bullet killed her. It doesn't make any difference to Brad King. It doesn't make any difference to me. And it doesn't make any difference to you. Fact number two, a shell casing was found in the loft of the barn. Don't deny it. Nothing you can do about it. Those police officers went up there and they found that shell casing. Fact number three, they went back out there two days later—not that night, don't get it mixed up, two days later—and they found that gun. Right next to that gun, seven casings. Not going to say they didn't. Not going to say they didn't exist. Fact number four, one year later, on January 31, 1992, they arrest Bradford King. Not February 9, or February 11, or March the ninth or eleventh, not April or May or June or July or August or September or October or November or December. One year later. If that's all there is, why are we here? I'll tell you why. You knew I would," Sims said, smiling.

"What is this case? The power of the state arrayed against Bradford King. What you're going to see is that if they really want somebody bad enough, [they] can get them, whether [they] got the proof or not. It's the power of the state and every law enforcement agency you can find scouring the countryside. What is this case made of? Insinuations, innuendo, suspicions, opinions without any foundation in fact, guesswork, speculation, think-so, what-ifs, maybes, unanswered questions and questions without answers. It's all, as somebody once said, sound and fury signifying nothing. Who did it? They don't know. They can't prove who did it. No one will get on that stand and say Brad King shot her, I saw him do it. No one can get on that stand and say Brad King had a gun that day, Brad King held a gun that day and he pulled a trigger that day. What you're going to hear is a big resounding silence. He was on the property, folks. And when you got nobody else, if you can't prove anything, let's take the nearest suspect. And of course, the husband's always the suspect. What they're doing is attacking a man. They're going to show you they're defending their own phony-baloney jobs. The police will say, 'I gotta explain why I didn't do my job.' Let's find a patsy, there he is. I'm not going to bore you to tears with a long recitation of every circumstance that ever happened in Bradford King's life. But I'm going to suggest to you that what's going to happen here is an attempt at assassination of character. They're going to drag in everything we can to dirty up this case to make the jury confused, get them prejudiced in one way or another. They don't want you to do your job and try this case as you swore to do. They want you to get mad at somebody and take it out on Brad King because there's suspicions but no facts. You swore an oath to uphold the presumption of innocence until proven guilty beyond a reasonable doubt by the facts in this case. At the end of this dog and pony show, when this circus is over, I'm going to come out here and demand that you find him not guilty."

From the jury box, Marybeth Culverhouse listened to both openings and gave the nod to the defense. She wrote that night of Sahli's opening, "It was all very showy but no facts as to who done it!! I myself was not impressed with all that. Mr. Sahli in his opening remarks had led us to believe Mr. K. was a womanizer. So what? Lots of men are. That is no reason to kill her."

Now came the first of sixty-seven prosecution witnesses, each a link in a chain leading to Brad King. The paramedics, the coroner, and the first deputies on the scene took the stand during the first two days.

"We were somewhat bored listening to repetition of medics. My feelings are for the defendant. I don't feel they have proven anything," Marybeth Culverhouse wrote after the first two days.

As part of his presentation, Sahli flipped on his slide projector to show Diane dead in the driveway. Her lifeless form lay on the ground, with her hands outstretched and her head tilted slightly to the right. Then he showed another frame, which also had shock value. It was a picture taken during the autopsy, showing Diane's nude torso punctured by a bullet hole just above her genital area.

Darlene, seated in the second row of the courtroom, recoiled at the images and cried quietly. "All I could think of was her saying, 'Oh my God, my kids are watching me bleed. I don't want to die in front of my kids.' That haunted me all the time," Darlene said. Brad turned his back to the screen when Diane's pictures were presented. Occasionally, he grabbed a tissue from a box on the defense table and dabbed on his dry eyes.

When Trooper Lisle testified, Judge Sindt instructed the jury at Sims's request to consider the testimony with great care. It has little value as proof. It cannot be the sole evidence to convict. There must be other evidence to show guilt.

During the second week of the trial, Brad got some moral support. His mother, Marjorie Lundeen, flew in from Texas. Actually, she was called as a prosecution witness concerning the .22 caliber bolt-action rifle her husband had purchased years ago for her boys. "I assumed Brad had it," Marjorie said when asked what happened to the gun. Her testimony finished, she sat in the first row of the courtroom, directly behind her son. It was a terrible ordeal, listening to the charges and the damaging testimony against him. But her midwestern, WASPish spunk wouldn't allow her to show any negative emotions, at least not in public. Very little personal contact was possible in the courtroom, but Marjorie gave what support she could with eye contact, nods, and body language. And on Thursdays, which were visiting days at the Calhoun County Jail, she sat and talked to her son.

There was no plan to put Brad King on the stand in his own defense. But at the prosecution's request the tape-recorded statements Brad made to police were played by Detective Jack Schoder. They were of poor quality and extremely difficult to hear, so the courtroom was especially still when the microcassettes were played. In a sense, it was a way to get Brad on record saying he didn't do it, because a jury always wants to hear the defendant's version. And having Schoder on the stand during parts of two days allowed the defense to rip the police for royally bungling the early part of the investigation.

Schoder stumbled when he was shown the scrap paper on which Brad drew a crude map of where he was walking the night of the murder. Asked who wrote words on the paper, Schoder studied it for a time and said Brad did, then said maybe it was Trooper Lisle, and finally he said he just didn't know. That was the opening Sims needed to attack his credibility. "You were lying to me, weren't you?" the defense attorney sneered.

That set the stage for a brutal cross-examination as Sims questioned him about the letter Diane received.

"When you got that letter, of course, you sent it off to the FBI, right?" Sims asked Schoder.

"No, I did not," the detective replied.

"Well, did you wiretap the phone of the Kings or put a tracer on it?"

"No, sir, we did not."

"Did you put a tracer or wiretap on the phone at WUHQ, Channel 41?"

"No, we did not."

"Did you interview every employee at WUHQ, Channel 41?"

"No."

"Did you interview the friends and family of Diane King?"

"No, we did not."

"Did you go check out other people who had written to celebrities of that type about whether they had contact with Diane King?"

"I did talk to one person during the investigation."

"When was that? Before or after Diane King was dead?"

"I don't recall."

"It was after, wasn't it?"

"I'd have to check my report. I don't recall at this particular time."

"Did you investigate the personal lives of Bradford King and his wife at that time?"

"No. Did not, sir."

"Did you send the letter off to the Michigan State Police crime lab?"

"No, I did not, sir."

"Did you do spot checks on Diane King or surveillance around the clock at that time?"

"No, I did not."

"Do you know if anyone at the Calhoun County sheriff's department did any of those things?"

"Any of those things? No, sir."

Sims was clearly enjoying himself. Police witnesses are usually the strongest part of a prosecutor's case. You expect the police to be authoritative and professional. But Schoder had to account for his own actions. Now the questioning turned to Brad's denial of guilt, which Schoder characterized as soft because he didn't become irate or angry at the suggestion he killed his wife.

"If I count them, would you agree with me there are approximately twenty-seven denials by Mr. King?" Sims asked.

"I wouldn't disagree, counsel," Schoder said.

"Twenty-seven denials? And those are soft denials?"

"Yes."

"I take it if he only denied it ten times, he confessed."

"No, sir, I would not."

"I'm trying to get your scale here, sir. If twenty-seven is a soft denial, then five is a confession? If you say five times 'I didn't do it,' that's a confession?"

"No, sir."

"Does it get to be a moderate denial when you get to fifty?"

"No, sir."

"I suppose you would have preferred he got up and pounded you in the teeth and then you could have arrested him and held him in jail and sweated him some more, right? That would have been a strong denial, wouldn't it?"

Sahli finally objected that the question was argumentative, and the judge sustained the objection.

"Would it have been a strong denial if he got up and punched you in the teeth?"

Again, there was an objection.

"Did you call in the Michigan State Police crime lab that evening?" Sims continued.

"No, we did not," Schoder said.

"Did you impose security around the premises? Did you cordon it off?"

"No sir, we did not. Based on the information we had at the time, we had completed our search."

"You said you were there and you conducted a search and there was nobody there so you left. When you left, did you even bother to lock the door?"

"I don't recall. I don't believe I was the one that secured the house."

"So to your knowledge, nobody even shut the door."

"The doors were shut."

"How do you know?"

"I was there when we left."

"I thought you just said a minute ago that you weren't?"

"There were several of us there at the time, sir. When we left the property, I wasn't the one who pulled the door shut. The doors were shut when we left."

"But you didn't shut the doors."

"That's correct."

"Certainly, you didn't lock them."

"Correct."

"Didn't put a guard on the premises."

"That's correct."

"Didn't cordon off the driveway and put a police car out front to keep people from going out there."

"That's correct."

"You don't have any idea whether people came out there the minute you walked out of there, or five minutes after you left or not, do you?"

"That's correct."

"And you don't know who it might have been."

"That's correct, sir."

"Paraffin test? Did you even do that?"

"No, sir, we did not."

"You didn't make pictures or casts of the footprints that you were aware of out back."

"That's correct."

"Is your conscience bothering you?"

"No, sir."

Sims's final question went unanswered: "You just didn't do your job, did you?"

Out in the hallway during a recess, Schoder said to no one in particular, "I'm done." He was talking about his time on the witness stand, but he felt like a slab of roast beef that had just been cooked.

In the jury box, Marybeth Culverhouse wasn't the only juror who thought to herself, "The police botched it up so bad it wasn't even funny."

The day actually got worse for the prosecution. One of the jurors heard Schoder ask Brad on tape about taking a lie detector test and wondered what the response was. Brad failed to answer, but a polygraph is inadmissible anyway. The question wasn't answered, but Sims moved again for a mistrial.

Another of his mistrial motions had nothing to do with the testimony. One day, Diane's family showed up with buttons depicting a picture of her. It was their way of bringing Diane into the courtroom, a statement that she was not a figment of someone's imagination, but had been a living, loving human being. One of the worst experiences for the family of a murdered relative is the feeling of having had no control over what happened. This symbolic gesture, recommended by the Parents of Murdered Children, gave Diane's family some control back. When Sims noted the buttons, he angrily said it was a violation of his client's rights and was an illegal attempt to communicate with the jury. Judge Sindt allowed the buttons to be worn, since a picture of Diane had been shown on the slide projector. But he ordered them removed a day later.

A trial, like life, has its ebb and flow. And the prosecution knew it would have to absorb some setbacks. Sahli was having trouble presenting the case he wanted, and his face turned red when the frustration level was highest. He was unable to introduce the story about Brad reporting a breaking and entering on the day he was with Julie Cook.

A frustrating rhythm emerged during the trial. Whenever a point was raised about whether testimony was admissible under the rules of evidence, the judge would stop the proceedings and have the jury removed until the issue was settled. Then out of earshot of the people deciding the case, the lawyers would argue whether something should be allowed and the judge would make his ruling. The strict rules protect the defendant's rights. For example, what Diane King told friends about Brad was not heard because it was ruled hearsay; there was no way to cross-examine a dead person.

But sometimes testimony gets in a side door. When Joanne Karaba was on the stand testifying in front of the jury, she said Diane had become fearful about getting out of her car after the threatening letter was received.

"She just told me she was really scared. One time she said, 'I thought it was Brad playing a sick joke.' And we both laughed about that," Karaba said.

Sims was livid. He wanted to object immediately, but he knew if he said anything it would merely plant the statement deeper in jurors' minds. He waited a few minutes before halting the proceedings, and the jury was again removed from court while the arguments were made. Again, Sims demanded a mistrial. He accused Sahli of misconduct.

"The jury caught. She planted it. He went right ahead, forged a trail right in there and got it out. I could see this witness was attempting to volunteer information. Counsel knew full well she was going to blurt out exactly what she did. He went fishing for it and he got it. What do I do with this blurted out statement which is clearly inadmissible? I can move to strike it from the record, but I can't strike it from the jury's mind. I'm in a quandary."

The defense attorney wanted the jurors to ignore

Karaba's statement. But it's human nature that if you are told to ignore something, such as ignore the fact Brad is bald, the tendency is to notice it even more. Sims asked that the statement be stricken without calling specific attention to it. But the prosecution argued that only a precise statement can be stricken; otherwise, the jury might disregard everything. And on this point he won. When the jury was recalled, Judge Sindt had to tell them to overlook something they weren't supposed to hear in the first place.

"The record should reflect [the] statement, 'I thought Brad was playing a sick joke.' It is the order of this court that the statement be stricken in this matter. It is not to be considered by you as evidence in any way. And you are specifically instructed to disregard it. You are to give it no weight whatsoever in the consideration of this case. It is not evidence and must not be considered as such," the judge said.

Of course, he might as well have told them to ignore the fact that his robe was black. It couldn't be erased, and most of the jurors had written down Karaba's statement on their yellow legal pads.

But the prosecution's frustration level reached its peak on the day before Thanksgiving. Sahli called Barbara Elgutaa, Freida Newton, and Julie Cook that day, and he was prohibited from eliciting testimony from each of them that he thought was crucial to the case. Elgutaa was prepared to testify about how Diane said, in reference to a major blowup between her and Brad, "I could walk out of this marriage right now." Freida wanted to tell the court about Diane's plan to leave the kids behind the night she was murdered. She heard Diane say, "Boy, won't your daddy be surprised to see you kids." And as for Julie Cook, Sahli was told there could be no mention of Brad's affair with her.

"This is a necessary element of the people's case. You have to look at the overall picture," Sahli pleaded to the judge at one point, his face reddening.

"I've never ruled you can't introduce evidence of marital discord. You haven't presented any evidence at this point," Judge Sindt said. "What you're really offering is the defendant's state of mind. To admit that would be serious error. There's no one here to cross-examine the defendant."

At the end of the day, Sahli was crushed. It was the low point of his trial. He felt thwarted in trying to string together a chain of evidence that would hold against Brad King. He remembered his original sentiment about the case: "I have always felt it would be easier to defend than to prosecute."

The only bright spot was that he would have five days to recoup over the Thanksgiving break. One of the greatest assets he had was the team around him. Assistant prosecutor Nancy Mullett was a real expert in case law, and she was always there to shore him up when things got bad. The two investigators, Gary Hough of the state police and Jerry Woods of Sahli's office, helped smooth over the rough spots, too. And the prosecution had its entire case computerized. Not everything was lost. To this point, Sahli had presented testimony from Tanya Scott, who lived a quarter-mile from the Kings on Division Drive, that she heard two shots some seconds apart at about 6:25 or 6:30 the night of the murder. Several neighbors and other witnesses had testified they saw no suspicious characters in the area or on the property that night. A few had mentioned seeing a beige car parked along Division Drive that Saturday afternoon, but a resident named Terry Saylor came forward and said he was ice fishing at one of the lakes with his two boys until five P.M. He drove a 1985 beige Oldsmobile, and once lived at the farmhouse the Kings rented. Robert Cilwa, the ballistics expert, said the casing found in the loft definitely came from the rifle found in the creek, and the slugs removed from Diane King were consistent with having been fired from that rifle. The first connections between Brad and the gun were also made. Just as they had done at the preliminary hearing, Barbara Elgutaa, Tom Darling, and Christopher Sly spoke of seeing a rifle in the King household. Once again, Sly made the strongest remark: "That is the gun I observed." Marjorie Lundeen testified that Brad's father had bought a rifle for the kids, and that she "assumed Brad had it."

But even during the trial, Tom Darling couldn't escape the groundless rumors of his having had an affair with Diane King. At one point, out of earshot of the jurors, Sims asked Darling about those rumors. This was the gossip that had been circulating in Marshall, and now Sims brought it out in the open, at least in front of reporters and TV cameras. But even without hearing Darling deny being involved with Diane, the jury was theorizing on its own. When the panel returned to hear the remainder of Darling's testimony, they had questions for him that were submitted in writing and reviewed by the lawyers before they were read by the judge:

> Q. Did Brad know Darling and his wife were going out of town the weekend of the murder?
> A. No.
> Q. Did Darling know of any marital discord between Brad and Diane?
> A. No.

The jury, it was apparent, was fishing for a motive. And its frustrations were showing.

The jury had frustrations of its own. Because of the sensitive nature of some testimony, they were often led back to the jury room while attorneys questioned witnesses in a process called an "offer of proof." Judge Sindt bent over backward to be impartial, and he disallowed a lot of testimony the jury would have liked to have heard. Some days, they heard as little as two hours of actual testimony, and they were clearly angry they were missing so much. They wiled away the boredom time putting together a 2,000-piece jigsaw puzzle of the fishing port at Portofino, Italy, or playing games like Yahtzee or Flinch they had brought from home. "Aren't we supposed to hear all the evidence so we can make a decision?" Marybeth Culverhouse wondered.

If the day before the Thanksgiving recess was the prosecution's worst, the first day back was its best. After days of slim testimony, Jon Sahli regrouped and was on a roll. He didn't get in everything he wanted, but he got in a large chunk, not the least of which came from Ann Hill and Julie Cook.

"He's telling them he's a single parent. Lo and behold, as of February 9, he is a single parent. I believe it shows motive," Sahli argued in having the women testify about the state of his marriage.

Wearing a black dress over black stockings, Ann Hill sat in the witness chair and trapped Brad in his own lies. The scorned woman unleashed her own brand of fury. "He told me he was separated, going through a divorce and he had custody of his son. He said he was a single parent," Ann said in a steady voice.

She was with him for several hours on October 30, the day the letter arrived in Diane's mailbox. Two days later,

Brad said Diane was upset with him because he had been late picking up his son.

She was also with Brad the evening of November 20, the date Kateri was born. It was the first time he had ever mentioned the baby. About a month later, she walked past Brad and Diane at school while he was holding the baby. "Why didn't you stop and say hi?" Brad asked her. "He said it was the first time he had seen the baby since she was born. Diane had specifically brought the baby over so he could see her," Ann said.

She talked about visiting Brad's house on December 19, but she was not allowed to say they had sex that night. She talked about their January 7 meeting when Brad said Diane had frozen their bank accounts and that he wouldn't be able to pay for a class he wanted to take. She talked about the phone message she received from Brad on February 8—the day before the murder. And the tape she had saved from her answering machine was played: "Hi, Annie. It's Brad. If you get in tonight, give me a call at home. I won't be home tomorrow or the rest of the weekend. So if you get in tonight, give me a call." She returned the call at 11:44 A.M. on Saturday, but Brad told her he was just on his way out the door and wouldn't be back until late that night.

There was more. She said that in the fall of 1990 Brad had bragged about being an excellent shot with a rifle. He preferred hunting with a bow because there was no sport in shooting something with a bullet. When he went hunting with friends, he always shot deer for them because he could kill instantaneously. Brad also told her about the time he was tracking a deer and he sunk up to his knees in some soft mud. He was surprised that the ground was so soft in the winter, and the spot he described was not far from where the Remington rifle was jammed barrel first into the creek mud.

And several weeks after the murder, Brad spoke about the investigation. "He was upset it was focusing on him. He felt he was being singled out. He felt Calhoun County was on a witch-hunt. He had married an Indian, he claimed to be an Indian, and the sheriff was prejudiced against him," Ann said.

Julie Cook had some damaging remarks also. She wasn't allowed to go into details about her affair with Brad or holding hands at the movies. But she told about the phone call Brad made to Diane from her apartment and his lie about being a single parent. "He said technically, yes, he was married, but his wife had left him in November." And she concluded by saying how Brad put his wedding ring back on after Diane's murder.

The prosecution also got a break with two unexpected witnesses who linked Brad to the gun. When the Kings lived in their Battle Creek apartment, Lori Osten and Carol Mendez cleaned for them. After the trial had already started, someone overheard them discussing a gun they had seen in the apartment, and the tipster called police. Neither woman wanted to get involved in the King case, but they had no choice now. Mendez especially was reluctant; she had bad memories from a trial involving her murdered brother, and she got the creeps from Brad. But she testified: every time she vacuumed the basement steps, up until the Kings moved to Marshall, she had spied a rifle.

"I can recall seeing it every time we was there. It was a .22 rifle. Long gun. Dark stock," said Mendez who had purchased some rifles for her husband. "It had a skinny barrel and a dark wooden stock."

Brad's brother, Scott, also took the stand. He said the

rifle pulled from Talmadge Creek looked similar to a bolt-action .22 his father bought and which Brad kept after graduating from college.

Another witness who damaged Brad's defense was Virginia Colvin, the wife of the station manager at WUHQ. A number of people had testified about Brad's demeanor at the funeral, noting that his behavior seemed strange for someone whose wife was murdered. But Virginia was most telling about Brad's crying. "I relate it to my children. When they want something, they cry one way. When they're really hurt or injured, they cry another. I thought it was forced, like my children did when they wanted their way with something. A few minutes later he was smiling. I couldn't put the pieces together. It just seemed strange to me there was no anger or deeper hurt. I told my husband, 'If someone killed me, would you be angry?' "

Finally, there was Stella Pamp, the Native-American woman who witnessed Diane's security rituals. In the courtroom, she clutched an Indian talisman called a Dream Catcher, a ring with a leather web that is supposed to catch spirits; it expels the bad ones and captures the good ones. This particular Dream Catcher was made by Diane King for Cindy Acosta, whose best friend's son was stricken with cancer. After some treatments and with the help of the Dream Catcher, the boy's illness went into remission. Cindy brought it into the courtroom, and Barbara Elgutaa and Freida Newton clutched it when they were on the witness stand. And now it was Stella Pamp's turn. Two questions came from a juror. Did Diane indicate who she thought was making the calls? And did she think it was the same person making the calls and writing the letters. Pamp answered yes both times, and the inference to Brad was clear.

Of the remaining witnesses heard over the next two days, the most diverse were Shemane Nugent, the wife of rock star Ted Nugent, and Sister Ann Jeffrey Selesky, a Roman Catholic nun.

Shemane wore red in her dress, stockings, high-heeled shoes, earrings, and lipstick. Brad had called her and her husband two days after the murder to say Diane had been shot by a stalker. "We weren't particularly close. I was surprised he was concerned enough to call us," Shemane said. Diane's family was astonished, too, since Brad didn't call them.

Sister Ann, the director of Native-American ministries for the Diocese of Kalamazoo, wore her nun's habit and veil to the witness stand. She was at the farmhouse to see Brad's parents on February 18, but they had already gone back to Texas. So she and Brad spent several hours chitchatting about anything and everything. "I made a remark I had a .22 and liked to target practice," Sister Ann said. "He said, 'So do I, and I'm an expert shot.' "

The nun was the sixty-seventh and final prosecution witness; the state had rested its case.

Immediately, John Sims requested that Judge Sindt direct a verdict of not guilty because there was insufficient evidence for the case to go the jury. A motion like this is common in murder trials, but Diane's family was unaware it was coming. They feared that Brad would be set free, and they asked Sister Ann to pray with them in a room.

Sims argued there was no evidence of premeditation and that the gun could not be conclusively established as the murder weapon or as having been used or belonging to Brad King. Nor were there any fingerprints found. "The gun was found in a creek, but it can't be tied to this murder. Mr. King was somewhere on the property, and he can't be tied to this murder. What you have here is conjecture piled upon inference, and inference piled upon possibility. It's a nice theory. The problem with this cloth is that it tears too easily," Sims said.

Judge Sindt didn't buy it. He ruled there was sufficient evidence presented for a rational person to reach a decision beyond a reasonable doubt.

"I recognize evidence connecting the gun in the creek to the murder and connecting the gun in the creek to the defendant. There is significant evidence placing the gun in the possession of the defendant. The casing found in the loft indicates the person lay in wait. It was Diane King's habit and routine not to get out of the car unless the defendant was present. She was shot after she got out of the car. There is evidence the jury could conclude the defendant was present at the time. There is evidence the marriage was not intact—such as the defendant's own statements about separation and custody that a divorce was filed, that kind of thing. Considering all the evidence, although it is circumstantial, there is evidence to put this case to a jury."

For the defense, seven witnesses provided a total of an hour's worth of testimony. Five rebuttal witnesses were called by the prosecution. Interestingly, a tenant who moved into a house near the King farmhouse found a .22 caliber Remington Model 511 Scoremaster rifle in an attic room, the same kind that was used to kill Diane. But the ballistics, firing pin, and ejector marks were different. There was a stipulation by Frank Zinn, an attorney, that the rifle had been in his family since the 1940s and had been locked in a back room. The last time it was fired was on New Year's Eve about forty years ago. Christopher Sly was called back to the witness stand to differentiate between the two guns.

Should Brad have testified in his own defense? He had the absolute right not to, but the jury certainly wanted to hear him. Putting a client on the stand is almost always a no-win situation for the defense, and Brad's co-counsel, Virginia Cairns, explained it this way in an interview with *Court TV*.

"Brad King has been in jail for almost one year. The man is completely distraught. He knows that whoever killed his wife is probably never going to be arrested, and he knows he didn't do it. The emotional trauma he has been through, especially with this trial this last month, has been immeasurable. I can't tell you the negative effect it's had on him. He is too emotional. He sat during the trial and cried just about on a daily basis. He couldn't have done it, that's all."

As for her theory about what happened to Diane King, Cairns said, "I think she was a woman who had a certain degree of celebrity. I think other people picked up on that. I think she was tormented. I think someone was after her. . . . I think the identity of whoever did it will probably never be known, or his motivation. It could have been a stalker. It could have been someone breaking into the property. It could have been anyone, but it wasn't Brad King. There just isn't enough proof to convict him beyond a reasonable doubt."

There was one more piece of business for the jury before they heard the final arguments. At the prosecution's request, they were taken to 16240 Division Drive to get a firsthand look at the murder scene. On a cold, snowy, dreary, thirty-degree day, they piled onto a white bus that said Calhoun County Medical Care Facility—Adult Day Care. State police cars with flashing emergency lights blocked the road to traffic about one hundred yards in each direction of the driveway. Judge Sindt wore his arctic parka, John Sims had his ice-fishing coveralls and a University of Michigan stocking cap, and Jon Sahli donned a heavy sweater and his hiking boots. A portable plastic chair was provided for court reporter Val Smith so she could sit and take notes. It was so cold that Suzanne Sinclair, the judge's secretary, had to tug on the paper to feed it through Val's machine, which was freezing up. During the one-hour stay, the jurors went into the barn and up to the loft. They peered through the door where the sniper waited. The dark, dusty place had the smell of old straw and corncobs. From there, they proceeded left toward Talmadge Creek and the rickety bridge. Some inquisitive jurors bent on one knee to write notes on their yellow legal pads. Across the creek, the brush thickens up considerably. You have to crouch low and bend down to get through the tangle, and it's not a place a stranger would go in the dark if he didn't know how to negotiate the deer trails. In the boggy area where the gun was discovered, you could sink ankle-deep quite easily. Only seven jurors walked back to the hay piles where Brad said he walked. It took twelve minutes to walk from there back to the house; Brad said it had taken him thirty minutes.

CHAPTER 17

The prosecution got a fortuitous break with the timing of the trial. The final witness was heard on a Friday. Since Monday was an off day and the jury spent Tuesday at the murder scene, Prosecutor Jon Sahli had four days to prepare his closing arguments. He had earned a reputation as a strong finisher, and the extra time allowed him to summarize a complicated string of evidence. The courtroom was jam-packed on Wednesday, December 9, when the lawyers had their final appearance before the jury. Brad's mother, Marjorie, and his stepfather, Cliff Lundeen, took their customary seats in the first row behind the defense table.

"I'm doing awful. It's been a two-year nightmare. When you're seventy years old, you shouldn't have to go through this," a nervous Marjorie said. She had been a rock through the trial, listening to the monstrous charges against her older son and the testimony against him. She had nodded to him every day in court and had been present every Thursday evening when visitors were permitted at the Calhoun County Jail. Nothing to date had made her lose her dignity; she sat composed and reserved through it all.

Among the courtroom spectators and curiosity seekers were two dozen Native Americans who got the word through the Indian network to attend in a show of support for Freida Newton and the deceased Diane King.

Just as he did during his opening, Jon Sahli relied on the visual aids of slides, charts, graphs, maps, and a writing board. He laid out the story of Diane's terror after receiving the anonymous letter while Brad was spending time with Ann Hill and Julie Cook. "Here's our single parent again," Sahli repeated several times with damning effectiveness. He drove home the point of the lies Brad told to these college women and his wife. Defense attorney John Sims objected and moved for a mistrial on the grounds Sahli tried once again to show a sexual connection. Judge Conrad Sindt took the unusual step of removing the jury—again—while they argued the point. After finding no grounds for a mistrial, the summation in front of the jury continued.

Sahli hammered home the point that Diane had a security ritual in which she would never get out of the car unless Brad was home. "Why, on February 9, would she vary the practice?" he asked. "Diane King required that the defendant be there before she got out of the car. Diane King saw the defendant on February 9 and she got out and that was when she was shot two times—once through the heart and once through the vaginal area." Again, the slide projector roared to life to show the murdered form on the ground as Diane's family and friends wept spontaneously. "The fatal shot was the first shot as she was standing next to the Jeep Wagoneer. The second shot was fired while Mrs. King was lying flat on the ground. The second shot was inflicted outside that barn."

The defense attorney leaped up and moved for another mistrial. The jury—again—was led from the room. "Nobody has testified that the location of that shot couldn't have been by a stranger. To make that argument is impermissible under the circumstances here. It's exceedingly prejudicial. Once again I move for a mistrial. I think the cumulative effect of the particular line of argument is terribly prejudicial and without foundation. This last one is ridiculous. This is completely out of [left] field. This is improper," Sims roared.

Judge Sindt overruled him and called the jury back in. Given the green light, the prosecutor bored in.

"Ladies and gentleman, I submit to you the second shot is not the shot of a stranger, but the shot of someone who was close to Diane King. The shot of someone who was enraged with Diane King, a revenge shot if you will. The second shot was inflicted after the defendant was outside of that barn and after the wife was laying on the ground. I submit it was not a stranger or an obsessed fan, but the defendant. There is not one iota of evidence that a stranger or an obsessed fan killed Diane King."

Now Sahli picked up the Remington Scoremaster Model 511 rifle and waved it in front of the jury for emphasis. And he talked about Brad's behavior that night.

"His wife is lying in the driveway and he doesn't take his children from the car? If there was stalker on the property, would he leave his children in the car? There are no footprints heading back to the hay bales. The defendant was never there. The defendant was getting rid of the gun," Sahli said, slamming the barrel into the floor as he if were jamming the gun into the soft mud of Talmadge Creek.

The next point of emphasis was the gun. Six witnesses said the rifle was similar to one they saw in the King household. Young Christopher Sly said emphatically, "That is the gun I saw." Ann Hill and Sister Ann Jeffrey were told by Brad he was an excellent shot. And there was the crime scene and the work of Travis the tracking dog.

"This person hiding in the barn who shot Diane King would have left the barn, headed south in the area he had just seen the defendant walking. If you accept the theory it's a stranger who made his way through, wouldn't they have run into each other. Wouldn't the defendant have heard him making his way through the marsh?

"If it was a stranger or an obsessed fan, why would the track of Travis come into the driveway going back to the King residence? If it was a stranger or an obsessed fan, why would they run this track? Why not go to the automobile, take the gun with you and get out? How is the case ever solved with the gun in the car? If it's a stranger or an obsessed fan, you're going to get out of there. You want to get out of there," the prosecutor continued. "If Travis is following a deer, does a deer put the gun in the creek? Did a deer then fire the shots? That, of course, is ridiculous. If the defendant believed it was an obsessed fan, why did he return on February 10? If there is this stalker out there, you just return to the house?

"Ladies and gentlemen, look at everything. Put it in its place. When you do that, you will conclude the people have indeed proven beyond a reasonable doubt that the defendant Bradford J. King is guilty of murder in the first degree and guilty of being in possession of a firearm during the commission of a felony."

With that, Jon Sahli's two-hour summation was over. Jurors were observed nodding their heads in agreement as he lucidly built his case. After a brief recess, it was up to John Sims to wreck that logic.

"Brad King is innocent, and I told you that a long time ago in a galaxy far, far away," Sims said. "Bradford King was on the property and they don't have a butler, otherwise the butler did it. You want to know what it's all about, folks? That's what it's all about, right there. See it?" he said, pointing to the *Court TV* camera broadcasting the proceedings around the country.

"It's the big production. The Calhoun County prosecutor's office, in conjunction with the Calhoun County Sheriff's Department, the Michigan State Police, the Michigan State Police crime lab, the FBI, and every other police agency in this country have put together the big production. See the script? I've seen it. You've heard it. We've got screenwriters. We've got a big budget. It's a massive production. The big trial. And this dog and pony show, as I refer to it, is a circus act complete with its own magic. Because when you haven't got anything and you have the power of the state and you have the big production, you can get anybody you want. It makes for interesting viewing, good press, lots of grist for the author's mills. We're going to write books. Oh, yeah. We'll have commercials sold. TV audiences increase. But how do you critique this particular production? If you were Siskel and Ebert sitting back there in 'At the Movies,' there's lots of money, lots of witnesses, lots of time, fairly interesting topic, the story line is decent, you've got celebrity here. You've also got a mother and a wife who's died. But there's a real problem here, folks. And that is, the whole thing falls apart at the most interesting point. The plot just doesn't make it. Thumbs down. Because it's all fantasy. This whole case is based upon the fact that nobody saw anything so it happened this way. What did they expect? Some guy with a big sign saying, 'I'm the killer.' Whoever did it was there to be seen because they'd been there watching. There are holes in this theory, behind all the smoke and mirrors, behind the illusions and the twists. It's like those old sci-fi movies where you see the toy rocket ships with this wire attached to it. Once you've seen that, it sort of goes burst."

He tried to knock the bricks out of the prosecution's foundation, especially Christopher Sly's testimony and the trail of the tracking dog.

"I may be a nasty individual sometimes, but I didn't go charging after Mr. Sly, who's a young man. And only the young can be that certain, folks. When I was thirteen, my old man didn't know anything. By the time I got to twenty, I was amazed at how much he had learned.

"Travis is very suspect. Why? He's an animal. And as my daddy used to say, never bet on anything that eats. And Travis eats," Sims continued.

"What this prosecutor wants you to do is convict Bradford King of murder because he didn't act the way somebody might think it's appropriate at his wife's funeral. God forbid. The next thing that's going to happen is we're going to be finding people guilty because they're black, they're yellow, they go to the wrong church, they didn't behave right when they went to school.

"I'm not going to tell you there was a stalker. I'm here to tell you one thing and one thing only. They haven't proved their case. Not beyond a reasonable doubt. And you can't convict Bradford King because you think he doesn't look right. You can't convict him because he didn't act right at his wife's funeral. You can't convict him because he's not a very nice person. You can't convict him because you don't like the way he sits or the way he moves. You can't think him into jail.

"The major failing of this case is simple—the gun they found in the creek. Their own expert says he can't say positively this is the weapon that fired those bullets. No proof that it is, but we want you to infer that it is. And we want you to jump one more time and say it's Bradford King's gun. And then we want you to jump one more time and say Bradford King had that gun on February 9, 1991. You're not through jumping yet. 'Cause then you have to jump from that and say he was up there in that loft and fired the first shot. He went somewhere else and fired the second shot. And they want you to believe Diane King would have never gotten out of that car unless her husband was right there. And if Bradford King is such a whirlwind planner, and he knew that gun was out there on the tenth, why the heck not go get rid of it? Great plan. Great plan telling all these gals you're a single parent. Yeah, you're getting ready to off your wife and you're telling these people? How much more trouble could he have put himself in? Great plan.

"When the police arrived, they knew who committed this crime. They decided that night. This ain't Sherlock Holmes. This ain't Agatha Christie. This is where we decide who did it and let's go find out how we can make it look like he did. I swear to you, folks, I think that if Jack Schoder had seen some guy standing out in the middle of the street with a sign saying 'I Killed Diane King' with blood on his hands and a gun in his other hand, he'd have run him over trying to get Brad King down there to sweat him a little bit. 'Cause he had already made up his mind. Folks, the gun that killed Diane

King went with whoever killed her. They just didn't prove it, despite all the media and all the hoopla. Send this man back to what's left of his family."

In the Michigan judicial system, the prosecutor is allowed a brief rebuttal.

"The people haven't given you eighty-five or eighty-nine different theories. The people have given you one theory. The defendant shot and killed his wife. If it was a crime scene when he saw his wife there, why didn't he get his children out of the car then? If he didn't want to disturb the crime scene, why did he on Sunday go back to where he claimed to have walked. Why drive over where he had walked? To obliterate the fact that there were no footprints in that area. Your verdict should still be to find the defendant guilty of premeditated murder in the first degree. Because all of the evidence in this case points only to that verdict."

The courtroom was drained. Nothing more could happen until the next day.

The judge's instructions were all that remained, but a Michigan snowstorm delayed the process. Six inches of snow were on the ground that Thursday morning, and jurors trickled into the Hall of Justice after slip-sliding their way through the treacherous Battle Creek streets. Tentative plans were made to go get jurors who couldn't make it in on their own, but all of them had assembled shortly before ten o'clock.

Judge Conrad Sindt then gave the final instructions, which were taped so the panel could refer to them if necessary during deliberations.

"A person accused of a crime is presumed innocent, which means you must start with that presumption, which continues through the trial and entitles the defendant to a verdict of not guilty unless you decide beyond a reasonable doubt he is guilty. The defendant is not required to prove his innocence. A reasonable doubt is a fair and honest doubt growing out of the evidence or lack of evidence."

For a verdict of premeditated murder, jurors were told the act must have been thought out beforehand. Any reasonable person would have thought twice about the deed, and the killing would have been done willfully. To lie in wait, the defendant must have intended to kill Diane King. Lying in wait must have lasted only long enough to show reasonable doubt. Jurors were told to disregard any reference to lie detector tests and that every defendant has the absolute right not to testify. The defendant did not have to prove he was somewhere else, the prosecution must prove beyond reasonable doubt he was there.

"Use your own common sense and general knowledge in weighing and judging the evidence. Direct evidence is what we see or hear. For example, if we look outside and see rain falling, that's direct evidence it is raining. The facts can also be proved by circumstantial evidence. If you see a person coming in from outside wearing a raincoat that is wet, that is circumstantial evidence it is raining," Sindt said in a twenty-five minute talk.

One of the alternates had been dismissed earlier in the week when his son was killed in an auto accident. To determine who else should be dismissed, thirteen numbers—each corresponding to a juror—were placed in a wooden box. A capsule was withdrawn for juror number one, and Eloise Lehman was discharged. Judge Sindt, only half-joking, said her release may have been "an answered prayer" because she was no longer responsible for rendering a decision in a difficult case. She shook hands with the jury and left the notes she had taken. Finally, at 10:39 A.M., five weeks after they had been sworn in, the jurors deliberated the fate of Bradford King. All the puzzles and games had been removed from the room with a large table and a window to the outside; now it was strictly the business of justice.

The jury's first order of business was to elect a foreman, and Jerry Mayfield, a retiree, was picked. When they got down to business, the mood was contentious from the start. On their first polling, they deadlocked at six-six as everyone explained the rationale of his or her position. Within five minutes, the vote was seven-five to convict, and that's the way the day ended.

In the corridors of the Hall of Justice, spectators settled down in a tedious vigil. Marjorie Lundeen, Brad's mother, sat for a time on a bench, then heeded her son's advice and waited in private at her hotel. Diane's family huddled together in a witness room. A Dream Catcher hung from the window, and pictures and portraits of Diane were placed throughout the room. They wanted her in some sense to be there at the moment of truth.

The dismissed juror, Eloise Lehman, came back to the courthouse to see the trial through to its conclusion. It was as if she were pregnant but was denied a chance to deliver. "My mind was here. I wanted to see it through, or I wouldn't have come back. Part of me would like to be back there, but part of me is relieved not to be," said Lehman, who runs an interior decorating shop in Battle Creek. Like the judge said, maybe it was an answered prayer. "I called my thirteen-year-old granddaughter last night to grant us the wisdom to judge it clearly. She's deeply religious. She believes in God. I figured her connections were better than mine." In the end, Lehman was the answer to the prosecution's prayers.

By Friday, the jury had all of the exhibits in the deliberating room: Brad's taped statements to Jack Schoder, the slides, the map of the dog track, the gun, both slugs, the eight shell casings, Diane's bloody clothes, and her appointment book. The jury also asked to hear the testimony again of Deputy Guy Picketts, the first person on the scene, and the direct testimony of Jack Schoder. Picketts's testimony was read by court reporter Val Smith; Schoder's was pulled from the transcript and printed for the jury to see on Monday.

Two jurors made up their minds to convict that day, Jerry Mayfield and Marybeth Culverhouse. Now the split was nine-three.

"I couldn't sleep that night. I listed pros and cons, and I remembered the judge said to use common sense. Everything pointed to him," Marybeth said. "He was the only one on the property who could have done it. Nobody else was there. It only pointed in one direction. I didn't think there was a stalker. I thought it was a prefabricated story. The police botched it so bad it wasn't funny. They didn't even cordon off the property. If it hadn't been for the tracking dog, they never would have found the gun. And the one thing that cemented it for me was the gun."

Marybeth brought a big boom-box radio in from home to listen to Brad's statements rather than rely on the poor quality of the microcassettes, and that helped in her decision. "You could hear his voice change every time he talked about his wife and kids," she said.

Motive was a question mark, however. The question of marital discord was obvious from references to the Oakridge Center for marriage counseling that Diane had marked in her book. And the jurors knew that Brad had been fooling around. "Sex? It was obvious. We're adults.

We're married. I didn't care. That happens every day," Marybeth said. "I wish they would have called Brad to the stand. I wanted to get to know him better. We did not have an easy time. There was a lot of hostility in that room. The boxing gloves were on from the word go."

Still, the weekend approached without a verdict. The feeling was that if nothing happened quickly, the wait was likely to be very long indeed. But the people in the deliberating room didn't want to be rushed into anything. They were salt-of-the-earth types, Middle Americans wrestling with their consciences. No one wanted to send an innocent man to jail for the rest of his life, but no one wanted to see a man get away with murder, either.

Among the three holdouts was Claude Oxley, forty-nine, a retired U.S. Air Force master sergeant. Oxley was the one juror who didn't take a single note; he didn't want to miss any expressions or nuances from witnesses. It had been a long, complicated case. And he wanted to have the weekend to mull it all over.

"I felt the guy deserved a fair amount of deliberation. The consequences were very severe, after all. I was trying my case in his favor. I think I was the best friend he had in that courtroom. I wouldn't want to be responsible for sending an innocent man to prison. I was trying to look at it from another perspective, that it was a stalker. It could have been somebody else. I do not think anybody had him convicted on pretrial publicity. I adhered to the judge's instruction that the man was presumed innocent throughout the course of trial. I certainly kept an open mind and did everything possible to find the man innocent. It just wasn't there," Oxley said.

Oxley reached his decision after listing the reasons why Brad was guilty versus why he should be acquitted.

He came up with twenty-two reasons for a conviction, and he brought the list into the courtroom on Monday.

1. Brad King denied owning a .22.
2. Five witnesses said that the gun looked similar to a gun Brad King had in his possession.
3. Two witnesses, his brother and his mother, said it was similar to the gun his father had.

"At first I was thinking, nobody has specifically identified this gun. But when you get to thinking about the fact he denied he owned it, five people testified they had seen a .22 in his home, his mom and brother said it looked similar to one he owned—that's good enough," Oxley said.

5. Brad King said he walked to a small group of hay bales, an area in which there were snowdrifts. But there were no footprints. That's an impossibility.
6. Another killer would have had to have been extremely lucky—not knowing when Diane King was returning home, sneaking in on the property, and taking the chance of waiting days on end.
7. All of the testimony that it was her practice not to exit the car unless Brad appeared. Why did she exit the car that particular evening without seeing him?
8. How did the killer get past Brad King when he ditched the gun and fled the property?

"If it was a stalker, he would have had to have seen Brad walk south. I wouldn't walk in that direction. I'd walk in the opposite direction. It didn't make good logic that he'd go in same direction," Oxley reasoned.

9. In December, Ann Hill said Brad King had fallen into the creek and sunk up to his knees. A stalker would have been extremely lucky to ditch the gun in that spot. Of the 500 acres back there, he picked the one spot where the gun would sink down in the creek bed.

10. Brad King had the opportunity to murder.

11. Only Brad King knew when Diane would arrive home.

12. Brad owned a watchdog who didn't bark.

13. Brad King didn't seem to be too concerned about Diane's dilemma.

14. Brad King and Randy Wright drove back on the Sunday after the murder. Why? Were they really looking for deer? How many husbands or spouses have a desire to go look for deer when their wife is just murdered? That didn't add up.

15. Lack of concern for his children's safety. Maybe he panicked. These children were in the car for 45 minutes to an hour. You would just not leave those children in that car. He could have asked the police to remove them.

16. Demeanor. I never heard that word demeanor so many times in all my life. His demeanor at the murder, funeral, gravesite, and after the post-funeral dinner. Who knows how anybody's going to respond to death? I didn't put whole of stock in it. But when you add everything up, it was something that didn't go into his column.

17. He didn't mention her. It was like she never existed. There was not much discussion about her after she was murdered.

18. If he was a former cop and not happy with the investigation, why didn't he do investigative work on his own? Brad King didn't seem angry or frustrated. He rather appeared to be boasting that an arrest hadn't been made, like he was proud rather than angry.

19. Prior to October 30, Brad quite often accompanied his wife. After she received the letter, she always went alone to visit her mother and her sister. He didn't seem to have a whole lot of concern. Two and two didn't seem to make four.

20. Why didn't he call the family and inform them of Diane's death? He called others, including Ted Nugent's wife, whom he had only casually met. This isn't normal behavior.

21. At the approximate time of death, a neighbor heard two shots. Why did Brad King only hear one gunshot?

22. Why did Brad King go for a walk when he knew his wife was coming home?

"It all pointed right back to Brad King. The only two things I came up with in his favor were there were no fingerprints found and nobody specifically identified that .22," Oxley said. "One reason I had such a hard time was that he was a former police officer and instructor of criminal justice. How could he screw things up so bad? Why was he so foolish to use that firearm if other people knew it existed? He made a lot of mistakes for somebody that was a former police officer. I figured the person calling Diane was not Brad King, but an admirer or fan. Brad King then used this information to his advantage to plot the murder to make it appear to be a stalker. It was a good game plan. It sure got fouled up in the process. Did the police botch it? That was a fiasco. But if Brad was an innocent man, why didn't he take the stand in his defense? If he didn't have anything to hide, why didn't he testify? Once I convinced myself, then I didn't have a problem with it. The judge gave the defendant every break he could."

When Oxley presented his reasons on Monday, another juror switched over with him. Now it was eleven-one to convict. But the lone holdout was adamant. "Why do I have to prove him innocent. They have to prove him guilty. I don't care if hell freezes over," said the lone holdout.

At eleven A.M., the jury passed a note to Judge Sindt that said: "At this point, we are a hung jury and need further instruction."

It was too early to throw in the towel with a hung jury, which meant Brad might have to be tried all over again in front of a different panel. Judge Sindt asked them to resume deliberations, reading a standard instruction: "Talk things over in the spirit of fairness and frankness. Reason the matter out. You can change your mind, but none of you should give up your honest beliefs," he said.

The jury went out again at 11:29 A.M. The defense was clearly encouraged at the prospect of a hung jury. And Brad, smiling, told his attorney: "Oh, it's almost time for lunch anyway."

The tension that had been building in Diane's family boiled over in Darlene. "I'll buy your lunch. I hope you have fish everyday for the rest of your life," she said, loud enough for him to hear.

Without anybody to support him, the lone holdout was vulnerable. Over lunch, the juror's mind was changed and the juror agreed on a guilty verdict of second-degree murder. But the other jurors argued. How could it be second degree if Brad waited in that loft? It was premeditated or nothing.

"It's cut-and-dried. He was laying in wait for 102 days from the time he planted that letter on October 30 until February 9," Claude Oxley said.

That swung it. At 1:55 P.M., word spread rapidly

through the courthouse: a verdict was in. People raced in to the courtroom, only to be led out so deputies could parade everyone through a metal detector for security reasons. Few events match the pure drama and raw emotion of a jury reaching a decision in a murder trial.

Brad was in the holding cell where he was locked up during deliberations. It was a sparse accommodation, with a tile floor and a combination metal sink and toilet in the right corner. On the beige-painted walls were two bits of juxtaposed jailhouse graffiti. One said "Jesus Saves," the other said "Fuck You." On the left wall was a concrete slab that doubled as a bench and bunk. When court officers came to retrieve Brad, he was asleep on the rigid cement.

Three deputies in their chocolate-brown uniforms stood between Brad and the spectators; two more armed guards were to his right. Diane's family filled the second bench, holding hands and uttering their final prayers. Freida Newton and her daughter, Darlene, wore leather medicine bags containing the Indian sacred herbs of tobacco, sage, cedar and sweet grass. Freida's face was buried in a tissue. "I couldn't look at Brad. That was the worst moment," she said.

Judge Sindt stilled the buzz in the room with a caution: "There must not be any kind of an outburst whatsoever."

Then at 2:07 P.M., jury foreman Jerry Mayfield rose from his seat in the back row and announced the finding. Marybeth Culverhouse was crying in her seat, and the man to her right gently rubbed her shoulder. Her knees were shaking. "We the jury find Bradford King, as to count one, guilty of first-degree premeditated murder, and as to count two, guilty of carrying a firearm in the commission of a felony," he said firmly. The finding was read back to him to make sure it was correct, and he answered, "Yes."

At the defense table, Brad had nervously rubbed his head and what hair he had left before he placed his hands palms down on the table. The pronouncement went through him like a shot. His head bowed slightly, then he sagged silently back into his chair. His face was blank. Defense attorney John Sims comforted him by placing his right hand on Brad's back; it was the first time he had touched his client during the trial. Then Sims requested the polling of the jury. Suzanne Sinclair asked each of them: "Is your verdict as stated by the foreperson?" Twelve times, the answer came back "Guilty" or "Yes, it is." Brad was placed in the custody of the sheriff.

With the proceeding over, the courtroom exploded. Twenty-two months of anguish lifted from a family's collective shoulders. Freida hugged Jon Sahli and Gary Hough, telling them, "You did a perfect job." Darlene stomped her foot and clenched her fists. "First degree! First degree! That son of a bitch is gone," she said.

"I feel weak. I feel deflated. Like my knees want to go down. It's an awful grief to lose a daughter. But at least now we have those two children. We wouldn't care if he walked away as long as we had the kids," Royal Newton said as he drifted out to the hallway.

In the back corridors, Brad was placed in restraining cuffs and chains. He had saved half of his Italian steak sandwich for the afternoon recess. Since he wouldn't be needing it now, he gave it to Deputy Guy Picketts. He had one request: a meeting with county jail chaplain Dave Mason. "He didn't say one other word. He was really crushed. I think he expected to beat it," said Deputy Lee Beebe. Brad was allowed a special visit from his parents, but he was placed on a twenty-four-hour suicide watch, a routine procedure for someone convicted of first-degree murder. He would be stripped naked and given only a heavy blanket, something that would be hard to tie into a noose.

On his way out of the back of the Hall of Justice, Brad passed Edith Cupples, Diane's aunt and the godmother of Diane's daughter. She was on the phone to family at the Kahnawake Reserve in Canada. "Oh, here comes Brad. Except he don't have that big smirk on his face no more," Edith said into the receiver.

Defense attorney John Sims said he would file a motion for a directed verdict and a motion for a new trial.

"There'll be an appeal. Absolutely. I believe there has been error in this trial. There's reversible error in just the buttons themselves. That was a horrible mistake by the people who wore them," he said. "I have not been able yet to figure out what it was that the jury hung their hat on. It was a totally circumstantial case. I guess they accepted the theory. I feel sorry for the jury for what they've been through. They had a very tough decision. Those people struggled with their own souls back there. That's the most I can ask. If I got them to do that, if what I did helped a little bit. I think I tried this case as well as anybody could have tried this case. And I'm very pleased with my effort. And I don't hold my head down for that at all. Brad is holding up. He and I have been preparing for this possibility for a long time. It's kind of tough to have twelve people say you did something that you totally maintained that you never did. It's kind of tough to look at what he's looking at as a mandatory sentence here and still not fall apart."

With the grueling business of a murder trial behind them, Diane's family gathered at Moose Lodge 676 in

Marshall. The brick building is on the road leading to Division Drive, just a few miles from the murder scene. Freed from the pressure and courtroom decorum, prosecutor Sahli danced with Edith Cupples to the jukebox music of Bob Seeger's "Old Time Rock 'n' Roll." Before he departed, the family and his associates assembled around him and sang "For He's a Jolly Good Fellow."

The mood was one of joy, relief, and reflection.

"Nothing's going to bring Diane back. This doesn't change anything. But I wanted those kids. They're really orphans now. He made orphans of his kids," Freida Newton said, never once mentioning Brad by name. "He thought he committed the perfect crime. I want him to spend every day of his life behind bars. His freedom is gone."

Freida had formed secret plans to whisk Marler and Kateri to the Kahnawake Reserve in Canada had the verdict been different. It would have been nearly impossible to enforce a court order on ground that is considered sovereign in a different country. "I might have been a prisoner for the rest of my life, but I wasn't going to give them up," she said.

In one corner of the Moose Lodge hall, a big-screen TV broadcast a replay of the verdict being announced. "Justice. Justice is served," said Gordon Marler, pumping his fist with satisfaction. Just a few hours earlier, a feeling of despair had washed over him. He had gone outside the courtroom with a prayer for a verdict when the news came back the jury was deadlocked. "No, Lord, don't do this," Gordon said. His heart lifted when the jury returned in the afternoon. "Now I realize God was just telling me in a different way. My prayer was answered. The jury had to come in so the judge could tell them to keep going. I used to be in favor of capital punishment. Now I see the light. I really want to see him suffer. He has to suffer every day of his life from now on for killing Diane."

Just by chance, this was the day the Moose Lodge had scheduled its Christmas party. A Santa Claus came in, distributing candy and gifts in a hall decorated with lights and season's greetings. "Christmas came early. We couldn't ask for a better present," Royal Newton said.

Elsewhere, the mood was decidedly more sober. Eloise Lehman, the dismissed juror, wondered how the verdict was reached. "I could never have arrived at that verdict. There would have had to have been more proof," she said.

And still, some felt Brad was a scapegoat.

"It just infuriates me. My son has lost a life," said Marjorie Lundeen, barely able to speak through her shock. "I think it's just terrible."

Brad also still had allies in his first wife, Gail Heitzger, and his daughter, Alissa.

"I think he got an unfair trial," said Gail. "There should have been a change of venue. I don't see how he could have gotten a fair trial in that community. Personally, I think the police botched the investigation. They focused on him so early they didn't look for anyone else. I feel for Diane. I feel sorry for the children, who are essentially orphans. But I don't think he did it. He's not a violent person. He never showed anything like that in all the years I've known him, and we had some heavy-duty arguments during the divorce. I don't see how he would plan something like that. If he was unhappy he would have just left. He would have left the house one day and never came back, leaving her with the kids and the bills. I feel like I'm in a movie. It's hard for me to imagine this is really happening. I remember him as a young man, when he was nineteen and had so much potential. That's one of the things that makes me the saddest. He had all that potential. I certainly don't see him as a monster, although I'm sure some people do."

Alissa also said it was against Brad's nature to do something that would essentially leave him responsible for raising two young children by himself. "I don't think he could have done it. It wasn't his style to sit down and plan this out. He always looked for the easy way out, and it wasn't the easy way out to have to take responsibility for those two kids."

Some friends in Colorado also remained loyal to Brad. "As far as I'm concerned, he's being railroaded for the murder of his wife, which we believe he didn't do. The two guys who did are running around Marshall, Michigan, somewhere. It's a conspiracy," said Susan Van Vleet. "We strongly believe the real murderers are still out there. For us, this is insane. Brad did some stupid things. It was stupid for him to have affairs with those college students. But nothing we know of either one of them makes sense. We've been living this nightmare since the day she was murdered. I'm still his friend. Because he's in jail I should stop being his friend? We're going to pretend we don't know this guy? This is when you need your friends."

Alex Galant in Denver couldn't make sense of it either. "There's not a chance Brad could be angry long enough to plan anything like this or do anything to cause long-term trauma to his children. I don't care what this bozo brigade says. He would have had to become stupid overnight to do something like this."

The final legal step for Bradford King was a formality. Under Michigan law, the sentence for premeditated murder is life without possibility of parole. Yet he had to come into the same courtroom where he was found guilty to hear Judge Sindt pronounce his term. Three of the jurors who judged him sat in a front row. As an inmate, Brad wore the prison "pumpkin suit," white socks, and blue slippers. He was chained at the waist and ankles, and what was left of his hair was mussed. He was allowed to speak, but first came a request by his attorney that he serve his time in a federal prison because, as an ex-cop, his safety would be threatened in a state institution. Diane's family was also permitted to make an impact statement.

"There is nothing that I can say that is going to change the sentence mandated by law," defense attorney John Sims said. "But I would say that the outcome of this trial was in no uncertain manner impressed by the pressure presented to Mr. King and the community by the public opinion in this case. There was immense pressure in this matter for conviction. It was compounded by an institutional insistence for trial here in this county. It's my own personal opinion there was pressure by the media and public opinion to the point where it was impossible to obtain a fair trial which would be uncolored by, either consciously or unconsciously, the media pressure and public opinion in regards to my client. It was a close case, and I think the court's very well aware of that. That type of pressure, observed and felt by the jury, either consciously or unconsciously, created an insurmountable task for the defense to establish that somebody else did it. The burden of proof shifted, in my opinion, your honor. Given my client's past experience as a police officer, I urge you strongly consider the recommendation to place him in federal prison to protect him from individuals who may have scores to settle with him."

Nothing the family could say could settle a score with

Brad. But Denise Verrier, Diane's younger sister, approached the podium with her handwritten remarks to vent some pent-up emotions. She cried throughout her remarks, which were part heartfelt grief and part biblical discourse.

"We were all devastated by Diane's death. We miss her dearly. Diane was always so chipper and full of life. Every trip to Battle Creek, I half expect to see her walk through the door and hear her say, 'I'm here. Let's go to lunch.' We were not able to be at her side the night she died. It was all so confusing and unbelievable. She laid there all alone in the hospital. Diane was devastated by the death of her father. And now ironically, her children have to suffer the very loss that she hated so much. But her children have lost two parents. The death of her father affected her whole life and who she was. She was never really happy until she learned the gift of serving others. If there was a soup line nearby, Diane was right there helping. She wanted her children to grow up with that same spirit of giving of themselves.

"Diane had so many plans for her children and how she wanted to raise them. She had put in an order for a baby lamb for Marler to raise. Mom planned to give him some laying hens for his third birthday. Diane's mind was busy; at one time planning to fill the barn with life, a lifestyle she had as a little girl with her own daddy. She wanted to be home with her children. Diane wanted to plant wildflowers down the lane where she could walk when showing everyone the deer on the property. She was so proud of that farm that she wanted to make a home for her children.

"Diane was sensitive and compassionate. She was never late or one to forget your birthday. My phone will never ring on my birthday with Diane's voice wishing me a happy birthday. We will not be sending her a birthday card or calling her every year. Instead we will be visiting her grave. When we take the kids to the zoo, it's won't be a fun day with Diane and the kids because Diane won't be there. A family reunion was planned by Diane. She looked forward to seeing some cousins and other relatives she had not seen in years. The reunion did not take place and Diane won't be able to be at the next one. I was not able to share the same mirror while putting on our makeup the way we always used to do for our brother's wedding. I'll never be able to see her face in the mirror again. She was so excited to go to her brother's wedding. She bought a new dress to wear during her time here the weekend she was murdered. Instead of celebrating her brother's wedding in it, she wore it at her funeral. She was still beautiful as ever.

"Our lives have been affected in so many ways. I have nightmares of her struggling, trying to turn over to get to the car to protect her children. Only last night I dreamed Diane did not die and she put my hand on her wounds. It was so real. If only it were real—she would be here for her children today. I'm sure for the rest of my life I will look out the window every year on February 9 at six-fifteen or six-thirty and remember her and how alone she was out there on the cold gravel drive—all alone, with only her crying children to be heard. In light of the events that have taken place this past two years, I have asked why. When there was no arrest, why do the wicked go unpunished? Why do the innocent suffer so many times? One thing I came to realize was through all this there comes a time to stop asking why and start trusting. And that's what we did. I know this may sound simplistic, but I do feel this is really what God wants. We are people called to live by faith. There is nothing wrong with inquiry, but the enemy loves to have us linger and doubt our God who says, 'Though they join forces, the wicked will not go unpunished'—Proverbs 11:21.

"Seven things the Lord hates: 'a proud look, a lying tongue, hands that shed innocent blood, a heart that devises wicked plans, feet that are swift in running to evil, a false witness who speaks lies and one who sows discord among brethren.' Part of me desires vengeance on the perpetrator, the other part fears greatly the judgment of God on this type of crime. I have thought that perhaps this man will be caught, sentenced, and after much hardship, repent and be saved. Perhaps this man will never be caught and will never repent and be hardened in his sin because the Lord is reserving him for judgment. Only one thing is for sure, and the very heavens and earth would have to pass away before His Word fails when it says, 'Take note; you have sinned against the Lord; and your sins will find you out'—Numbers 23:32. And again the Word says, 'Vengeance is mine and recompense; their foot shall slip in due time; for the day of their calamity is at hand and the things to come hasten upon them'—Deuteronomy 32:35.

"I know that an impact statement is meant to make an impact on deciding the sentence of the defendant. In this case, by Michigan law, his sentence is mandatory life in prison—no parole. We are grateful for that. He should not win an appeal and be released because of a mere loophole."

Now for the first time in the entire trial, Bradford J. King rose to speak in his own behalf. He shambled to the podium with co-defense counsel Virginia Cairns at his right side. He was defiant and accusatory, not remorseful or contrite. He spoke angry words, but his tone was flat, not outraged, as he read words handwritten on a yellow legal pad. He saw himself the victim of everyone else's incompetence.

"Presumed innocent. The basic tenet of the justice system. Presumed innocent did not exist in this case. The prosecutor's zealousness for the public's right to know obliterated the foundation of justice. What occurred throughout the investigation and the trial is a conspiracy to convict at any cost, otherwise known as vigilantism. The obvious victims of this farce are my wife, myself, our children, our families, and our friends. The not so obvious victims are the citizens of this county and the justice system. My heart is saddened and angered at the loss of my wife and my freedom, and the effect this has had on our children, family, and friends. For those who have to live with a corrupt justice system, I should have pity. I don't. You have the ability to change your justice system, and you deserve what you have until you change it. This statement is harsh, but it explains my position," he said.

Addressing Judge Sindt, he continued, "First, you forced a trial in this county on me. You forced a jury on me, a jury with considerable prior knowledge of this case and obvious opinions. Second, you allowed the prosecutor, your friend, to continue to attempt to enter inadmissible testimony in this trial. Third, you remained the trial judge while you knew that you were biased for prosecution. Fourth, you knew that to ensure a conviction the only way was to cover the incompetence of the investigation into the death of my wife. Fifth, this case carried a lot of media coverage and political impact. Control of the trial process was necessary in order to ensure a conviction. Why were these points carried on in this trial? To cover your guilt and the conspiracy to convict. To cover your guilt and the travesty of justice you knew this to be.

He also shared his feelings about the twelve people

who rendered the verdict. "To the jury, I charge you with failure to follow the court rules. I charge you with lying during the selection process. I charge you with willful misconduct. You also threw out the basic tenet of presumed innocent. I say you chose to act in the manner you did for your comfort and not in the interest of justice. I have nothing but contempt for you.

"Finally, I stand here a proud man. I did not kill my wife. I am not guilty. I am taught that all things are related. Everything is a part of a greater whole. I have asked the Great Spirit to guide me, to help me to restore balance and peace in my life. I am taught that your actions are not actions of true humans, and you have forgotten about me as you acted as you did toward me. I forgive your actions, but this does not erase your responsibility for the perpetration of this travesty," he said.

The Native Americans present shook their heads and groaned at the mention of the Great Spirit by a WASP who had been convicted of killing a Native American.

Judge Sindt listened impassively to Brad's speech. He had no response to his charges other than having the final word. Sindt told Brad he would spend the remainder of his life behind bars, plus two years as a coup de grace for using a gun to commit a felony. Because Brad had served 342 days in the Calhoun County Jail, that time would be credited to his sentence. With that, Brad was off to the state prison at Jackson, Michigan, for quarantine and orientation. The Department of Corrections would have to rule on the recommendation to place him in federal prison.

"I don't think anything he said would be worthy of a comment," said prosecutor Jon Sahli, who said nothing during sentencing. "He's a little angry. I don't think he helped himself by saying that." As for his thoughts on

Brad's blaming everyone but himself for what happened, Sahli said, "I think he's been that way for forty-six years."

Jury foreman Jerry Mayfield disputed Brad's contention that the jurors lied when they said they were impartial. Like the others, he wrestled with his conscience in the deliberations. "It wasn't that we just found him guilty. We called it as we saw it. We found him guilty based on the evidence that was presented. There were no winners here."

Defense attorney John Sims was now finished with the case, too. A court-appointed attorney would handle Brad's appeal.

"The fact of the matter is he has no money, and his family has no more money," Sims said. "I think he has an excellent chance for retrial in this matter. He just feels he got the raw end of this deal. I think the thing that bothers him the most is that he was forced to trial in this county, where the public opinion was strongly against him. I think the biggest plus the prosecution had was getting the case tried in this county. That's why Brad believed this judge was in on it. I sure would have liked to try it in a different place. If this case had been tried in Detroit, it would have been over in fifteen minutes."

And what about the justice of the sentence? "That's the law. Justice has nothing to do with the law," Sims said.

CHAPTER 18

The antisocial personality is typically cynical, ungrateful, disloyal, and exploitative. He has no empathy or fellow feeling and therefore cannot comprehend on an emotional level how his actions hurt others. Other people are there to be used. As for giving or receiving love, these are beyond his capabilities. As a consequence of his lack of strong feelings the sex life of the antisocial personality is typically manipulative and faithless.

—James F. Calhoun,
*professor of abnormal psychology**
Current Perspectives

Of all the loose ends in the murder case of Diane Marie Marler Newton King, the two major unresolved questions are (1) what exactly happened on February 9, 1991, and (2) why? Even the investigators aren't in total agreement on the precise events of the murder, so what follows is a composite hypothesis.

Brad had known for two weeks that Diane was going to Detroit for a Salvation Army event, and that she was taking the kids for a three-day stay. He had spent his free time with Julie Cook and his other college women. He and Diane had obviously argued over the phone that Friday night when Diane was at Regina Zapinski's house. She was upset enough to exclaim, "I could walk out of this marriage right now."

On the day of the murder, he told Ann Hill he was leaving for the day and wouldn't be back until late. But he stayed at the farm, puttering around with fixing up the porch, except for a trip to McDonald's and the video store to get *Next of Kin,* which he himself described as a "nice violent cop movie." He was reclining on the couch when his mother-in-law called at four-thirty P.M. to say Diane was on her way home. According to the theory, he had plotted this scheme for some time, to the point where he was stealing .22 caliber bullets that no one could trace to him. And he lugged the rifle up to the second story of the barn to wait, with cold calculation, the way a hunter waits for his prey to enter the killing zone. Diane King was being stalked all right, but not by an obsessed fan who was infatuated with her. She was stalked by the person who knew her every move with intimate detail, the person who shared her bed and her life, the person who played a deceitful game by sending that note and exploiting her fear—her husband. He knew she wouldn't get out of the Jeep unless she knew he was there. He must have yelled to her, "Diane. Up here." When she got out and faced the barn, a bullet destroyed her heart. He ejected the spent casing and chambered another round, hurrying down the steps and out the barn door. When he was within seven to fifteen feet of her fallen form in the driveway, he pulled the trigger again while aiming at a specific target—her genitals. The second shot was meant to ravage her womanhood as surely as the first one was meant to take her life. Cops have a name for the second bullet. It's called the "bitch shot," as in, "Take that, bitch." The experts said it was the only emotional sign to the crime, his only expression of the anger pent up inside him. If he could have gotten rid of the gun according to plan and reported finding her in the driveway much later that night, you wouldn't be reading this. (And no autopsy can accurately pin down the exact time she died.) But now to his horror, he noticed the kids were in the Jeep he liked so much. They were strapped in their car seats facing the front, unable to see anything behind them but having seen their mother fall. Now the plan went out the window because he couldn't just leave the kids there. As his brain races nine hundred miles per hour, he improvises. The first impulse is to head back onto the property in a southerly direction to ditch the gun. He's not sure what to do, which is why police noticed one bootprint facing north and a second one going south. He remembers the bog is soft enough to swallow a gun, and he races along a familiar deer path through the heavy undergrowth to a point in Talmadge Creek where he jams the gun into the muck. What about the seven casings thrown into the water? Perhaps he used them for target practice as he was zeroing in his shooting eye and he tossed them to dispose of them. The casing in the barn? It either slipped his mind or he couldn't find it in the straw. Now he comes back to the house, crossing to the far side of Division Drive so no motorists will spot him until he gets back to the driveway. He never counted on the tracking dog, or people being able to link him to a gun he thought was untraceable. Back in the house, when he hit zero on the phone and called for help through the operator, he was crying—not for his wife, but because his plan went down the drain. He never touched his dying wife, never attended to her or administered first aid when he found her in the driveway. And he left his kids in the car. Some investigators even believe his two recorded interviews with Jack Schoder were to make a tape for himself.

But why? It wasn't for financial gain. There was no huge insurance policy, and Brad couldn't cash the one Diane had because of the murder investigation. He was seeing other women, but he didn't kill her because he was in love with someone else. Financial pressures had reached a breaking point, with the IRS and bill collectors on their backs. There was the new baby, another person to share attention with. Diane was a demanding woman who wanted to relinquish her role as a breadwinner, meaning Brad was being pushed to get a job that would make him give up his life of campus freedom. Sure, Brad had divorced one woman without having to kill her, but he never struck that one when she was pregnant, either, the way he did Diane. Why wouldn't he just walk away again? It came down to a question of control. He had lost control of his relationship with Diane, and he was more dependent on her than he had been on his first wife. He liked the celebrity of being Mr. Diane King, but it was almost as if he had lost his own identity in her. Did he take on the role of martyr willingly, or did Diane demand that he do that? Either way, resentment can build to uncontrollable levels. The mix can be devastating if resentment is teamed with a deep denial of what you want to be doing or should be doing. Then again, if your identity is in another person, and if you perceive you may lose that person, then it's a matter of your own survival. The fear of abandonment by the person you need is the most threatening and scary thing imaginable. For a man who once told Kristina Mony "Nobody crosses me," he had been worked into a corner. And the worst thing you can do to a psychopath is corner him.

In the past four decades, mental health experts have recognized a personality type known variously as a psychopath, sociopath, or antisocial personality. Such a person has no real personality but has learned to project the image of whatever is required to blend in. He can emulate emotions when it fits his needs, but he has no real feelings. He knows what the rules are and can parrot them, but they have no meaning to him. No one seems so convincingly normal. Others can be charmed by him but are ultimately disappointed. He is cool and sure in situations where others would tremble and fear.

Dr. Hervey Cleckley, clinical professor of psychiatry at the Medical College of Georgia, described sixteen psychopathic characteristics in his book, *The Mask of Sanity:*

1. Superficial charm and good intelligence—The typical psychopath will seem particularly agreeable and make a distinctly positive impression. Alert and friendly, he tends to embody the concept of the well-adjusted, happy person. He looks like the real thing. He seems normal and pleasant with high abilities.
2. Absence of delusions—He is free of signs or symptoms regarded as evidence of a psychosis. He can foresee the consequences of injudicious acts, outline acceptable plans of life, and criticize in words his former mistakes.
3. Absence of nervousness—He has a relative immunity from anxiety and worry as might be judged normal

or appropriate in disturbing situations. His relative serenity is noteworthy even in circumstances that would cause others embarrassment, confusion, acute insecurity, or visible agitation. He is almost as incapable of anxiety as of profound remorse.

4. Unreliability—He gives the impression of being thoroughly unreliable. On many occasions he shows no sense of responsibility whatsoever, no matter how binding the obligation, how urgent the circumstances, or how important the matter. He may appear happy and gracious with his wife, then cuff her, or he might suddenly throw a glass of ice tea in the face of his small son.

5. Untruthfulness and insincerity—The psychopath shows a remarkable disregard for truth, but he is a skillful liar. Overemphasis, obvious glibness, and other traditional signs of the clever liar do not show in his words or in his manner. During the most solemn perjury, he has no difficulty at all in looking anyone tranquilly in the eyes.

6. Lack of remorse or shame—He cannot accept substantial blame for the various misfortunes which befall him and which he brings down upon others. He usually denies all responsibility and directly accuses others. His career is always full of shameful exploits, yet he shows almost no sense of shame or regret.

7. Inadequately motivated, antisocial behavior—He is not only undependable, but he cheats, deserts, fails, and lies without apparent compunction. He will commit theft, forgery, adultery, fraud, and other deeds for astonishingly small stakes. He will commit such deeds in the absence of any goal at all.

8. Poor judgment and failure to learn by experience—Despite excellent rational powers, he throws away excellent opportunities to make money, to achieve a rap-

prochement with someone important to him, or to gain other ends he has sometimes invested considerable effort toward gaining. It might be said he cares little about success, financial or otherwise.

9. Pathologic egocentricity and incapacity for love—His self-centeredness is unmodifiable and all but complete. Although plainly capable of casual fondness, he has an absolute incapacity for love. He is skillful in pretending a love for women or simulating parental devotion to his children. His absolute indifference to the financial, social, emotional, physical, and other hardships he brings to those he says he loves confirms his true attitude.

10. General poverty in major affective reactions—He sometimes gets excited and shouts as if in a rage or weeps bitter tears or speaks eloquent and mournful words. But it dawns on those who observe him carefully that it is a readiness of expression rather than strength of feeling. Absurd and showy poses of indignation are within his emotional scale. But wholehearted anger, true indignation, honest grief, sustaining pride, deep joy, or genuine despair are not likely to be found. He does not grieve as others grieve.

11. Specific loss of insight—He has absolutely no capacity to see himself as others see him. He blames his troubles on others with elaborate and subtle rationalization. No affective conviction is there to move him.

12. Unresponsiveness in general interpersonal relations—He shows no consistent reaction of appreciation except superficial and transparent protestations. For example, a man who causes his parents hardship and his wife anguish by sordid affairs might sit with a bedridden person, or do some such act of ostentatious charity, so as to gain admiration and gratitude.

13. Fantastic and uninviting behavior when drunk and sometimes when not—He is given to pranks and buffoonery. Lowered inhibitions are the oil that lubricates his engine but neither furnishes the energy for progress nor directs it.

14. Suicide rarely carried out—He does not take this final step even though he throws away or destroys the opportunities of life. Suicidal threats are nearly always empty.

15. Sex life impersonal, trivial, and poorly integrated—Sexual desire is like a simple itch that is seldom intense. He never seems to find anything meaningful or personal in his relations or to enjoy significant pleasure beyond the localized or temporary sensations. What is felt for the prostitute, sweetheart, casual pickup, or wife is all the same. He feels no loyalty to anyone. His familiar record of sexual promiscuity is related to an almost total lack of self-restraint.

16. Failure to follow any life plan—He does not maintain an effort toward any far goal at all. He seems to go out of his way to make a failure of life.

Motive is a subject that may always haunt the case.

"I cannot understand why. He didn't have to kill her. All he had to do was walk away. She wouldn't have asked him for anything," said Nancy Gwynne. "He ruined so many lives. The children are going to have to live with this terrible truth for the rest of their lives. It's always going to be there. It's never going to go away. He took everything from them. He was like a child. As long as he could have all the candy and eat it, too, he was fine. Diane was his meal ticket. Then she said, 'We can't do this anymore.' I think it was pure hate. He had evil eyes. I can't explain it any other way. If you saw them at a gathering, Diane always had the spotlight. He'd look at her with those evil eyes as if to say, 'It's supposed to be me out in front.' He just didn't know how to get there."

Elaine Wash figured that Brad was always influenced by dominating women, beginning with his mother, and he got fed up with it. "Diane was so organized. She knew what she needed to do. She did what she wanted to do in life. She left lists for him. She structured his life, told him what to do every day. To me, it was like he resented her. He resented her being popular. He resented she did so well in her job. He learned to resent her and despise her. It turned to hate. I'm sure Diane nagged at him, prodded him. He was under pressure to produce and be a total person. She was just another person in his life pushing him, and not letting him do what he wanted to do. Why didn't he just leave?"

Julie Cook theorized Brad was playing a game. "She walked all over him. He felt trapped. I think he did it because he could get away with it, just for the thrill of the hunt. He got tired of her. That was his way of having control."

Theresa Nisley weighed everything over and over before she settled on her own answer. "I think he got tired of being Mr. Diane King."